Defining Battles of World War II
© 2025 Future Publishing Limited

Future Books is an imprint of Future PLC
Quay House, The Ambury, Bath, BA1 1UA

A catalogue record for this book is
available from the British Library.

ISBN 978-1-80521-903-3 hardback

The paper holds full FSC certification
and accreditation.

Printed in China by C&C Offset Printing Co. Ltd.
for Future PLC

GPSR EU RP (for authorities only)
eucomply OÜ Pärnu mnt 139b-14 11317
Tallinn, Estonia
hello@eucompliancepartner.com
+3375690241

**Interested in Foreign Rights to publish this title?
Email us at:**
licensing@futurenet.com

Group Editor
Dan Peel

Art Editor
Perry Wardell-Wicks

Contributors
**Josh Barnett, William F Buckingham,
Nik Cornish, Duncan Crook, Marc DeSantis,
Tom Garner, Charles Ginger, Rebecca Greig,
Mike Haskew, Martin King, Will Lawrence,
Scott Reeves, David Smith, Jonathan Trigg,
William Welsh, Steve Wright**

History of War Editor-in-Chief
Tim Williamson

History of War Senior Designer
Curtis Fermor-Dunman

Senior Art Editor
Andy Downes

Head of Art & Design
Greg Whitaker

Editorial Director
Jon White

Managing Director
Grainne McKenna

Production Project Manager
Matthew Eglinton

Global Business Development Manager
Jennifer Smith

Head of Future International & Bookazines
Tim Mathers

Cover image
Getty Images/W. Eugene Smith/The LIFE Picture Collection

MIX
Paper | Supporting
responsible forestry
FSC® C008047

DEFINING BATTLES OF
WORLD
WAR II

6

On 1 September 1939, Hitler's army marched into Poland. Two days later Britain and France declared war on Nazi Germany. Just over 20 years after the end of the Great War, in which 20 million people died, the world was back in the clutches of a global conflict that would become the deadliest in history. For more than five years, battles raged around the globe, from Europe and Asia to the Atlantic and Pacific. In Defining Battles of World War II we take an in-depth look at some of the most significant campaigns and key battles of the conflict, from early German maneuvers in Western Europe and Hitler's fateful decision to invade the Soviet Union, to the Japanese attacks on Pearl Harbor and Singapore. We discover how the United States took control at Midway, the Soviets stood firm at Stalingrad, and the British won the day at El Alamein, as well as the Allies' final decisive victories as the war drew to a close. In addition to the fascinating features, we also bring you stunning battle maps, iconic imagery, and explore the key events and defining moments that led the world to war once again.

CONTENTS

A sea of fervent Nazis stretches before Hitler and party leadership at Nuremberg in 1934

RISE *And the road to World War II*

For two decades after the end of the Great War, the lengthening shadow of the Nazi Party – hypernationalist and seeking redress for the oppressive terms of the Versailles Treaty – and Allied tactics of appeasement brought another world war ever closer

WORDS MIKE HASKEW

VERSAILLES TREATY SIGNED

The Versailles Treaty ends World War I, saddling Germany with blame and harsh reparations

In the Hall of Mirrors at the Palace of Versailles on the outskirts of Paris, the major warring parties sign the peace treaty ending World War I. Although the terms are unfavorable to Germany and the other former cohorts of the Central Powers, the defeated nations' representatives are compelled to comply. The harsh terms impose monetary reparations on Germany that eventually exceed 132 billion Reichsmarks, or the equivalent of $33 billion. Article 231, known as the "war guilt clause", further forces Germany to accept full responsibility for initiating the global conflict.

The treaty requires Germany to vacate approximately ten per cent of its territory, including the establishment of an Allied occupation and demilitarized zone in the Rhineland. The German Army is limited to only 100,000 men, while naval vessels are restricted to a maximum of 10,000 tons, and the country is prohibited from maintaining an air force or possessing certain types of weapons. The Treaty of Versailles is economically crippling for Germany, and its imposition becomes a catalyst for post-war civil unrest, the rise of the Nazi Party, and the coming of World War II 20 years later.

The Big Four: Britain's Lloyd George, Italy's Orlando, France's Clemenceau and the US's Wilson

Hitler with the other defendants in the Beer Hall Putsch trial

BEER HALL PUTSCH

An ill-fated attempt to seize power leads to prison for Hitler

Led by Adolf Hitler and General Erich Ludendorff, a hero of World War I, the Nazis attempt a coup d'etat to seize power in Munich and Bavaria, intending eventually to oust the weak government of the Weimar Republic. Nazi marchers are confronted by 130 policemen, and 16 Nazis are killed or wounded, while four police officers lie dead following an exchange of gunfire.

Hitler is injured, and the abortive attempt fails. The Nazi dead become martyrs, and the Beer Hall Putsch is the origin of the revered 'Blood Flag'. Arrested and tried for high treason, Hitler uses the court proceedings as a platform to launch a tirade against the existing government. Rather than being deported to his native Austria, Hitler is sentenced to five years in prison, actually serving about eight months.

NAZI PARTY FOUNDED

The Nationalist German Workers Party meets

Emerging on the political far-right as a product of nationalism, economic discontent, and bitterness over the terms of the Versailles Treaty, the German Workers Party meets in the Bavarian city of Munich and adopts a new name, the National Socialist German Workers Party. Popularly known as the Nazis, the group is initially a fringe movement but gains popularity among former members of the German Army who develop a paramilitary culture, while the leadership begins a systematic program of blaming Jews, Communists, and other elements of German society for the "stab in the back" that resulted in defeat during World War I. The Nazis further promote the notion that the Germanic peoples are an 'Aryan' or master race. Adolf Hitler, ordered by the Reichswehr to infiltrate the party, is influenced by Anton Drexler, a leading member, and actually joins the organization as its 55th member, rising to leadership in July 1921.

Nazi Party leader Adolf Hitler and members of his inner circle render a Nazi salute

Nazi stormtroopers parade with their swastika-emblazoned standards

18 July 1925

MEIN KAMPF PUBLISHED

Released through the Nazi central publishing house

During his confinement in Landsberg Prison in Bavaria following conviction on charges of high treason stemming from the failed Munich Beer Hall Putsch, Adolf Hitler dictates the text of *Mein Kampf*, his manifesto and autobiographical discourse of life events that have led him to personal conclusions supporting the Nazi world view, to associate Rudolf Hess, future Deputy Führer of Germany. *Mein Kampf Volume I* sells fewer than 10,000 copies in its first year; however, *Volume II* follows in 1927. The basis for the Nazi Party's political and ideological future, *Mein Kampf* rails against the forces Hitler believes have brought suffering to post-World War I Germany, particularly the influences of international Jewry; France, Germany's traditional enemy; the communists and other political parties; and the need for Lebensraum, or living space, in the East. Hitler further promotes the notion of the Aryan, or master, race and totalitarian National Socialist government. In 1933, the year Hitler becomes Chancellor of Germany, the book sells over a million copies.

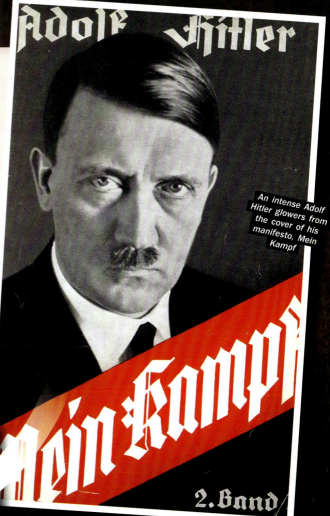

An intense Adolf Hitler glowers from the cover of his manifesto, Mein Kampf

Hitler delivers a speech during the 1932 election, which he lost to Hindenburg

1928-1932

NAZI ELECTORAL TIDE

The Nazis gain political influence during critical national elections defining the future of Germany

At first, the Nazi Party exists as a fringe group on the political periphery of post-World War I Germany. However, during a series of national elections the party advances from virtually no representation in the Reichstag, the national assembly, to a majority in just four years. During the Reichstag election of 1928, the Nazi Party receives three per cent of the vote and gains the attention of other German political parties. In 1930, the Nazis receive six million votes, increasing their number of seats in the Reichstag from 12 to 107. Hitler challenges World War I hero Paul von Hindenburg in the 1932 presidential election and loses. However, the Nazi candidate receives 37 per cent of the vote. In the Reichstag elections in July, the Nazis garner 13.7 million votes, gaining a majority with 230 seats.

Hitler with SA Leader Ernst Röhm, a former friend assassinated during the blood purge

NIGHT OF THE LONG KNIVES

As Hitler moves to consolidate power, support of the German Army is essential. However, military leaders become concerned with the strength of the Sturmabteilung (SA), or Stormtroopers, the paramilitary group of Nazi thugs led by Ernst Röhm which greatly outnumbers the army. Although a longtime ally of Hitler whose SA has played a key role in achieving the Nazi grip on Germany, Röhm is suspected as a rival for party leadership.

Therefore, Hitler authorizes Operation Hummingbird, popularly called the Night of the Long Knives, sending SS (Schutzstaffel) and Gestapo personnel to accomplish a blood purge of the SA. The murders are carried out swiftly, and other political enemies, including former Chancellor Kurt von Schleicher, are also eliminated. Many of the SA leaders are arrested at the resort of Bad Wiessee and summarily executed. Röhm is among the dead.

30 January 1933

A PROBLEMATIC PACT WITH HITLER

In a dramatic shift of power, the German establishment offers Hitler to office

Following the rise of the Nazi Party in recent elections and the party's achievement of a majority in the Reichstag, former chancellor of Germany Franz von Papen leads a group of advisors in recommending the appointment of Adolf Hitler as chancellor in the government of President Paul von Hindenburg. The appointment is an attempt to exert political control over Hitler and minimize Nazi influence in the future of Germany. Papen comments to close advisors, "Within two months we will have pushed Hitler so far in a corner that he will squeak." On the contrary, it is Hitler who dupes the political establishment with a ruthless rise to power that eventually results in absolute rule in Germany. Even though party infighting led by a splinter movement under Gregor Strasser contributes to some losses in the 1932 Reichstag election.

Hitler and top Nazis broker a deal with former Chancellor Franz von Papen (seated right)

Hitler salutes marching Nazis during the 1935 rally in which he proclaims the Nuremberg Laws

2 August 1934

DEATH OF HINDENBURG

With the death of Germany's president, Hitler proceeds to consolidate power in himself as dictator

The death of 86-year-old Paul von Hindenburg, president of Germany and hero of World War I, removes the last substantial barrier to Hitler's consolidation of power as Nazi dictator. With the support of the German armed forces secured following the Night of the Long Knives, Hitler authorizes a plebiscite to decide the question of merging the offices of chancellor and president. The German people approve the measure resoundingly with 90 per cent of the vote in the affirmative, and Hitler assumes the title of Führer. Further exercising his authority through the Enabling Laws, Hitler sanctions and energizes the state sponsorship of a virulent campaign of anti-Semitism, and his personal popularity soars as the economic hardships of the Great Depression ease somewhat. Further, the Nazi regime continues to suppress political opposition in Germany and Hitler prepares to embark on an aggressive campaign of redress against the oppressive terms of the Treaty of Versailles.

Chancellor Hitler bows subserviently to the elderly President Paul von Hindenburg in 1934

15 September 1935

NUREMBERG LAWS ENACTED

The Reichstag passes laws restricting rights of German Jews and fueling Nazi ideology as state policy

The Nuremberg Laws, placing severe restrictions on the civil rights of the Jewish population in Germany, further broaden the legal basis for the Nazi persecution of the nation's Jews and other minorities as a matter of policy. The principal regulations include the Law for the Protection of German Blood and German Honor and the Reich Citizenship Law. The first prohibits extramarital sexual intercourse and marriage between Germans and Jews and the employment of German women under 45 years of age by Jewish households. The second proclaims that only those people of German or related blood are citizens. Other individuals are stripped of their citizenship. A subsequent law imposed later in the year defines who is considered a Jew based upon ancestry, and the law is soon expanded to include other ethnic populations. The Nuremberg Laws follow Hitler's 1933 enactment of a national boycott of Jewish businesses and other Nazi activities to isolate the Jewish population in Germany.

German tanks at a Nazi Party Congress following the start of rearmament

16 March 1935

HITLER REPUDIATES VERSAILLES TREATY

In a major foreign policy stroke, Hitler formally announces the renewal of military conscription in Germany

Although the German armed forces have been conducting a covert program of rearmament for years, much of it with the assistance of the Soviet Union, Adolf Hitler announces to the German people and the world that the Third Reich will no longer abide by the military disarmament restrictions of the Treaty of Versailles.

"For in this very hour, the German Government renews its resolve before the German people and before the entire world that it will never step beyond the bounds of preserving German honor and the freedom of the Reich," Hitler proclaims, "and in particular shall never make of the German national arms an instrument of warlike aggression, but an instrument confined exclusively to defence and thereby the preservation of peace."

Hitler's proclamation reintroduces general military conscription and lifts the secretive veil from military training and arms manufacture.

The German Army is projected to increase to 12 corps and 36 divisions, significantly beyond the Versailles restrictions. The news is alarming, but the former Allied nations take no meaningful steps to curb the increasing threat of German rearmament.

The Führer stands with government officials after announcing German rearmament on 16 March 1935

Riding into the Rhineland on horseback, a German soldier accepts flowers from a welcoming woman

1 August 1936

THE 1936 OLYMPIC GAMES

Berlin hosts the Games of the XI Olympiad

The eyes of the world focus on a new and apparently prosperous Germany as Berlin, the Nazi capital, hosts the games of the XI Olympiad. Hitler opens the games amid great pageantry, and foreign visitors and dignitaries are treated with courtesy and deference. The Nazi persecution of the Jews and other minorities has been fully implemented, but all vestiges of the program are temporarily suspended to hide the truth from the outside world.

Although the Nazis have repudiated the Versailles Treaty, reconstituted a strong military, and occupied the Rhineland, they view the games as a tremendous propaganda opportunity, projecting a veneer of goodwill. A new 100,000-seat stadium has been constructed along with six gymnasiums and other facilities. Acclaimed filmmaker Leni Riefenstahl produces a stunning documentary, and the games are the first to be televised. In keeping with Hitler's hopes for 'Aryan' success, the German team leads in overall (89) and gold medals (33). However, American Jesse Owens, an outstanding African-American track-and-field athlete, wins four gold medals to Hitler's chagrin.

7 March 1936

GERMAN TROOPS OCCUPY THE RHINELAND

In direct violation of the Treaty of Versailles, German troops march into the Rhineland, an area designated as a demilitarized zone, in western Germany. Hitler's bold move effectively renounces the Locarno Pact of 1925, which had reaffirmed the provisions of the Versailles Treaty, permitted the entry of Germany into the League of Nations, and led to the withdrawal of Allied occupation troops in the Rhineland, which is accomplished in 1930. Although the German move is provocative and Hitler is prepared to pull back rapidly if the Allied nations respond with force, his calculated risk pays off. The Allies, particularly France, do nothing of substance to compel the Nazis to withdraw. The successful gamble sparks tremendous support for Hitler's aggressive posture and emboldens the Führer to make further territorial demands in Europe.

African-American athlete Jesse Owens won four golds during the 1936 Olympics in Berlin

Prior to Anschluss, a jubilant crowd greets Hitler as he enters the Austrian capital of Vienna

13 March 1938

ANSCHLUSS WITH AUSTRIA

In a triumph of his efforts to unite ethnic Germanic peoples and territories outside Germany into a greater Reich, Hitler proclaims the union, or Anschluss, of Germany and Austria, his native country. The annexation of Austria is preceded by subversive activities of Austrian Nazis and Hitler's coercion of Austrian Chancellor Kurt Schuschnigg, who meets with the Führer in the vain hope that his nation might remain independent but is instead forced to appoint Austrian Nazis to key posts in his government. After calling for a national plebiscite to decide the question of union with Germany on 9 March, Schuschnigg is forced to resign two days later. Hitler crosses the Austrian frontier with German troops on 12 March and returns triumphantly to the capital of Vienna, a city where he spent much of his youth in disillusionment. He appoints a new government and proclaims the Anschluss complete the following day.

28 May 1937

CHAMBERLAIN BECOMES PM

Prime Minister Chamberlain presides over final drama leading to World War II

With the retirement of Stanley Baldwin, Conservative politician Neville Chamberlain accedes to the office of Prime Minister of Great Britain. Amid the growing threat of war with Nazi Germany, Chamberlain continues a foreign policy of appeasement, offering concessions in exchange for assurances that armed conflict may be averted. Chamberlain is best known for acquiescing to German demands for the annexation of the Sudetenland, a region of predominantly German-speaking inhabitants in western Czechoslovakia. The agreement is negotiated during a meeting in Munich, Germany, and Chamberlain returns to Britain confident that war has been averted.

Prime Minister Neville Chamberlain meets the Führer in the city of Munich in September 1938

17

30 September 1938

MUNICH PACT

Chamberlain, Daladier, Hitler and Mussolini pose for a photograph during the Munich Conference of 1938

Chamberlain of Britain and Daladier of France sign away sovereign Czech territory to appease Hitler

In the vain hope that another world war may be avoided, British Prime Minister Neville Chamberlain and French Prime Minister Edouard Daladier travel to Munich, Germany, to meet with the Nazi Führer Adolf Hitler and Benito Mussolini, the Fascist Italian dictator. Hitler demands that the Sudetenland, a region in western Czechoslovakia, be ceded from the sovereign Czechoslovak nation to greater Germany due to its German-speaking population. Czechoslovakia is not represented at the conference. Chamberlain and Daladier sign the Munich Pact, giving in to Hitler's demands and eventually sealing the fate of all Czechoslovakia, which the Nazis occupy the following spring without firing a shot. Chamberlain returns to Britain and receives a warm welcome. Addressing the crowd and waving a document that bears the signatures of the various leaders, he proclaims, "Peace for our time." The Munich Pact stands to this day as stark evidence of the failed Allied doctrine of appeasement that contributed to the outbreak of World War II. Some observers, among them future British Prime Minister Churchill, complain that the agreement is a diplomatic defeat.

Nazi troops enter the Prague Castle grounds during the occupation of Czechoslovakia in March 1939

9 November 1938

THE NIGHT OF BROKEN GLASS

Kristallnacht, the Night of Broken Glass, spreads like an ill wind across Nazi Germany as violence erupts against the nation's Jewish population. Synagogues are torched, businesses are ransacked, homes are destroyed, and 100 Jews are killed in the rampage while authorities ignore the atrocities. Approximately 30,000 Jewish men are arrested and transported to concentration camps as the Nazis use the murder of Ernst vom Rath, a German diplomat in Paris, as an excuse for the pogrom.

Until Kristallnacht, much of the persecution against German Jews has been in the form of boycotts and anti-Semitic legislation. However, this escalation of tension and violence signals to the world a warning that Nazi malevolence may not be contained within the nation's borders. The violence continues into the following day, and the *New York Times* reports, "Large crowds filled the main streets this morning to gaze on the destruction wrought in last night's riots..."

Ordinary German citizens walk past the gutted storefronts along a Berlin street following Kristallnacht

15 March 1939

GERMANY OCCUPIES CZECHOSLOVAKIA

After annexing Sudetenland, Nazi Germany extends its territorial gains as troops occupy all of Czechoslovakia

After annexing Sudetenland the previous fall, Nazi Germany sends troops across the frontier to occupy all of Czechoslovakia. Hitler completes his bloodless conquest of the country after intimidating Czech Prime Minister Emil Hacha with threats of bombing the capital city of Prague. Hacha has previously offered concessions to Hitler, but none are satisfactory. In the evening, Hitler arrives in Prague to a tumultuous crowd. With the occupation, the powerful Czech Army is rendered inert, while tremendous resources, including substantial coal and iron deposits and steel production facilities, come into the possession of the Nazi government. The Skoda Works, which produce outstanding, modern weaponry, is now at the disposal of the German military. Slovakia is declared independent, although it remains a Nazi puppet state, while Bohemia and Moravia are designated a German Protectorate.

Images: Getty

PACT OF STEEL

Nazi Germany and Fascist Italy sign an alliance that openly threatens peace in Europe

Although Italian Fascist dictator Benito Mussolini initially opposes the rise of Hitler and the Nazis in Germany, particularly due to the Führer's aggressive territorial demands, the two leaders discover common ground in their lust for empire. In fact, Hitler has considered Mussolini, his senior, as something of a role model for the emergence of the totalitarian state in Germany. By the spring of 1939, the two leaders have directed their foreign ministers to conclude an agreement known popularly as the Pact of Steel and specifically as the Pact of Friendship and Alliance between Germany and Italy. The agreement pledges diplomatic and military cooperation between the two countries.

Italy's Count Galeazzo Ciano and Germany's Joachim von Ribbentrop sign the treaty in Berlin, and the pact includes a secret supplementary protocol that provides additional mutual covert economic and military assurances. Originally, Japan has been a probable signatory, but the European partners wish to focus on Britain and France, while the Japanese are preoccupied with concluding an agreement offering security against the Soviet Union. Japan later joins Germany and Italy in the Tripartite Pact of 1940.

Hitler alongside German Foreign Minister Joachim von Ribbentrop at the signing of the Pact of Steel

GERMANY INVADES POLAND

German forces invade Poland, and World War II erupts as Great Britain and France declare war

After fabricating a so-called border incident with the Polish military, German forces roll into Poland and unleash the Blitzkrieg, or Lightning War, as they press toward objectives including the capital city of Warsaw. German troops, tanks, artillery, and aircraft overwhelm the Polish Army, which mounts a heroic but futile resistance. Luftwaffe bombers devastate Warsaw. Soviet troops launch their own invasion of Poland from the east on 17 September, while the German campaign of conquest is concluded in 35 days.

Meanwhile, British Prime Minister Neville Chamberlain addresses the nation on 3 September, stating somberly, "...This morning the British ambassador in Berlin handed the German government a final note stating that unless we heard from them by 11 o'clock that they were prepared at once to withdraw their troops from Poland, a state of war would exist between us. I have to tell you now that no such undertaking has been received, and that consequently this country is at war with Germany..."

Both Great Britain and France formally declare war on Nazi Germany on 3 September 1939, plunging Europe into World War II.

Adoring Nazis roar their approval as Hitler announces the invasion of Poland in the Reichstag

NAZI-SOVIET NONAGGRESSION PACT

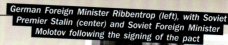

German Foreign Minister Ribbentrop (left), with Soviet Premier Stalin (center) and Soviet Foreign Minister Molotov following the signing of the pact

Nazi Germany and the Soviet Union, the bastion of communism, shock the world with the announcement of a nonaggression pact that pledges peace between the two countries. The news is particularly startling in the West, which has understood that the communists are Hitler's sworn enemies. Actually, the Soviet Union and Nazi Germany have cooperated for years during the covert program of German military rearmament in violation of the Versailles Treaty. The countries have further engaged in substantial economic trade. Signed in the Soviet capital of Moscow, the agreement stipulates that neither country will ally itself with or aid an enemy of the other. It also includes a secret protocol, which acknowledges respective spheres of influence and sets the stage for each country's invasion of neighboring Poland, triggering World War II. Hitler shreds the agreement in June 1941, taking advantage of a naïve Soviet Premier Joseph Stalin, and launching an invasion of the Soviet Union.

WORLD AT WAR

SIEGE OF WARSAW

When Germany launched its invasion of Poland, few expected the capital city to fall in less than a month

WORDS DAVID SMITH

German infantry advance into the outskirts of Warsaw, using a tank for cover

In the early hours of 1 September 1939, the German battleship Schleswig-Holstein fired the first shot of World War II. The German campaign plan, 'Fall Weiss' (Case White) swung into action and the world was introduced to a new form of warfare that would later be recalled as 'blitzkrieg' (lightning war). Although debate continues over how meaningful the term is, and how deeply rooted in German planning it was, there can be no doubt that speed was the defining characteristic of the invasion of Poland. On the seventh day of the campaign, German tanks were approaching the outskirts of Warsaw and the stage had been set for a brief yet brutal siege.

The seeds of World War II had been planted at the end of the Great War, with Germany aggrieved by territorial losses to Poland, including the 'Pomeranian corridor', which split East Prussia from the rest of Germany, and the designation of the port of Danzig as a free city.

By 1939, Poland was counting on protection from France and Great Britain as Germany made increasingly bellicose attempts to regain its territory. An initiative to pull the Soviet Union into an anti-German alliance failed due to Polish misgivings over Russian intent and on 25 August 1939, the stunning Molotov-Ribbentrop non-aggression pact placed Poland between two rapacious and suddenly cooperative powers.

The invasion force

In 1939, the German Army was not quite the smooth-running machine it is often characterized as being. As war approached only a fraction of the army had been mechanized and the bulk of it still relied on horses, bicycles and its own feet.

By concentrating all of its mechanized and motorized divisions on Poland, however, Germany was able to create massive local superiority. An advantage in tanks of 2,511 to 615 would no doubt have proved decisive enough, but the German plan allowed them to enjoy a better than eight-to-one advantage at the points of attack.

The tanks involved were not the powerful behemoths of the later war years. Tanks were utilized in an anti-infantry role and the majority were Panzerkampfwagen types I and II, armed with machine guns or 20mm cannon respectively. There were less than 100 of the more powerful PzKpfw III, armed with a 37mm gun, while the 75mm-equipped PzKpfw IV was used as a fire support platform.

The Germans also enjoyed a significant advantage in artillery, with 5,805 guns to 2,065 for the Poles.

"BY CONCENTRATING ITS MECHANIZED AND MOTORIZED DIVISIONS ON POLAND, GERMANY WAS ABLE TO CREATE HUGE LOCAL SUPERIORITY"

What differentiated the German use of armor was its massing in panzer divisions (combined arms units with tanks as well as motorized artillery and infantry). The use of high-quality radios was of critical importance, as it allowed for a great flexibility in movement and rapid responses to problems.

The Germans also enjoyed an advantage in manpower of at least 1.5:1, although in reality it was greater as Polish mobilization was never really completed.

The birth of 'blitzkrieg'?

Germany wanted, and needed, a quick victory. With Britain and France declaring their support for Poland, the campaign would need to be fought and won before the Western powers could react. German divisions could then be rushed westwards to face an anticipated French offensive.

Polish planning took this into account. Believing they needed only to buy enough time for the French to mobilize and launch a massive offensive against Germany, their entire strategy was flawed from the start. Compounding this flaw was the fact that France believed Poland would be able to hold out for at least three months.

The Poles therefore called for an initial defense of their western territory, followed by a planned withdrawal to defensive positions along the Vistula River. Such a defense would not only signal that Poland was willing to fight (and therefore worthy of its promised support from France and Britain), but also give time for mobilization of its forces to be completed.

The German plan threw all of this into confusion. Whether or not there was a coherent acceptance of the concept of blitzkrieg (the term itself was almost certainly coined by a journalist, not a general), German commanders accepted the need to move quickly. This paramount objective would overwhelm Polish resistance in a matter of weeks.

Invasion

German forces aimed to converge on Warsaw from two directions. From the north, Army Group North, under Fedor von Bock, marched with

Above: Luftwaffe raids destroyed or damaged many buildings throughout the city

Left: The view over the wing of a German bomber as it circles Warsaw during the siege of September 1939

15 divisions. From the southwest came Army Group South, 26 divisions strong, under Gerd von Rundstedt. With 630,000 and 886,000 men respectively, the two army groups significantly outnumbered the Polish defenders.

Warsaw was a target from day one. The Luftwaffe was tasked with bombing the city, but weather conditions on 1 September were far from ideal and the spirited defense of the Brygada Poscigowa, the 'Pursuit Brigade', took the German airmen by surprise. The majority of Poland's squadrons had been allocated to support its various field armies, but the 54 planes of the Pursuit Brigade, mostly obsolete PZL P.11 fighters, downed 16 Luftwaffe aircraft on the first day of the war.

Losses in the Polish Air Force were catastrophic, however, and against the vastly superior Messerschmitt Bf 109 and the newly introduced Bf 110, as well as defensive fire from bombers, the PAF was to lose around 85 per cent of its aircraft during the short war.

German propaganda insisted that the Polish planes had been destroyed on the ground in the first two days of the fighting, but in fact the Poles had wisely scattered their aircraft and only unserviceable wrecks had been caught on the ground at their main airfields. Nevertheless, air defense quickly became limited to anti-aircraft guns as the PAF was driven from the skies. The stage was set for the sinister Stuka dive-bomber to write itself into history.

Relatively slow (it would perform disastrously in the later Battle of Britain against Hurricanes and Spitfires), the 340 Stukas of the Luftwaffe reveled in the open skies above Poland, attacking lines of communication, trains, railway lines, and other key tactical targets at will and becoming in many ways the symbol of blitzkrieg.

The German plan was not running as smoothly as their propaganda claimed, however. Coordination between the panzer and infantry divisions was patchy and the Poles were enjoying success with their 37mm anti-tank weapons, even employing obsolescent armored trains effectively.

Below: Hitler watches on as the battle for Warsaw unfolds

Polish cavalry was still useful due to its rapidity of movement, but it was never used in full-scale charges against panzers, as German propaganda claimed (a successful charge was mounted against an infantry unit, but was then repelled by advancing German tanks).

Warsaw under attack

Following the confusion of the early days of the war, the Germans began to make serious advances. Most worrying for the defending Poles was that they were unable to retreat as quickly as the Germans were advancing. Pressure on two Polish armies, Army Lodz and Army Prusy, resulted in a gap developing between them, wide enough for the Germans to race through. By the afternoon of 7 September, elements of 1st and 4th Panzer Divisions had reached Warsaw.

By now, Luftwaffe raids were having more of an effect, and the rubble of destroyed buildings dotted the landscape. Distressing though this was for the civilian population, it actually helped with the preparation of defenses – the bombed-out buildings provided excellent cover for the placement of anti-tank guns and artillery pieces.

In addition to this, ditches were dug, rail lines ripped up and planted into the ground to form rudimentary tank traps, and barricades built. Tram cars were toppled over to block roads.

On 8 September, as the defenders waited, the rumbling sound of advancing tanks began to build as the first units of 4th Panzer Division advanced cautiously into a hostile and unfamiliar environment. The tanks, mostly Type I and II panzers, were thinly armored and unable to withstand anything more substantial than machine-gun fire. The 37mm and 75mm shells fired at them, often at point-blank range from behind the improvised defensive works on the streets of Warsaw, easily tore through the thin armor. Many of 4th Panzer Division's tanks were destroyed in this way before the attack was called off.

The Poles had served notice that they would not give up their city without a fight, but how determined that fight would be was up for debate.

The evening before, the Polish commander, Edward Rydz-Smigly, had taken a fateful decision. Convinced that Warsaw was about to be surrounded by the rapidly advancing Germans, he ordered the bulk of the army command apparatus to relocate to Brzesc-nad-Bugiem (Brest-Litovsk). At the worst possible moment, with its armies reeling under the German onslaught, the Polish command structure disintegrated.

The tanks of 4th Panzer Division attacked again on 9 September, but were again repulsed. Polish defenses had been strengthened overnight and the 'Children of Warsaw Brigade' had been recalled to the city, launching a series of small night-time raids to keep the Germans off balance.

The Polish counterattack

One area in which blitzkrieg left the Germans vulnerable was in their susceptibility to counterattacks on their exposed flanks. As their divisions raced along as fast as they could, it was inevitable that some would become strung out, and with their focus on what was immediately in front of them, a force on their flanks might be overlooked.

Just such a situation had arisen with Army Poznan. Bypassed by the advancing German armies as they had streamed past to the north and south, its commander, Tadeusz Kutrzeba, had begged for permission to hurl his fresh troops against the flank of the advancing divisions. Repeatedly, Rydz-Smigly had refused but now, with the situation becoming desperate, he finally acquiesced.

The German Eighth Army was the target, blissfully unaware of the danger as intelligence had mistakenly reported Army Poznan retreating to Warsaw. As evening approached on 9 September, three Polish infantry divisions, flanked by two cavalry brigades, attacked two German infantry divisions along the Bzura River. After 24 hours of fighting, the Germans were forced to withdraw and around 1,500 men were taken prisoner.

It was a small victory, but it achieved its primary goal – that of buying time for the defenses of Warsaw to be strengthened and for more units to make it safely back to the city. Epitomizing this was the recall of 1st and 4th Panzer Divisions from Warsaw to join in an encircling movement on Army Poznan.

The good news for Warsaw was, of course, bad news for Army Poznan, which was quickly surrounded. Kutrzeba had hopes of fighting his way through to the east, which would have allowed the army to reach Warsaw, but instead was forced to turn northwards in the face of overwhelming enemy forces.

On 16 September the Luftwaffe sent 820 planes against the trapped Poles in the 'Bzura pocket', who were also being pummeled by artillery fire, while panzer forces closed in. The end was inevitable, and although some units did manage to break through a weak spot in the German cordon, Army Poznan was virtually annihilated. A staggering 120,000 men were taken prisoner.

It had been a brave diversion, but the inferior communications systems of the Poles had proved to be a major handicap. It had also only held up the German advance from one direction. Out of the north came the two armies of Army Group North, closing in once more on Warsaw.

The city

Warsaw was a city of 1.3 million inhabitants, including the largest Jewish population outside New York – 350,000 Jews called Warsaw home, and most were to suffer a horrendous fate in the years that followed the German capture of the city.

Ironically, the belief that France would quickly launch an offensive on the opening of

"AIR DEFENSE QUICKLY BECAME LIMITED TO ANTI-AIRCRAFT GUNS AS THE PAF WAS DRIVEN FROM THE SKIES. THE STAGE WAS SET FOR THE STUKA DIVE-BOMBER TO WRITE ITSELF INTO HISTORY"

German soldiers parading in Warsaw following the invasion

the war had not only misled the Poles, it had also hampered German planning. Unwilling to have its forces committed too far to the east in case they needed to respond quickly to a French attack, German commanders had been tentative about crossing the Vistula River. By the middle of September, reality was dawning – the French were not about to move quickly and the armies engaged in Poland were free to roam at will. Bock's Army Group North was therefore able to move southwards on both sides of the Vistula, posing a much more serious threat to the Polish defensive positions. Third Army was in the vanguard as German units again pushed down towards Warsaw.

In the beleaguered city at the time was an American journalist, Julien H Bryan, who remained to document the assault. Armed with a still camera and a Bell & Howell cine camera, he captured images of the city under the hammer of the German war machine. In particular, the incessant air attacks had become a monotonous terror. "By the 12th day," Bryan reported in his documentary film 'Siege', "it was absurd even to sound alarms, for there was always an air raid." Bryan's film, smuggled out after the city fell, gave a glimpse of the work undertaken to construct defenses and the devastating effects of German incendiary bombs, which turned whole blocks into infernos.

The siege of Warsaw

The Polish plan was still to hang on until help arrived from France, so keeping field armies intact was of paramount importance. On the same day that Rydz-Smigly had shifted the Polish command center from Warsaw, he had issued an ominous order – men within a certain age range were also to leave the city.

The inevitable conclusion was that Warsaw was being left to its fate, with manpower shifted further eastwards, out of reach of the advancing Germans. The order was so frightening, in fact, that it was ignored, with the general in charge of the defense of Warsaw, Walerian Czuma, agreeing with the mayor, Stefan Starzynski, that the men were needed to defend the city.

For the population, it was a terrifying time. There was no doubt that the war was going badly, even disastrously. Alexander Polonius, trapped in the suburbs of the city as the noose tightened, told later of the hopelessness experienced in the face of German military superiority: "At the beginning of the war," he noted, on 8 September,

"we were always trying to distinguish the colors and markings of the planes to see which were the enemy; but now few even took the trouble: whatever airplanes were heard we took it for granted that they were German."

On the same day, Rydz-Smigly had issued an order that resistance was to continue. Posters appeared in the city, urging the citizens to arms (Do Broni) and declaring that it would be defended to the last man. Retreating units were finding their way into the city and there was little doubt that events were reaching their critical point.

The city was not yet surrounded, however. German forces were closing in from the north, but to the west, the Bzura counterattack was still tying up Rundstedt's armies. To the south, there was hope in the form of four fortifications, Forts Szczesliwicki, Mokotowski, Dabrowski and Czerniakowski. The forts were old, though, and Mokotowski had been partially dismantled in preparation for being converted to a storage facility. They were a comforting presence for the civilian population, but they could not hope to hold back modern German forces for long.

Keeping the civilian population under control was becoming increasingly difficult as the nightmarish reality of a siege began to sink in. Polonius wrote of bakeries being broken into by hungry mobs, while Bryan, the American journalist stuck in the city, filmed the bodies of women machine-gunned by German planes while foraging for potatoes. "Sleeping is a peace-time prejudice," Polonius wrote in his diary on 10 September. "I spent the night in hearing the stunning din of heavy vehicles on the road, as the rows of lorries and armored cars passed through the village." Later he would write of the terror as his house was bombed and strafed.

By 19 September, the city was flooded with refugees, begging in the streets and being directed to aid stations which were, in Polonius's words, "sheer mockery. There is invariably an enormous queue, but no food or drink." The stench of rotting corpses began to fill the air.

The fall

Fittingly enough, in what Polonius described as "this speediest of all wars", the end for Warsaw came quickly. As the Bzura counterattack fizzled out, German forces completed the encirclement of the city by 21 September, committing 12 divisions to the task.

The short, sharp lessons learned by the panzer forces in the earlier street fighting, had helped persuade the German command that the capture of the city would be best left in the hands of the artillery and Luftwaffe. A thousand guns were amassed around Warsaw to pummel the city, while the air force continued its air raids.

On 23 September, a major assault was beaten back by the desperate Polish defenders, but two days later resistance appeared futile in the face of a huge artillery bombardment, accompanied by bombing raids featuring 1,200 planes. Warsaw disappeared under a pall of smoke, which actually made it difficult for Luftwaffe planes to spot their targets, resulting in numerous 'friendly fire' casualties among German ground units.

The forts to the south of the city fell the next day, after determined infantry assaults. Fort Mokotowski, home to the Polish Broadcasting Station, had kept transmitting up to the 25th despite being repeatedly targeted from above by German bombers. Resistance was still an option, as fresh reserves of ammunition had been transported into the city via locomotive, but the cost was becoming too high.

"I feel that I am growing abnormal," Polonius wrote as the siege neared its inevitable conclusion. "When the guns are firing I feel quite assured and light of heart, but I am afraid of the silence." Polish troops had arrived at his house on the 26th, setting up a new defensive perimeter as the Germans closed in, but the following day the soldiers were just as suddenly withdrawn. The city had surrendered.

The aftermath

As many as 40,000 civilians had died during the siege of Warsaw. Following its capture, the Jewish population was to suffer most at the hands of the German occupiers, first forced to live in a cramped ghetto (where an estimated 83,000 would die of disease and starvation) and later transported to death camps for more organized extermination.

Warsaw's capture had never been in doubt from the moment it was fixed as the target of the German offensive, and events elsewhere had ensured a similar fate for the entire country.

The Ribbentrop-Molotov pact, signed just before the opening of the war, had called for the partition of Poland between Germany and the Soviet Union. As Poland hung grimly on, waiting for the promised assistance from its allies in the west, Russian forces massed along its eastern border.

This army was far inferior to the one that had rolled over Poland's western borders a few weeks earlier. The Soviet army was badly led and organized, but it did not need to do much more than occupy the territory allotted to it under the terms of the Molotov-Ribbentrop pact – Poland had shifted almost all its forces to the west to face the Germans. The two great armies, unaware that they would shortly be pitted against each other, calmly divided Poland between themselves.

The cost of defeat for Warsaw was immense. At the end of the war, when Soviet forces 'liberated' the city, they would find a population of just 174,000.

SIEGE OF WARSAW
1-27 SEPTEMBER 1939

04 THE NORTHERN APPROACH
By 15 September the Germans are back, this time approaching the city from the north, along both banks of the Vistula River. The suburb of Praga, on the east bank, is the focus of the assault.

06 BLACK MONDAY
The city is surrounded by 12 German divisions. On 25 September a huge artillery bombardment, along with bombing raids by 1,200 Luftwaffe planes, rocks the city.

05 THE FLIGHT OF ARMY POZNAN
Having staged a brave but doomed counterattack, the remnants of Army Poznan fights its way into Warsaw. The attack has bought precious days for the organization of defenses in the city, but the situation is increasingly desperate.

Vistula

08 THE FINAL SURRENDER
With Hitler ordering that no civilians are to be allowed to leave the city, Polish commanders recognize the pointlessness of further resistance. On the evening of 26 September talks open with the Germans and the city surrenders the following day.

07 FALL OF THE FORTS
A string of obsolescent forts to the south of the city, which offer more comfort to the civilian population than concern for the Germans, are overwhelmed by infantry assaults on 26 September. The southern route into Warsaw lies open.

FORT CZERIAKOWSKI

FORT DABROWSKI

FORT MOKOTOWSKI

02 THE POLISH COMMAND WITHDRAWS
Fearing that an encirclement of Warsaw is inevitable, Polish commander Eduard Rydz-Smigly orders the removal of the Polish command headquarters, sparking a temporary panic in the city.

03 THE PANZERS ARRIVE
On 7 September, German tanks arrive on the southwestern outskirts of the city. The following day they push into the suburbs at Ochota, but are repulsed by anti-tank and artillery fire. The panzers are then withdrawn to help deal with a Polish counterattack.

01 THE LUFTWAFFE STRIKES
On the first day of the war, the Luftwaffe bombs Warsaw, but determined defense from the two squadrons of the Polish 'Pursuit Brigade' (which shot down 42 German planes in the first six days of the war), along with bad weather, limits the effectiveness of these initial air raids.

FORT SZCZESLIWICKI

E
N
S
W

BATTLE OF THE ATLANTIC

Discover the key role played by the US in the
longest campaign of World War II

WORDS SCOTT REEVES

Below: *The 1,301 survivors of the Athenia sinking were taken to Galway Harbor*

THE BATTLE BEGINS

3 SEPTEMBER 1939

Just hours after Neville Chamberlain told the British people they were at war with Germany, the first shots of the conflict were fired. Those on board the passenger liner SS Athenia were unaware it was being tracked by the German submarine U-30. Two torpedoes were fired when the liner was 200 miles off the northwest coast of Ireland, causing it to sink in 14 hours with the loss of 117 lives, including 28 Americans.

The targeting of the Athenia indicated Germany was adopting a policy of unrestricted submarine warfare. According to the accepted rules of war, the U-boat commander should have searched the liner and only captured or sunk it if it was engaged in military activity or refused to stop. The Battle of the Atlantic had begun in a particularly cruel manner.

A U-boat shells an unknown merchant vessel in the Atlantic – action like this served to increase hostility to the Nazis in America

OCCUPATION OF GREENLAND

9 APRIL 1941

President Roosevelt created the protectorate of Greenland to ensure that the US neutrality zone in the western Atlantic remained intact.

BISMARCK SUNK

27 MAY 1941

Just days after it had destroyed HMS Hood and damaged HMS Prince of Wales, Bismarck, one of the largest battleships ever built by Germany, was sunk.

THE BATTLE IS NAMED

30 SEPTEMBER 1940

In Missouri's *St Joseph News-Press*, journalist Ernest Lindley became one of the first to refer to "the Battle of the Atlantic".

MERCHANT SHIPS TARGETED

21 MAY 1941

SS Robin Moor, an American merchant ship, was carrying general cargo when it was stopped by the German submarine U-69 750 miles west of Sierra Leone. Despite flying a neutral flag, the 46 crew and passengers were given 30 minutes to board the lifeboats. Once they were safely in the water, the submarine fired a torpedo at Robin Moor's rudder and shelled the bridge. The lifeboats were abandoned by the submarine with only four loaves of bread and two tins of butter to sustain them until their rescue, days later.

American merchantmen now feared an unprovoked raid from beneath the waves. Hitler feared that the actions of his U-boat commander might provoke the US into war and ordered similar attacks to cease, but it was too late to prevent the growth of anti-German feeling in the US.

THE SINKING OF USS REUBEN JAMES

31 OCTOBER 1941

President Roosevelt had tried to ensure US neutrality through the creation of the Pan-American Security Zone, a region of the western Atlantic in which acts of war would not be tolerated. To enforce the zone, the US military conducted sea and air patrols. Stretching the definition of 'neutral' to the limit, from 1941 US Navy ships escorted Allied convoys across the Security Zone to ensure no belligerent acts took place in it.

On Halloween 1941, US destroyer Reuben James was on convoy escort duty when it was struck by a torpedo fired by U-552. An explosion in the forward magazine ripped apart the bow and the ship sank immediately with the loss of 115 of the 160-man crew. The sinking of the first US Navy ship, before the nation had officially joined the war, further increased tensions between Germany and the US.

OPERATION DRUMBEAT

13 JANUARY 1942

The first U-boats reached US waters in Operation Drumbeat, a patrol targeting Allied shipping off the North American coast.

The torpedo that sank Reuben James was probably intended to strike one of the merchant ships it was escorting

Dixie Arrow, one of many American tankers lost off the East Coast in 1942

DECLARATION OF WAR

11 DECEMBER 1941

The US and Germany declared war on each other, officially making America a combatant in the Battle of the Atlantic.

SECOND HAPPY TIME

6 FEBRUARY 1942

In just 24 days, the five U-boat commanders involved in Operation Drumbeat sank 156,939 tons of shipping off the North American coast without a single submarine loss. They encountered large numbers of unescorted ships with their lights on and crews chatting over the radio. Coastal towns were reluctant to impose blackouts because it was bad for tourism and navigational beacons remained on. No wonder the submariners referred to this period as the Second Happy Time.

The Type IX U-boats who patrolled the American coast returned to base in early February and exclaimed how easy their successes had been. Wave after wave of new Type IX submarines followed until US defenses improved with the introduction of destroyers and naval convoys.

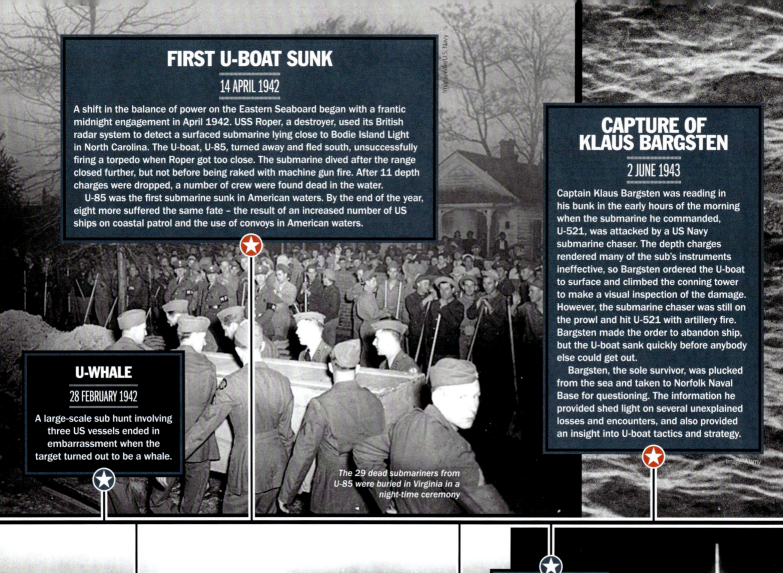

FIRST U-BOAT SUNK
14 APRIL 1942

A shift in the balance of power on the Eastern Seaboard began with a frantic midnight engagement in April 1942. USS Roper, a destroyer, used its British radar system to detect a surfaced submarine lying close to Bodie Island Light in North Carolina. The U-boat, U-85, turned away and fled south, unsuccessfully firing a torpedo when Roper got too close. The submarine dived after the range closed further, but not before being raked with machine gun fire. After 11 depth charges were dropped, a number of crew were found dead in the water.

U-85 was the first submarine sunk in American waters. By the end of the year, eight more suffered the same fate – the result of an increased number of US ships on coastal patrol and the use of convoys in American waters.

CAPTURE OF KLAUS BARGSTEN
2 JUNE 1943

Captain Klaus Bargsten was reading in his bunk in the early hours of the morning when the submarine he commanded, U-521, was attacked by a US Navy submarine chaser. The depth charges rendered many of the sub's instruments ineffective, so Bargsten ordered the U-boat to surface and climbed the conning tower to make a visual inspection of the damage. However, the submarine chaser was still on the prowl and hit U-521 with artillery fire. Bargsten made the order to abandon ship, but the U-boat sank quickly before anybody else could get out.

Bargsten, the sole survivor, was plucked from the sea and taken to Norfolk Naval Base for questioning. The information he provided shed light on several unexplained losses and encounters, and also provided an insight into U-boat tactics and strategy.

U-WHALE
28 FEBRUARY 1942

A large-scale sub hunt involving three US vessels ended in embarrassment when the target turned out to be a whale.

The 29 dead submariners from U-85 were buried in Virginia in a night-time ceremony

U-848 attempts – ultimately without success – to escape US Navy Liberator from which this photograph was taken

BLACK MAY
24 MAY 1943

The U-boat campaign was temporarily halted after one-quarter of operational submarines were sunk in the month of May.

BX AND XB CONVOYS
20 MARCH 1942

A new system of convoys is initiated between Boston and Halifax to counter the U-boat threat along North America's East Coast.

Image: Alamy

THE MID-ATLANTIC GAP CLOSES
18 MARCH 1943

The battle reached a turning point in the spring of 1943 as U-boat losses increased while their tallies of victims decreased. Part of the reason submarines became less effective was the closing of the mid-Atlantic gap, a strip of ocean previously unreachable by aircraft, leaving convoys more vulnerable to underwater wolfpacks.

In the middle of March, President Roosevelt issued the second of only two direct orders during the war (the first was to give Operation Torch precedence over other campaigns). Roosevelt ordered his chief of naval operations to transfer 60 B-24 Liberators from the Pacific to the Atlantic. These aircraft were stripped of armor to give them a longer range and were able to attack surfaced submarines. The 'Black Pit' of the mid-Atlantic was no longer quite so dangerous.

Captured submariners like this one from April 1943 were a rare source of intelligence – two-thirds of U-boats sunk that year left no survivors

SURRENDER OF GERMANY

8 MAY 1945

The German admission of defeat brought to an official end the longest continuous campaign of World War II.

CONVOY HX 300 ARRIVES SAFELY

3 AUGUST 1944

On 17 July, 102 merchant ships – 76 of which flew an American flag – set sail from New York with a naval escort. Over the next three days they met up with merchant ships sailing from Canada, creating the largest convoy of the war. During the tense crossing of the Atlantic, all eyes were on the water, keeping a watch for prowling U-boat wolfpacks. However, three weeks later, every ship had docked without a single submarine attack having occurred.

The vast majority of the American vessels were Liberty ships, a low-cost, mass-produced cargo ship churned out in great number by American shipyards during the war. American industry was able to vastly exceed the losses suffered at the hands of the U-boats – in total, 2,710 Liberty ships totaling 38.5 million tons were constructed during the war.

Convoys offered greater protection than single ships; the numbers in them grew as the war progressed

CAPTURE OF U-505

4 JUNE 1944

U-505 was captured by the US Navy – the code books and machines on board helped the Allies crack the Enigma code.

PAUL HAMILTON SINKS

20 APRIL 1944

The German threat in the Battle of the Atlantic was not confined to submarine warfare. One of the most deadly attacks occurred when Paul Hamilton, a Liberty ship transporting troops and high explosives, was attacked by Luftwaffe bombers.

The flight of 23 Junkers Ju 88 that sank Paul Hamilton sighted the ship – voyaging from Hampton Roads to Gibraltar – when it was 30 miles off the coast of Algeria. Being a veteran of four previous convoys meant nothing when the bombers dived low and fast to avoid anti-aircraft fire. A successful torpedo strike ignited the high explosives on board, causing a massive explosion. When the smoke cleared, no trace of the ship remained.

Image: Wiki/US Coast Guard photo

D-DAY

6 JUNE 1944

The heavily defended U-boat bases in France were bypassed by the Allied liberators as they were not considered targets of strategic value.

Image: Wiki/US Coast Guard Photo No. NRL(MOD) 29402

LAST ACTION IN AMERICAN WATERS

6 MAY 1945

By the last months of the war, submarine attacks had reduced to little more than inconveniences. On 5 May, the final American merchant ship was sunk in the war when U-853, lying in wait off Point Judith, Rhode Island, fired on the coal ship Black Point. The attack led to an overnight search and destroy mission in which a US destroyer, two destroyer escorts, and a frigate dropped over 100 depth charges. Aerial support came in the guise of two airships the following morning.

When planking, life rafts, clothing, and an officer's cap floated to the surface, the destruction of the U-boat was confirmed with the loss of all 55 men on board. The same morning, U-881 was destroyed by depth charges dropped from USS Farquar off the coast of Newfoundland. The U-boat threat was finally over.

Depth charges explode in the hunt for U-853 off Rhode Island

580 were killed when the Paul Hamilton was destroyed, making it one of the costliest Liberty ship losses of the war

THE FALL OF FRANCE

10 MAY – 25 JUNE 1940

Poland had fallen quickly, but everyone expected France to put
up stiffer resistance – until the Germans attacked

WORDS DAVID SMITH

*German troops march towards the
Arc de Triomphe following the Nazi
occupation of France in 1940*

The style of warfare unleashed by Nazi Germany at the start of World War II was not new. The shocking demolition of Poland's armed forces had been breathtaking and bold, but it followed long-established German strategic principles.

Germany could not afford to engage in protracted wars of attrition. World War I had proved what the outcome of such a conflict was likely to be. The nation did not have the natural resources required for a war effort lasting years, while its limited coastline made blockades easy to enforce. Germany had always needed to seek a quick knock-out blow, and the plans for World War I had conformed to that need, before it had become bogged down in static trench warfare.

Nevertheless, the world saw Germany's tactics as something new, and would christen it blitzkrieg – 'lightning war'.

Following the fall of Poland, Europe braced itself for the next blow. When it came, it would be on a scale unseen before. What was most remarkable,

however, was not the methods employed by the Germans, but the sheer audacity of a small group of commanders. Men like Heinz Guderian simply ignored the misgivings (and sometimes the direct orders) of their superiors.

The German Army as a whole had no faith in or understanding of the tactics championed by Guderian. Repeatedly, the commanders of Germany's massive army groups would caution against advancing too quickly or stretching lines of communication too thinly. Men like Gerd von Rundstedt, commander of Army Group A, were not disciples of blitzkrieg, and were openly hostile to the plans put forward by Guderian. Their misgivings seem misplaced in hindsight, but at the time there were solid reasons for their doubts.

The plan to smash the Allies in the opening phases of the invasion of France was breathtaking in its scale. An entire army group, Army Group B, was to be used as a diversion, attacking through northern Belgium and the Netherlands and drawing the

Heinz Guderian, the Germans' visionary proponent of blitzkrieg

Allies northwards to meet them. Meanwhile, Army Group A would move through the Ardennes into Belgium and Luxembourg.

There were reasons why the Allies were likely to fall for this ruse. Firstly, an attack through northern Belgium was anticipated. Secondly, the Germans would devote much of their air power to the feint, to both destroy Allied air forces and reinforce the deception. Thirdly, the Ardennes were believed to be impassable to large armored formations.

On the march

The German troops that opened the German campaign, Case Yellow, on 10 May 1940, were not the unstoppable war machine of common perception. Only ten of the 135 divisions allocated to the offensive were mechanized. The vast bulk of the men were plodding infantry, marching on foot or on horse-drawn carts.

Where Guderian's plan excelled was in its concentration of force. The cutting edge of the newly formed armored divisions were the panzers, but they required infantry support. Rather than allowing the infantry to slow his tanks down, Guderian mounted them in vehicles of their own, so the entire division could move at high speed. There were limited resources, ten armored divisions would make up the spearhead of Army Group A for the thrust through the Ardennes, with a corps commanded by Guderian himself, comprising three panzer divisions, the tip of the spearhead.

Superb communications would be key (German tanks were equipped with excellent radio systems), as would the initiative-allowed junior commanders. Rather than sticking to rigid orders, they would be free to think on their feet and react to developments.

Speed of movement would be the Germans' secret weapon. Army Group A planned to cover the 100 miles from Germany's border to the banks of the Meuse River in just three days. It was scheduled to cross the next day and then keep moving, pushing all the way to the English Channel.

Senior army commanders either smirked at the ambition of such a plan, or expressed genuine concern, but Guderian had the utmost faith in his own tactics. Reserve panzer crews were carried on vehicles to make sure the tanks did not need to stop. Refueling depots were set up along the route of march and supplies were carried by the vehicles themselves. Amphetamines were liberally supplied to the men who would be expected to remain awake and able to fight for three consecutive nights after crossing the Meuse.

The Allies were well equipped, in terms of men and materiel, to counter the German offensive. There were less than 2,500 tanks in the German armies, while the Allies had over 4,000. Importantly, the Allied tanks were often superior in terms of armor and weaponry.

Air power was fairly equal. The Luftwaffe had 2,500 planes available at the opening of the campaign. The French had 900 and the British added 500, in addition to the air forces of Belgium and the Netherlands.

Where the Germans held the advantage was in choosing their point of attack. With the Allies dispersed to guard against many different scenarios, there was a window of opportunity. If the German advance stalled for any reason, the ponderous Allied armies could converge and stop it in its tracks.

Air strikes began on the morning of 10 May. Equally matched in the air, the Germans concentrated on destroying Allied planes on the ground, wiping out the bulk of the Dutch Air Force in this manner. By 13 May, the Germans had reached the coast of the Netherlands.

A German landing force prepares to cross the River Meuse on 26 May

Images: Getty

DELIVERANCE AT DUNKIRK

The war had opened in shocking fashion, but Dunkirk allowed the British to fight another day

Dunkirk is hailed as a triumph, but although rescuing nearly a quarter of a million men from death or capture was a major feat, the BEF had suffered an extraordinary defeat at the hands of the Germans.

Relatively small, it was nevertheless an extremely modern army, equipped as well as the Germans. All that changed when the soldiers were evacuated. Left behind were 66,426 men, 25,000 of whom were dead or wounded. Fewer than 5,000 of the nearly 67,000 vehicles taken to the continent with the BEF made the return journey. Artillery was a similarly disastrous story, with 2,472 of the 2,794 guns of the BEF abandoned. As an invasion of Britain loomed, there were 54 anti-tank guns left in the entire country.

The Royal Navy lost six destroyers during the evacuation, and 19 more were damaged. More than 400 fighters had been downed, among total losses of around 1,000 planes.

Despite this, there was a feeling of huge relief that most of the men had been brought home. The prime minister recognized this relief, but was cautious not to overstate it.

"We must be very careful," Winston Churchill warned, "not to assign to this deliverance the attributes of a victory. Wars are not won by evacuations. But there was a victory inside this deliverance, which should be noted."

The RAF had just 524 fighters available in June 1940. These few planes would bear the brunt of the next phase of the war.

British soldiers on board a ship during the evacuation of Dunkirk

The bulk of Germany's invasion force marched on foot or under horsepower

Race to the coast

To the south, the move through the Ardennes had become a near farcical mess as divisions crossed each other and got caught in a 170-mile traffic jam. Critically, enough of the armored divisions had got through to reach the Meuse and make a crossing ahead of schedule. Guderian now pushed on, flogging his men and machines in a race to the coast. It was risky in the extreme, as he was moving past the bulk of the French Army and was highly vulnerable to a flank attack, but the French moved with agonizing slowness. Where they did get close enough to engage the Germans, they were badly mauled. The French 1st Armored Division, with 170 tanks, found itself reduced to just 36 tanks in one day of fighting. Although the French often had superior machines, the Germans integrated their anti-tank guns far more effectively with their panzers, effectively running circles around the French, isolating their tanks and destroying them in huge numbers.

Total disaster soon faced the British Expeditionary Force, enclosed in a shrinking pocket around the port of Dunkirk. Tens of thousands of French soldiers were trapped as well, but now the German high command betrayed Guderian and his exhausted men.

"AIR STRIKES BEGAN ON THE MORNING OF 10 MAY. EQUALLY MATCHED IN THE AIR, THE GERMANS CONCENTRATED ON DESTROYING ALLIED PLANES ON THE GROUND"

Hitler's infamous 'Halt Order', delivered on 24 May, forced the panzers to stop. Guderian could ignore the orders of his commanding general, but not the Führer himself. A mistaken belief that the terrain around Dunkirk was unsuitable for tanks, and the boasts of Hermann Göring that he could finish off the Allies at Dunkirk with his Luftwaffe, persuaded Hitler to call off the tanks. The British were able to evacuate the bulk of their men, as well as 122,000 French soldiers, but the Battle of France was far from over.

There were still thousands of British troops in France, as well as a significant air force, and a new defensive line was established, this time running along the Somme and Aisne rivers. Almost incredibly, Britain sent more troops back over to France just days after plucking men from Dunkirk. Almost all of the rescued French were also repatriated. But France was a spent force. Germany switched to Case Red, which

planned for the complete destruction of France's armed forces, but the job was already mostly done. Having lost more than a million men, dead, wounded or taken prisoner, France was staggering, with just 64 divisions left to face the German invaders. Many of the units were also in a terrible state as far as morale was concerned.

Two days after the Germans occupied Paris, on 14 June, Britain staged a second major evacuation, lifting 124,000 men from France. A desperate plan to merge Britain and France as a single united country to continue the fight came to nothing, and France signed an armistice with Germany on 22 June.

The fall of France had happened more quickly than anyone had dreamed possible. Anyone, that is, except the visionary commanders like Guderian, who had proved that blitzkrieg could bring a major power to its knees in a matter of weeks.

French colonial troops surrender to German soldiers

The British Expeditionary Force was small at the start of the campaign but well equipped

Supermarine Spitfires, the most famous RAF planes of the entire war, bask in the sun's rays

BATTLE OF BRITAIN

JULY – OCTOBER 1940

Following the fall of France, Germany set its sights on Britain, and only the men of the Royal Air Force stood in the way

WORDS DAVID SMITH

Few battles have names that resonate as much as that attached to the fighting over the skies of Britain at the end of 1940. At the time, the public viewed the actions of the Royal Air Force both as a stirring testament to the grit of the nation, and as a last stand against the might of Nazi Germany.

The fighting between Messerschmitt and Spitfire, and between Hurricane and Heinkel, did not take place in a vacuum. Both the Germans and British knew that it was just the preliminary stage of the planned invasion of England. If the RAF cracked, Britain faced the same fate as Poland, Belgium, the Netherlands, and France. A few hundred fighter planes were all that held the German war machine at bay across the Channel.

Despite its importance, the dates encompassing the Battle of Britain are difficult to pin down. Debate continues over when it started and when it finished. This is partly because it blew up and then petered out like a storm, with the most intense and recognizable action taking place through August, September and October of 1940. But Germany's air campaign had started before then, and would continue afterwards.

Further confusion is added by the shifting nature of the campaign. As the Germans looked for a weak spot, they continually changed their emphasis, giving the battle several distinct phases. Battle of Britain Day is commemorated on 15 September, but settling on a definitive start and end date is all but impossible.

In July, Hitler was still hoping that Britain would come to the negotiating table and thrash out the terms for peace. RAF planes were bombing Germany in a disjointed and haphazard manner (41 missions were mounted in July), but the period was mostly devoted to recovery. Following its exertions in the Battle of France and the retreat from Dunkirk, Fighter Command was gathering itself for the next test. This was expected to come in August.

For the campaign, the Luftwaffe amassed 3,358 planes, with more than a thousand of them fighters. The RAF could counter with similar numbers, but the Germans

A Spitfire pilot after returning from a sortie

had a slight edge in ready-to-fly fighter planes, with 805 compared to the RAF's 715. The resonant phrase 'the few' could fairly be attributed to both sides.

Taking to the skies

German plans anticipated that the campaign proper would start on 13 August. Hermann Göring spoke of the 'attack of the Eagles' in ominous tones, but missions had actually started the previous month, and 10 July is often put forward as the real start of the battle. It was an uncertain and tentative start. The Luftwaffe took time to feel out Britain's defenses, launching exploratory raids on the coast in daylight and venturing further inland under cover of darkness.

The Germans undoubtedly gathered useful intelligence from this opening phase of the battle, but the RAF arguably learned more. Most importantly, British pilots discovered that their doctrine of flying in threes was too rigid when pitted against the loose, two-plane formations of the Germans. Luftwaffe pilots hunted in pairs, with one plane hanging back and covering its partner. The RAF pilots quickly adjusted.

In turn, the Germans learned that their flight formations were faulty. The bombers initially went in with a fighter umbrella above and behind them. This created the opportunity for the bombers to be mauled before the German fighters closed in, so they eventually drew closer to their bombers, until they actually flew in front and on the flanks of their formations. These were just the first of many moves and counter-moves that would punctuate the battle.

"A GERMAN PILOT SHOT DOWN OVER BRITAIN WOULD EITHER DIE OR SPEND THE REST OF THE WAR IN A POW CAMP, WHILE AN RAF PILOT HAD A CHANCE OF BEING BACK IN A PLANE THE NEXT DAY"

In August, the Luftwaffe was tasked with degrading Fighter Command's combat ability by concentrating attacks on its bases, rather than on the planes in the air. It was a potentially devastating tactic, but one that was swiftly countered by the RAF. Bad weather prevented the wholesale implementation of the initiative until 18 August, but 12 August to 6 September saw some of the most intense fighting of the battle. A total of 32 raids were mounted against Fighter Command bases during that period.

The results were surprising. Only 56 British fighters were destroyed on the ground. Initial successes quickly prompted the RAF to disperse their planes, adopt improved camouflage techniques and even house planes at remote airfields. A significant portion of the available fighter strength was also dedicated to protecting the bases, with patrols mounted to limit the possibility of surprise attacks (the planes of 10 and 12 Groups were held back to guard the airfields, while those of 11 Group tackled the raiders).

Importantly, the Germans believed their attacks had been far more effective than they actually had. With an invasion date of 15 September in mind, they congratulated themselves on putting eight Fighter Command bases out of action. In reality, although several bases were damaged and forced to cease operations for short periods, none were permanently knocked out.

Overestimating their successes perhaps led the Germans to persevere with a failing tactic for too long. By September, they believed they had whittled British fighter numbers down to just 100. In truth, there were 701 fighters available on 1 September, and this number was steadily rising. It reached 738 on the 6th of that month.

The numbers game

In reality, neither side found it possible to accurately track enemy losses, but British overestimations were a boost to morale, while German errors obscured the futility of their methods. In fact, it was a remarkably even contest, and both sides were finding themselves worn down by the ceaseless fighting. RAF fighter numbers may have been rising, but that was only because production of new planes was holding at an impressive level. New pilots were also funneled into the maelstrom at the rate of more than 300 per month.

A view from the
nose of a Heinkel
He 111 bomber
during the battle

By the end of August, it was German pilots who were showing signs of 'nervous exhaustion'. Their losses were also harder to make good. A German pilot shot down over Britain would either die or spend the rest of the war in a POW camp, while an RAF pilot had a fighting chance of being back in a plane the next day. This reality led to the practice of German pilots machine-gunning their RAF counterparts as they parachuted down to earth. Though an unpleasant facet of the battle, both sides agreed that it was acceptable under the rules of war.

Much has been written on the superiority of British planes to those employed by the Germans. An early casualty of the battle had been the fearsome Stuka. A propagandist's dream, the screaming divebomber had been the scourge of continental Europe, but was unsuited to tackling RAF fighters. Devastating losses saw it pulled out of the fray in August.

Elsewhere, things weren't so clear-cut. The Spitfire was certainly an exceptional aircraft,

but during these early stages of the war it had its weaknesses. Most obvious was its reliance on .303 machine guns. Packing four in each wing sounds formidable, but such small bullets often had little effect on a target, especially if fired from long range. To make matters worse, a Spitfire only carried enough for around 15 seconds of firing.

The Messerschmitt Bf 109, by comparison, had a pair of 20mm cannons, as well as machine guns, and carried significantly more ammunition. It was also the superior flying machine at high altitudes. The result was that the RAF lost a higher number of fighters than the Luftwaffe, but the Germans also suffered crippling bomber losses. From the 7th to the 15th September, the Luftwaffe lost almost 300 aircraft. Less than 100 of those were fighters, while the RAF lost 120 fighter planes.

The Blitz

By this point, the battle had entered another new phase. On 4 September, Hitler ordered

Hermann Göring, the most senior soldier in Germany, promised Adolf Hitler that his planes could batter the RAF into submission

45

Luftwaffe attacks to focus on British cities. This was not a concerted terror campaign. Targets were limited to legitimate industrial and military installations, but accuracy was impossible with the technology of the day. Damage to civilian buildings was inevitable, and the death toll among the British population began to climb.

On 15 September, the Luftwaffe mounted a massive raid, with 200 bombers and an armada of fighter escorts. The RAF claimed to have shot down 185 aircraft – a wildly optimistic number that may simply have been made up for propaganda purposes. In fact, 60 German planes were lost (34 bombers and 26 fighters), but even this lower level of attrition was unsustainable. The German high command took the only option now available: it switched to night-time raids.

As the Battle of Britain merged with the Blitz, the greatest weakness of the Luftwaffe became apparent. The lack of a heavy bomber was critical. Germany's medium bombers lacked the hitting power of the monsters the Allies would unleash over German cities later in the war. Despite this, German losses dropped as their formations now had to compete with less impressive British night-fighters, including the Bristol Blenheim, the Boulton-Paul Defiant and the Bristol Beaufighter.

By this point, however, the Battle of Britain had been won and lost. German invasion plans were shelved, never to be realized. The exact end of the battle is as debated as the exact start, but with the invasion called off, the ultimate goal of Nazi Germany had been denied.

Losses had been astonishingly even, with the RAF losing over 1,700 planes and the Luftwaffe more than 1,900. The Blitz would see tens of thousands of civilians die, but Hitler would become distracted by his plans to invade the Soviet Union. His great effort to crack the British and knock them out of the war had failed.

"GERMANY'S MEDIUM BOMBERS LACKED THE HITTING POWER OF THE MONSTERS THE ALLIES WOULD UNLEASH OVER GERMAN CITIES"

Image: Getty

THE WONDERFUL MADMEN

RAF pilots hailed from all corners of the globe, but one nation made a special contribution

The RAF was desperately short of fighter pilots as the Battle of Britain opened. No fewer than 284 pilots had been lost in France, but help was at hand from a variety of sources. Canadians, New Zealanders and Czechs, among many other nations, played their part, but no country was more important than Poland.

Originally dispersed among mixed squadrons, Polish fighter pilots were soon organized into four dedicated units. The men of 303 Squadron would emerge as an elite force, described as "wonderful madmen" by one impressed observer.

Having been trained to fly Hurricanes, 303 Squadron entered the fray on 31 August, claiming six kills on its first day of action. On 5 September, the nine Hurricanes the squadron was able to put in the air shot down eight German planes for the loss of just one. Out of 37 Polish pilots who fought with the squadron (there were two British, one Canadian, one Slovak and one Czech pilot as well), nine lost their lives in six weeks of fighting during the Battle of Britain. They shot down 126 German planes, the highest number achieved by any squadron in the RAF during the battle.

BATTLE OF CRETE

20 MAY – 1 JUNE 1941

The Germans launched the first ever mass airborne invasion
in history to seize the island from Greek, British and
Commonwealth forces

WORDS JONATHAN TRIGG

ixty-two miles from the mainland, Crete is the second-largest of the Greek islands, a strip of land measuring 160 miles from east to west and just 7.5 miles at its narrowest. Dominated by the White Mountains that form its spine, it has a rich history of invasion and occupation, with the Romans, Arabs and Venetians among others all having left their mark, especially on the likes of Khania, Rhethymnon and Heraklion on its more populated northern coast. Historically fought over, it had been a relative backwater for years until WWII erupted and thrust it center stage in the spring of 1941.

The Mediterranean war

Fascist Italy took the lead for the Axis in the Mediterranean, its military weakness exposed by the December 1940 British offensive in the western desert that almost wiped out Mussolini's forces in North Africa and saw more than 130,000 dispirited Italians shuffle into captivity. However, with total victory within its grasp, British Middle Eastern Command was ordered by London to send its best troops to Greece, where an earlier failed Italian invasion had forced Hitler's hand. There, on the morning of Sunday 6 April 1941, Generalfeldmarschall Wilhelm List's 12th Army crossed the Greek frontier and proceeded to drive the British into a hasty retreat that ended just over three weeks later with the evacuation of the British force back to Egypt.

Not all, however, arrived in Alexandria – some were dropped off in Crete instead. There, they joined the existing garrison and provided a much-needed reinforcement in numbers, but not much else, the defeat in Greece having cost the already miserly equipped British and Commonwealth forces 8,000 vehicles, 233 guns, 104 tanks and most of the rest of their heavy equipment. Most disastrous of all, the Royal Air Force had lost 209 irreplaceable aircraft in the skies above Greece, meaning it had barely a handful of modern fighters and bombers to support the ground troops and Royal Navy.

Imperial Lion vs Nazi Eagle

Nevertheless, the British Prime Minister Winston Churchill thought he had an answer – General Sir Bernard Freyberg VC. Freyberg was a living legend. A New Zealander nicknamed the 'Salamander' by Churchill for his determination to be in the heat of the action, he had won a Victoria Cross in World War I and commanded the 2nd New Zealand Division in the Greek campaign. Courageous, honorable and tough, he was also prone to

General Kurt Student thought the attack on Crete would be a walkover – he was wrong

Allied soldiers surrender after their position was overrun

mood swings and trapped in a World War I mentality that led him to believe the threat to Crete would be from a seaborne invasion.

His opponents would be Kurt Student and Julius Ringel. The latter a bearded Austrian and fervent Nazi, whose 5th Gebirgsjäger (mountain) Division was a late addition to a plan wholly of the making of his ambitious fellow general, Student. Operation Mercury – as the invasion of Crete was coined – was Student's dream, the zenith of his belief in the ability of airborne forces to achieve victory through mass air and glider drops. Having only been formed in the late 1930s, Nazi Germany's fallschirmjägers (paratroopers) had achieved glory by carrying out a series of daring attacks during 1940-41, including the capture of Europe's strongest fort – Belgium's Eben-Emael – by a handful of glider-borne troops. Now, a year later, he was determined to show the world what his paras could do.

Briefed to his commanders in a second-floor suite of Athens' Hotel Grande Bretagne, Student's Mercury was a colossus. Split into three groups, the nearly 11,000 men of 7th

Flieger Division would land and seize Khania, the nearby airfield at Maleme, and then Rhethymnon and Heraklion further along the coast. They would be reinforced by Ringel's mountain troopers, who would both fly into captured air strips and be ferried in by sea. Student's intelligence head, Major Reinhardt, assured the assembled group that there were only around 5,000 defenders and the Cretans themselves would welcome the invaders – it would be a walkover. He would be wrong on all counts.

20 May: invasion day

Well before dawn thousands of paratroopers heard the command: "To the aircraft, march!" Each man held the metal clip end of the long static cord in his mouth, leaving his hands free to pull himself up into the belly of the aircraft. Then, he fastened the clip onto the jump-wire running at head-height inside the plane. Each then took their seat, armed only with a pistol, all their other weapons and equipment packed into the four containers already loaded into the bomb bay. The containers would be dropped with them, but until they reached them the paras would be virtually defenseless.

The Luftwaffe had concentrated the bulk of its transport fleet of Ju 52s – Auntie Jus as they were nicknamed – and as the 500 aircraft headed south the sky brightened, promising a hot sunny day. Just after 0800hrs, as the Allied garrison stirred, Major Humphrey Dyer of the New Zealand Maori Battalion heard "a continuous, low roar. Above the horizon there appeared a long black line as if a flock of migrating birds… We looked, spellbound." On board the armada the bulkhead lights were red – two minutes to go – then they changed to green.

BRITISH, ALLIED & COMMONWEALTH FORCES

BERNARD FREYBERG

Commander of the New Zealand Expeditionary Force in the Battle of Crete, Freyberg had been the youngest general in the British Army when he served during the First World War. Freyberg bounced back from defeat in Crete with successful campaigns in the North African theater, including at the Second Battle of El Alamein.

ANDREW CUNNINGHAM

As Commander-in-Chief of the Mediterranean fleet Cunningham was in charge of several key naval battles during World War II and protecting supply lines in the region. He was made First Sea Lord in 1943, a role he held until his retirement in 1946. He was also Lord High Steward for the coronation of Elizabeth II.

GERMAN AND AXIS FORCES

KURT STUDENT

The German Luftwaffe general was a pioneer of the use of airborne forces and was in charge of developing the Nazis' elite paratrooper force, which played a key role in the Battle of Crete in 1941. After the war, Student was put on trial and convicted for committing war crimes for how his men mistreated and murdered Crete prisoners of war.

WALTER KOCH

Koch was the commander of the German paratrooper branch, called the Fallschirmjäger, and led the first wave at the Battle of Crete. However, he publicly opposed Hitler's Commando Order (that insisted Allied commandos be killed without trial even if in uniform or surrendering) and died in Berlin shortly afterwards in an automobile collision.

FRANCESCO MIMBELLI

The Italian naval commander was in charge of the torpedo boat Lupo that successfully defended most of a convoy of German troops against seven British ships. He was later given command of Italy's Black Sea forces and after the war was promoted to rear admiral and commander of the Italian Naval Academy, finally retiring in 1964.

What followed was a slaughter. The slow transports made perfect targets, with the aircraft riddled by fire and dozens of paratroopers dying before even jumping. Those that did manage to jump were shot at as they floated down, unable to steer themselves due to the design of their parachutes. Many that did reach the ground were killed before they could arm themselves. The 750 Germans in gliders were supposedly better off than their aircraft-borne comrades as they were fully armed and so could fight from the moment they touched down, but their wood and fabric gliders drew horrendous fire.

Large as the air armada was, it still wasn't enough to take in all the paratroopers in one wave, so that afternoon a second assault went in, to the east. They met the same fate. By now alerted to what was coming, the Allied defenders mauled the slow-flying transports.

In the balance

Miraculously, some fallschirmjägers survived the carnage and began to fight back. In isolated groups they took cover wherever they could and fought it out with Freyberg's men and Cretan civilians, who, far from welcoming them, were determined to wipe them out.

Heartened by reports from across the island, Freyberg signaled Middle East Command that, although a hard day, his men had seen off the German threat. But a lack of effective communications and an inability to understand the type of battle that he was actually fighting blinded him to the reality that it was far from over, and in fact was being decided at the far west of his line at Maleme. Maleme's airstrip was the Germans' main objective that first day of the invasion. Take it and they would be able to fly in the reinforcements and materiel that would win them the battle. Student knew this implicitly and threw everything he had at it.

The key to Maleme was Hill 107, a feature rising up to the west that dominated the area. Held by a single battalion, the 22nd New Zealand, it came under sustained attack from the start. Eugen Meindl – the senior German officer in the landings – gathered up every paratrooper, gun and mortar he could find and desperately tried to take it. Under immense pressure, and in a welter of poor communication and misunderstanding, the New Zealanders' commanding officer – the VC-holder Leslie Andrew – withdrew off the hill that night, and with it the battle was lost. Counterattacks to retake it were later launched but not followed through – one supported by two Matilda tanks failed when one of the tanks broke down and the other's turret mechanism jammed at the same time as the crew realized

Heraklion

BATTLE OF CRETE
20 MAY – 1 JUNE 1941

01 GRUPPE WEST ATTACKS MALEME
Split into three, Gruppe West is the largest of the fallschirmjäger assaults and is led by the most senior German officer involved in the landings, Generalmajor Eugen Meindl. Casualties are catastrophic, with one battalion of 600 men losing 400 killed during the landings.

02 GRUPPE MITTE (CENTER) ATTACKS RHETHYMNON
Landing in the first wave on the morning of 20 May, Gruppe Mitte is leaderless from the start of the battle when its commander – Wilhelm Süssmann – is killed along with his staff when their glider crashes onto the island of Aegina on the way to Crete.

03 GRUPPE OST (EAST) ATTACKS HERAKLION
Scattered on landing, Gruppe Ost's commander – Oberst (Colonel) Bruno Bräuer – gathers as many men as he can and tries to capture the city, only to be beaten back by the Highlanders of 2nd Battalion Black Watch.

STRENGTHS 20 MAY

British Commonwealth Troops

NZ Division 7702
Australian...................6540
Royal Marines...........1941
British Army............15063*
                 31246

Greek Troops 10258

*MNBDO: Mobile Naval Base Defense Organization

German Parachute & Mountain Troops

Parachute 10100
Glider........................... 750
Seaborne 7000*
By Air Transport........5000
                22850

*Failed to arrive

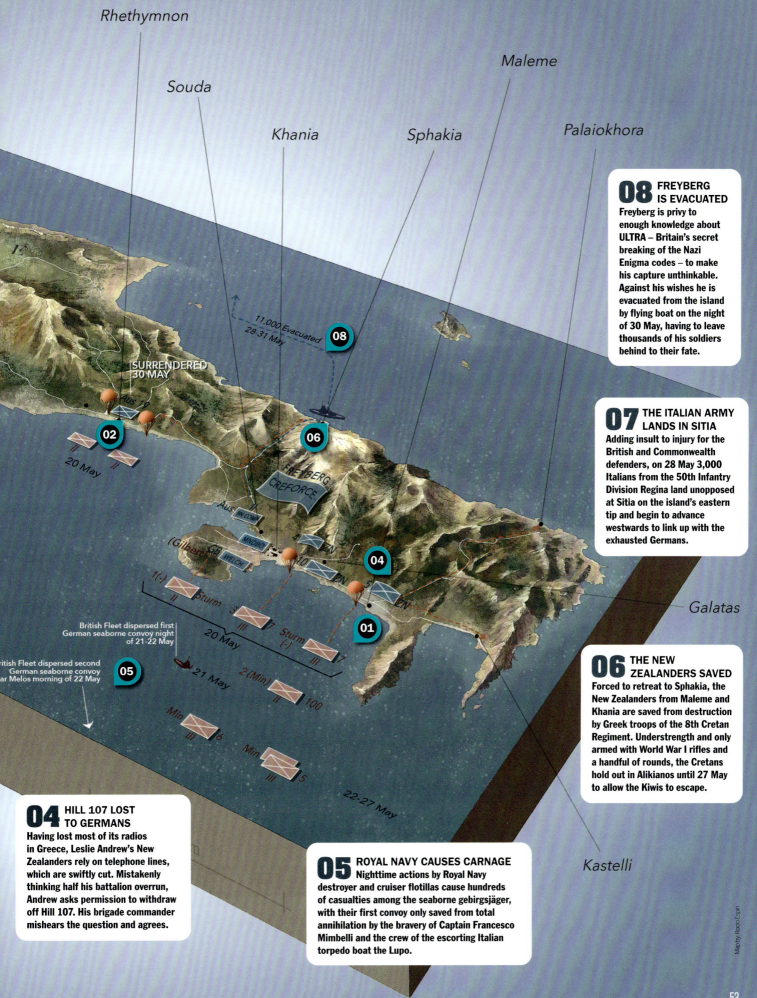

Rhethymnon

Souda

Khania

Sphakia

Maleme

Palaiokhora

Galatas

Kastelli

11,000 Evacuated
28-31 May

SURRENDERED
30 MAY

Aus 19

02

20 May

FREYBERG
CREFORCE

Aus IN COMP

(Gilbert)

GB WELCH

MNDSO

EN

04

EN

01

EN

08

06

1(-) Sturm 3

II

Sturm
(-)

17

20 May

British Fleet dispersed first
German seaborne convoy night
of 21-22 May

British Fleet dispersed second
German seaborne convoy
near Melos morning of 22 May

05

21 May

2 (Min)

100

Min
6

Min
5

22-27 May

08 FREYBERG IS EVACUATED
Freyberg is privy to enough knowledge about ULTRA – Britain's secret breaking of the Nazi Enigma codes – to make his capture unthinkable. Against his wishes he is evacuated from the island by flying boat on the night of 30 May, having to leave thousands of his soldiers behind to their fate.

07 THE ITALIAN ARMY LANDS IN SITIA
Adding insult to injury for the British and Commonwealth defenders, on 28 May 3,000 Italians from the 50th Infantry Division Regina land unopposed at Sitia on the island's eastern tip and begin to advance westwards to link up with the exhausted Germans.

06 THE NEW ZEALANDERS SAVED
Forced to retreat to Sphakia, the New Zealanders from Maleme and Khania are saved from destruction by Greek troops of the 8th Cretan Regiment. Understrength and only armed with World War I rifles and a handful of rounds, the Cretans hold out in Alikianos until 27 May to allow the Kiwis to escape.

04 HILL 107 LOST TO GERMANS
Having lost most of its radios in Greece, Leslie Andrew's New Zealanders rely on telephone lines, which are swiftly cut. Mistakenly thinking half his battalion overrun, Andrew asks permission to withdraw off Hill 107. His brigade commander mishears the question and agrees.

05 ROYAL NAVY CAUSES CARNAGE
Nighttime actions by Royal Navy destroyer and cruiser flotillas cause hundreds of casualties among the seaborne gebirgsjäger, with their first convoy only saved from total annihilation by the bravery of Captain Francesco Mimbelli and the crew of the escorting Italian torpedo boat the Lupo.

Map by Rocio Espin

German paratroopers landing in Crete

they had the wrong caliber of ammunition. Freyberg, still obsessing over a seaborne attack, failed to see that with Maleme the Germans already had a beachhead.

Battle at sea

The seaborne armada Freyberg so feared was a paper tiger. With the Kriegsmarine having no real presence in the eastern Mediterranean, Ringel had been forced to cobble together a makeshift force of some 63 vessels – mostly requisitioned Greek fishing caïques powered by a sail and a small auxiliary engine – escorted by a single Italian torpedo boat, the Lupo. Putting to sea, they crawled towards Crete at a sluggish seven knots, until on the night of 20/21 May they were found by Rear Admiral Irvine Glennie's three cruisers and four destroyers. The German fleet was effectively destroyed and hundreds of men were drowned.

However, while the Royal Navy ruled the waves during darkness, it was a different story when the sun came up. With no air cover the Luftwaffe hunted Glennie and the rest of Admiral Andrew Cunningham's force across the sparkling waters of the Mediterranean. HMS Greyhound was the first to be sunk, followed by two cruisers: the Gloucester and Fiji. Darkness brought respite, but not for long as five destroyers under the command of Lord Louis Mountbatten found themselves pounded by Stukas the following dawn. The Kelly and the Kashmir were sent to the bottom in quick succession, and with their loss Cunningham felt the Navy's defense of Crete was untenable.

21 May: invasion day + 1

Hauptmann Kleye – an officer on Student's staff – was sent by his boss to find out what was going on and landed at Maleme at around 0700hrs on the morning of 21 May. Although he came under fire, he reported the airfield as usable and from then on a steady stream of aircraft began to arrive, ferrying in desperately needed ammunition and supplies, but more importantly reinforcements and heavy weapons. Most of those fresh troops were Ringel's gebirgsjägers and, supported by masses of Luftwaffe firepower, they began to roll up the British and Commonwealth positions from west to east.

Having come within an ace of losing the battle and the Third Reich's only parachute division, Student was left kicking his heels as the cautious and methodical Ringel took over the campaign. Freyberg's command was effectively split into three, with the troops in Rhethymnon and Heraklion caught in their own struggles as the courageous New Zealanders fought on in Khania.

The efforts of Mahlke and his comrades were decisive. Constant air attack caused terrible losses and robbed the remaining defenders of any ability to coordinate their efforts and counterattack, and even if they had it begged the question: with what? They had hardly any heavy weapons, with most of their artillery being captured Italian and French models, many without sights or more than a few rounds. Almost all their armor had already been destroyed or rendered unusable, they had no air cover, and even rifle ammunition was running out.

Crete abandoned

The same morning that Mahlke made his ground attack the exhausted Freyberg cabled Cairo: "In my opinion the limit of endurance has been reached by the troops under my command… our position here is hopeless." Shocked at what they regarded as a sudden turnaround in fortune, permission was reluctantly given to evacuate the island. The surviving troops from Khania headed south on the single road to the small port town of Sphakia, mercilessly bombed and strafed by the Luftwaffe as they went. As thousands of dispirited British and Commonwealth troops streamed south, those at Rhethymnon and Heraklion fought on.

Even as the retreating men reached Sphakia, the Royal Navy was steeling itself to run the gauntlet and save as much of the garrison as it could. In a heroic effort worthy of the finest traditions of the senior service, starting on the night of 28 May, Cunningham's warships evacuated almost 11,000 men from the southern port, and another 4,000 from Heraklion on the northern coast.

By the morning of 1 June it was over. British and Commonwealth losses included just under 2,000 dead and the same number wounded, with another 5,000 left behind to trudge into captivity, one of whom was Campbell, whose mighty defense of Rhethymnon counted for nought as the Navy was unable to reach him and his gallant men, forcing them to surrender.

Terrible though these figures were, they were overshadowed by the German tally. Some 6,580 men were killed, wounded or missing, half of this number being paratroopers killed on the first day of the operation. The Germans also lost some 150 transport aircraft, which would be sorely missed in the upcoming invasion of the Soviet Union. But it was the heavy losses among the ranks of the elite fallschirmjäger that were the most damaging. One of the best-trained and best-equipped spearhead formations in the entire Wehrmacht had been gutted in less than a fortnight.

Heraklion was severely damaged in the bombing campaign during the German invasion

Fallschirmjägers move into action after touching down in Crete. Dozens were blown out to sea on 20 May and drowned, while some landed in a bamboo thicket and were impaled

German troops prepare a military glider for Operation Mercury at an airfield near Athens

OPERATION BARBAROSSA

SOVIET UNION 22 JUNE – 5 DECEMBER 1941

Germany's invasion of the Soviet Union was Hitler's greatest gamble of WWII and the bloody realization of his most ambitious dreams

WORDS CHARLES GINGER

A Wehrmacht soldier takes cover during the winter of 1941. Barbarossa claimed the lives of around 200,000 German troops

In the summer of 1940, with much of Europe crushed beneath the boot of a rampant Wehrmacht, Hitler had every reason to be euphoric. His pact with the Soviet Union, signed in August 1939, had held, enabling his forces to sweep through Poland before surging into Western Europe. By late June of 1940, only the British remained to stand against them, the narrow escape of over 300,000 troops from Dunkirk scarred into the national consciousness. And yet despite a torrent of victories that led Field Marshal Wilhelm Keitel to label Hitler as "the greatest warlord in history", the Führer was not entirely satisfied.

Britain's refusal to acknowledge Germany's triumph and submit to peace talks puzzled Hitler. After all, he had always been open about his desire for peace, going so far as to "appeal to reason" during his annual speech in the Reichstag on 19 July 1940. To Hitler's chagrin, Churchill and the British people remained resolute, leading Hitler to surmise that Britain was pinning its hopes on the Soviet Union. Hitler's delusions led him to reason that only the complete annihilation of the Soviets would force Britain to recognize that her cause was lost.

During a conference with his military commanders at his lair in Berchtesgaden, Bavaria, on 31 July 1940, Hitler outlined his most ambitious plans yet: Germany would invade the Soviet Union the following year. "The sooner Russia is crushed, the better," he

explained. "If we were to start in May 1941, we would have five months to finish the job."

However, while there were strategic motives behind Hitler's determination to destroy the USSR, arguably the more pressing desires behind Hitler's greatest gamble were of an ideological nature. While the summer of 1940 may have witnessed the germination of an idea that would become Operation Barbarossa, a cataclysmic showdown with 'Judeo-Bolshevism' was something that Hitler had first mentioned while writing *Mein Kampf* in 1924-25.

When discussing the apparently pressing need for Germany to secure Lebensraum (living space) in order to ensure a future in which the nation would have ample space and resources, Hitler was characteristically blunt when outlining his intended targets. "If we speak of soil in Europe today, we can primarily have in mind only Russia and her border states." Describing the Slavs of Russia as "an inferior race", Hitler warned that "the end of Jewish rule in Russia will also be the end of Russia as a state."

Hitler viewed the fate of the human race as an endless struggle for resources in a finite space, one that would end, in his twisted view, in the eventual triumph of "inferior" races (namely the Jews) unless a "pure" race was willing to fight to prevent them. In his primal opinion, "nature knows no boundaries. She places lifeforms on this globe and then sets them free in a play for power."

Believing that every evil on Earth could be placed at the feet of Jews, Hitler sought to

tear down anything that he perceived as being a Jewish entity or system. Communism, he claimed, was one such policy, and it was this distorted belief that led him to state that it was Germany's duty to defeat the nation that had given communism a home: the Soviet Union.

Hitler's plans

Unswerving in his confidence that Britain was already beaten and thereby would not present a second front, Hitler directed the German High Command to begin planning the invasion. The operation was to be codenamed Barbarossa, in honor of the Holy Roman Emperor Frederick Barbarossa, a talented military commander.

Scheduled for 15 May 1941, the operation would see three army groups (North, Center, and South) pouring across the Polish-Soviet border under the respective leadership of Wilhelm Ritter von Leeb, Feodor von Bock, and Gerd von Runstedt. Von Leeb's forces were tasked with taking the Baltics and Leningrad; Bock's men were to head first to Smolensk and then onto Moscow; and Runstedt was to race to secure the "breadbasket" of Ukraine and the oil-rich Caucasus. Certain of victory, Hitler proudly boasted, "We only have to kick the door in and the whole rotten structure will come crashing down."

While Germany began to make the necessary preparations for Barbarossa, the target of its impending assault sat paralysed. In the wake of Stalin's ruthless purges in the late 1930s, which saw three-quarters of the Red Army's leadership executed or imprisoned, the forces of the USSR were woefully short on both morale and efficiency. To compound its already significant problems, Stalin insisted on controlling the placement of his divisions, further hamstringing the Red Army.

Laboring under the false belief that Hitler could only attack the USSR once he had dealt with Britain, Stalin was sure that any invasion was at least a year away. His obstinate refusal to accept the threat massing on his borders was further emboldened in April 1941 when Stalin received a letter from Winston Churchill warning of the Germans' intentions. Instead of heeding the British Prime Minister, Stalin discarded Churchill's correspondence as an Allied attempt to provoke the Soviets into launching a pre-emptive strike against their German allies.

Although Stalin's suspicions about Churchill's true motives may be understandable, his dismissal of the warnings of another, closer source were nothing short of catastrophic. In May of 1941, Richard Sorge, a Soviet spy working in Japan, informed Moscow that Germany was indeed planning to attack, information that he had received from none

"STALIN INSISTED ON CONTROLLING THE PLACEMENT OF HIS DIVISIONS, FURTHER HAMSTRINGING THE RED ARMY"

A German Wehrmacht soldier throws a stick grenade

German soldiers attack a Soviet bunker with a *Flammenwerfer*, which was capable of spitting flames up to 82 feet

THE BLOODY PURSUIT OF LEBENSRAUM

How the Ostheer blazed a trail through the plains and cities of Eastern Europe

04. Finnish assistance
10 July
While the Romanians plug away in the south, the Finnish army moves towards the Karelian Isthmus. In total, 300,000 Finnish soldiers join in the fight against the USSR.

01. The distant rumble of panzers
22 June
Barbarossa gets under way as German armored divisions race east to deliver what they hope will be a knock-out blow to the unprepared Soviet forces.

05. Smolensk
16 July
Another important city on the road to Moscow is taken by the Germans. Resistance lasts in the city until 5 August. By 1 September, the frontline has extended as far as Leningrad in the north and the Crimea in the south.

07. Operation Typhoon
2 October
An all-out assault on Moscow begins after much deliberation in the Nazi hierarchy. The Germans manage to fight their way to the capital's suburbs, but ultimately fail to take the city as winter sets in.

09. Winter takes hold
5 December
Horrendous weather conditions and fresh Soviet recruits take their toll on the exhausted Wehrmacht, which has no alternative but to turn back. Operation Barbarossa has failed in its objectives, however, Eastern Europe has fallen under the shadow of the Greater German Reich.

03. More cities fall
3 July
The onslaught continues as Volkovysk and then Minsk are both taken as German forces encircle the Red Army and take 324,000 prisoners.

06. The taking of Kiev
16 September
The capital of the Ukrainian Socialist Soviet Republic is the next settlement to fall as Soviet troops are trapped in a pocket east of the city. A month later, the Wehrmacht have advanced even further to Bryansk and Belgorod.

02. Romanian allies
22 June
It isn't just the Wehrmacht ploughing east, as two allied Romanian armies press into Ukraine heading for the city of Odesa.

08. Siege of Sevastopol
16 November
Crimea falls into the hands of the Germans after a lengthy siege that eventually results in an Axis victory. The area will be used as a launch pad for the drive to the oil fields of the Caucasus in Operation Blue.

LATVIA

LITHUANIA

BYELORUSSIA

GERMANY

HUNGARY

USSR

UKRAINE

ROMANIA

KEY
GERMAN ADVANCE
SOVIET COUNTERATTACK
SURROUNDED SOVIET FORCES
GERMAN TROOPS
SOVIET TROOPS

other than Colonel Eugen Ott, the military attaché at the German embassy in Tokyo.

Amazingly, even when Sorge provided a date of 20 June 1941 (just two days off the actual launch date of 22 June), Stalin remained implacable, the Soviet ruler insisting that Hitler was not "such an idiot" as to risk a war on two fronts. Less than a month after receiving Sorge's report, Stalin would be proven spectacularly wrong.

A five-week delay due to Hitler's decision to invade Yugoslavia in May 1941 after its pro-Nazi government had been toppled meant Germany was not ready to unleash its Eastern campaign until June. Barbarossa was to be a campaign of extermination, with the ruthless removal of the elites and mass starvation employed as a method of subjugating Soviet cities. In fact, the German High Command went so far as to devise a 'Hunger Plan' that would see food taken from the Soviet Union and given to German soldiers and citizens. (According to historian Timothy Snyder, approximately 4.2 million Soviet civilians were starved to death between 1941 and 1944.) No quarter was to be given.

The assault begins

At 3.15am on 22 June, thousands of Luftwaffe engines burst into life to signal the beginning of Barbarossa, the fleet sailing high over the German assault boats bobbing on the River Bug in anticipation. As the planes zeroed in on their targets (airfields lined with neat rows of stationary Soviet planes), thousands of German artillery pieces began to belch flame into the sky. Hitler was finally attacking the entity he loathed the most, and he'd gathered 3.8 million soldiers (including Romanians, Italians, and Slovaks) for the job, well-trained men supported by 600,000 vehicles, 3,350 armored vehicles, 3,000 aircraft, and 500,000 horses.

As millions of troops raced into the USSR, their counterparts radioed their superiors demanding to know what to do. Such was the shock of the assault that many border guards were gunned down in their nightwear, their homes and families engulfed in the flames of the bombardment. Despite this, Stalin was still – inexplicably – wary of some Allied trick and ordered that nothing be done to provoke the Germans.

In all their wildest dreams, the German commanders could never have dared to hope to find their adversaries so woefully off guard. Many of the Soviets' defensive positions lacked the weaponry needed to counter a concentrated Panzer attack, and they could

Soviet bombers soar over Moscow. Following horrendous losses in the early stages of the war, the Red Army Air Force gradually recovered and played a key role in offensive operations

"MANY BORDER GUARDS WERE GUNNED DOWN IN THEIR NIGHTWEAR, THEIR HOMES AND FAMILIES ENGULFED IN FLAMES"

not hope to rely on any aid from above; on the first day of the operation the Soviets lost around 1,800 planes to the Luftwaffe's 35.

Within two days of the start of the attack, many of the 49 German Panzer battalions selected for the invasion were 50 miles inside the USSR. By 28 June over 400,000 Soviet troops were encircled outside of Minsk as the Second Panzer Group, under the command of General Heinz Guderian, linked up with Hermann Hoth's Third Panzer Group.

To the north, General von Leeb was faring just as well, his troops hailed as emancipators by the violently suppressed peoples of the Baltics, many of them

actively helping the Germans by attacking Red Army positions. However, the invaders certainly didn't have it all their way.

Army Group South, charged with taking Kiev and then hurrying on to the priceless oil fields of the Caucasus, was finding the going difficult in the face of determined resistance. Rundstedt was doubly unfortunate as he was not only marching on the most heavily defended region of the frontlines, but his men were doing so as KV and T-34 tanks (the latter the best all-round tank of the entire war) rolled towards them. While the central and northern thrusts of the German army continued to slice into Soviet territory, Rundstedt found himself

Moscovites build fortifications to defend the Russian capital against the German offensive

Images Getty

increasingly bogged down. His failure to keep up with the rest would ultimately prove fatal for Hitler's hopes of a rapid victory. Yet as July approached, the overall picture from a German perspective seemed unexpectedly rosy.

Upon finally realizing that Hitler had betrayed him, Stalin had fallen into a stupor of despair that lasted for over a week. Now, with machinery being evacuated from Ukraine, Stalin finally began to emerge from his trance, and on 3 July he addressed the Soviet people as his "comrades" as he called on them to "selflessly join our patriotic war of liberation against the fascist enslavers".

While the idea the Soviet people were fighting to defend a communist utopia that upheld their rights and shunned the violence so freely used by the Wehrmacht (especially the SS divisions attached to it) is laughable, Stalin was not exaggerating when he referred to the threat of enslavement. From the outset

of the war, Hitler had expressed his desire to carve Germany's new Eastern territories into a series of states filled with Soviet slaves. A cruel and manipulative tyrant he may have been, but in his speech at the start of July Stalin was, for once, telling his people at least some of the truth.

On the same day that Stalin addressed the nation, German General Franz Halder, Chief of Staff of Army High Command, confided in his diary that it was "no overstatement to say that the Russian campaign has been won in the space of two weeks". In hindsight this statement reeks of hubris, but at the time German confidence was more than justified. By 13 July the German armies had advanced between 186 and 373 miles, incapacitated (either by killing, injuring, or capturing) over 589,000 enemy soldiers, and obliterated over 6,850 aircraft. The Wehrmacht was edging ever closer to Moscow, and the First Battle of Smolensk was about to finish with the entrapment of almost 760,000 Soviet troops. A glorious

triumph loomed. Then came a High Command directive that would change everything.

On 19 July, Hitler issued an order that the Soviet armies trapped around Smolensk (the 16th, 19th, and 20th) were to be utterly destroyed before Army Group Center advanced, not towards Moscow, but south to the outskirts of Kiev to aid Army Group South, which was still 50 miles outside of the Ukrainian capital.

Longing to continue the drive for Moscow, both Halder and von Bock were adamant that the city had to remain their priority, but Hitler was unmoved. And so, on 23 August, Army Group Center swung south. Three weeks later its southern counterpart started to drive north, and on 16 September two more Soviet armies were annihilated as the pincer closed east of Kiev. Stalin's order that the city be held at all costs had condemned over 700,000 Soviet troops to encirclement.

Still progressing steadily in the north, the forces under the command of von Leeb had sealed off the city of Leningrad eight days prior to the encirclement of Kiev. Hitler had

Red Army troops, clad in the winter clothing the Germans lacked, storm across a snow-blanketed field

THE SHADOW OF EVIL

Barbarossa was not just a military operation; it was a race war. The Nazis planned to ethnically cleanse Russia

The Einsatzgruppen (SS death squads) tasked with following the Wehrmacht into the Soviet Union were ruthless in the execution of their primary task: murdering civilians. From Soviet commissars to Jews and Romani, millions of innocent people were shot, hanged, or otherwise killed by the prowling SS commandos scouring the lands already scorched by the advancing German army. The predominant method of execution involved lining victims (including women, children, and the elderly) along the edge of pits they had been forced to dig themselves, then shooting them in the back of the head or neck.

One of the most famous examples of such a mass execution was the Babi Yar massacre of September 1941. Over two days German soldiers and Ukrainian police officers shot 33,771 people in a ravine north of Kiev, many of whom were forced to lie down on the corpses of those who had gone before them.

Aside from Poland, it was the Soviet nations (notably the Baltics) that witnessed the worst atrocities of the war. Estonia, just one of a group of countries that suffered the horrors of Hitler's genocidal war, lost almost 99 per cent of its Jewish population.

Within five months of the invasion of the Baltics, Einsatzgruppe A alone had slaughtered nearly 140,000 people. Yet such figures failed to satisfy Reichsführer-SS Heinrich Himmler, who in time decided that gassing "undesirables" would be a quicker and cleaner method. By the war's end, Himmler's charges had murdered approximately 1.5 million Jews along the Eastern Front and thousands of Romani.

A Jewish-Ukrainian woman tries to shield a child as a soldier takes aim. Many Ukrainians were complicit in the Final Solution

selected the city as a primary target during the planning of Barbarossa, and now his armies (with the support of Finnish troops sent to retake lands lost to the Soviets during the Winter War of 1939-1940) had provided him with the chance to put his hunger plan into action once more. Instead of bombarding the city, its people were to be starved into submission in a siege that would last until January 1944 and claim over 800,000 lives.

Battle for Moscow

Now that the resistance shielding Kiev had been removed, Army Group Center could once again turn its gaze on Moscow. Despite the panic that had spread throughout the city, Stalin had chosen to stay and invigorate the natives with his presence. He had placed the defense of the city in the hands of General Georgy Zhukov, a formidable figure who had overseen the desperate efforts to counter the Siege of Leningrad.

Zhukov wasted little time in putting the men and women of Moscow to work excavating defensive trenches and anti-tank ditches. The factories that continued to function

(much of the Soviets' industry had been evacuated east) were also turned to military tasks (a clock maker was asked to begin building mine detonators). If the Germans were to take Moscow, Zhukov was determined they would pay dearly for every street.

Codenamed Operation Typhoon, the assault on Moscow began on 2 October 1941. At the outset of the attack the Germans enjoyed a 2:1 superiority in tanks and troops and a 3:1 advantage in aircraft. It seemed that it would only be a matter of time before the Soviet capital fell. But there was one enemy the Germans failed to account for: Mother Nature.

Known as the rasputista (the time without roads), on 8 October a yearly deluge began, churning the roads into sucking quagmires that dramatically slowed the German advance. By the end of the month the Wehrmacht was still 50 miles from its target. Yet while the rain was a frustration, the freezing temperatures that followed in December were a death sentence.

By 5 December the Germans were forced to halt 19 miles short of Moscow as the conditions froze both men and machines, the lack of proper winter clothing (a result of

Hitler's assurances that the campaign would be over in weeks) condemning thousands to death.

On the same day as the Germans stopped their advance the Soviet armies behind Moscow (carefully husbanded by Zhukov and reinforced by soldiers transferred from Siberia once it had become clear that Japan was not planning to attack the region) were readying to unleash a merciless counteroffensive. Certain that the Red Army was all but beaten, the unfortunate German troops dug in around Moscow did not know what hit them when the Soviets began their attack with a massive bombardment. The moment the guns settled waves of T-34s poured across the frozen earth towards the German positions accompanied by a total force of over one million men and a resurgent Red Army Air Force.

Stunned by the sudden change in fortunes, Hitler demanded that every patch of ground be fought for, and in time the retreating German forces steadied themselves and consolidated their lines, but the threat to Moscow, built over months of fighting, had been eradicated in a matter of days. Now it was the Red Army's turn to advance.

PEARL HARBOR

OAHU, HAWAII, USA 7 DECEMBER 1941

Imperial planning and preparation for the surprise attack on Pearl
Harbor began months before the Sunday morning aerial assault

WORDS MIKE HASKEW

Just before sunrise on Sunday 7 December 1941, six aircraft carriers of the Imperial Japanese Navy's First Air Fleet under the command of Vice Admiral Chuichi Nagumo, turned into the wind, ready to launch a powerful striking force of 353 aircraft.

Nagumo's flagship, Akagi, and her consorts, Kaga, Soryu, Hiryu, Shokaku, and Zuikaku, set in motion the marauding strike force that would plunge the Pacific into World War II. Its target was the US Navy's Pacific Fleet, which was anchored at Pearl Harbor on the island of Oahu in the territory of Hawaii. Other US Navy and Army installations on the island, Hickam Field, Wheeler Field, Bellows Field, Ewa Marine Corps Air Station, and the naval air stations at Kaneohe and on Ford Island in the heart of Pearl Harbor were to be hit as well.

The opening blow was intended to cripple the American military presence in the Pacific; allow the Japanese armed forces to seize and consolidate strategic gains throughout the region; and bring the US government to the negotiating table where Japan would dictate favorable terms of an armistice. To that end, the Pearl Harbor raid was coordinated with attacks on the Philippines, Wake Island, Midway Atoll, and Malaya.

The gambit was all or nothing for Japan. Although senior Japanese commanders were confident of swift victory, at least some of them acknowledged that a prolonged war with the United States was a daunting prospect, considering the industrial might and resources at the disposal of their adversary. Years of rising militarism and imperialism in Japan had placed the island nation on a collision course with the United States, a preeminent power in the Pacific since the Spanish-American War. Japan's provocative military moves on the Asian mainland, particularly the occupation of the Chinese region of Manchuria and later of French Indochina, had brought the two nations to loggerheads. While negotiations were continuing, most observers on either side of the Pacific believed war was inevitable.

The British influence

At 9pm on the evening prior to the Pearl Harbor attack, Nagumo ordered all hands aboard the Akagi to attention. He solemnly read a message from Admiral Isoroku Yamamoto, commander-in-chief of the Combined Fleet. "The rise or fall of the empire depends on this battle. Everyone will do his duty to the utmost."

Yamamoto meant the communication not only as an encouragement to the Japanese sailors and airmen, but also as homage to naval esprit de corps. During the decades preceding World War II, the Imperial Japanese Navy had embarked on a lengthy program of expansion, modernizing and modeling itself on the finest naval tradition in the world – the British Royal Navy. The message from Yamamoto echoed one similarly flashed by

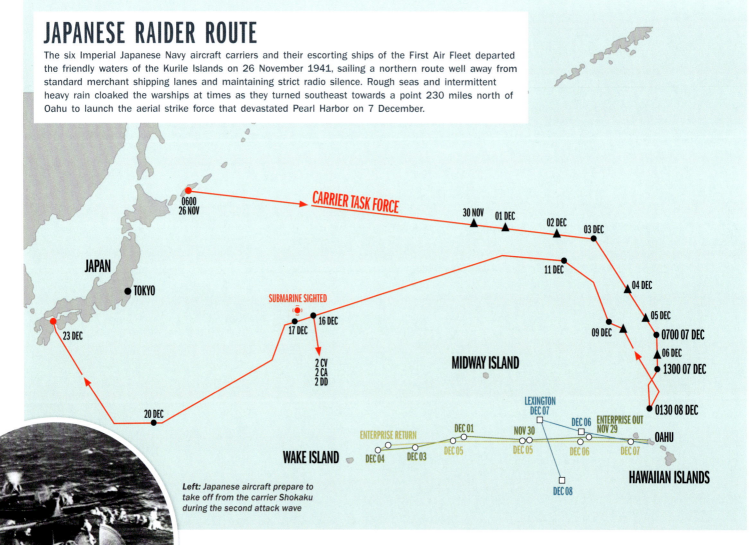

JAPANESE RAIDER ROUTE

The six Imperial Japanese Navy aircraft carriers and their escorting ships of the First Air Fleet departed the friendly waters of the Kurile Islands on 26 November 1941, sailing a northern route well away from standard merchant shipping lanes and maintaining strict radio silence. Rough seas and intermittent heavy rain cloaked the warships at times as they turned southeast towards a point 230 miles north of Oahu to launch the aerial strike force that devastated Pearl Harbor on 7 December.

0600 26 NOV

CARRIER TASK FORCE

30 NOV   01 DEC   02 DEC   03 DEC

11 DEC   04 DEC

JAPAN   05 DEC

TOKYO   09 DEC   0700 07 DEC

SUBMARINE SIGHTED   06 DEC

23 DEC   16 DEC   1300 07 DEC

17 DEC

2 CV
2 CA
2 DD   MIDWAY ISLAND

0130 08 DEC

20 DEC   LEXINGTON DEC 07

ENTERPRISE OUT NOV 29

ENTERPRISE RETURN   DEC 01   NOV 30   DEC 06   OAHU

DEC 05   DEC 05   DEC 06   DEC 07

WAKE ISLAND   DEC 04   DEC 03

DEC 08   HAWAIIAN ISLANDS

Left: Japanese aircraft prepare to take off from the carrier Shokaku during the second attack wave

Admiral Horatio Nelson, one of the greatest heroes in the history of the Royal Navy, prior to the epic battle of Trafalgar in 1805.

Japanese respect for the Royal Navy ran deep. Since the turn of the 20th century, some vessels of the Imperial fleet had actually been constructed in British and French shipyards, while Japanese training, operational standards, uniforms and rank insignia were similar to those of the British.

Following the outbreak of war in Europe, the Royal Navy again served as a role model for the Japanese. On the night of 11 November 1940, Fairey Swordfish torpedo bombers of the Fleet Air Arm flew from the deck of the aircraft carrier HMS Illustrious in the Mediterranean Sea and attacked the Italian naval anchorage at Taranto. The 21 obsolescent British biplanes sank one Italian battleship and damaged two others.

For the Japanese, the idea of a preemptive raid on Pearl Harbor had been discussed, tested during war games and shelved several

The battleship USS Arizona belches black smoke as its superstructure buckles after a devastating explosion during the Pearl Harbor attack

NAVAL AIR JUGGERNAUT

The Imperial Japanese Navy observed Western advances in naval aviation and welcomed military envoys to consult and train its pilots

The British Royal Navy pioneered many aspects of the development of naval aviation in the early 20th century and Japanese naval observers also recognized its potential. Intent on emulating the Royal Navy's successes, the Japanese received a British mission headed by Captain William Sempill in the fall of 1921. Sempill led 29 air operations instructors charged with assisting the development of the Japanese naval aviation program. By 1922, the Japanese had also constructed the Hosho, the world's first aircraft carrier purpose-built, rather than converted from another ship type.

Sempill, who was later exposed as a spy for the Japanese, hoped to secure substantial sales of British arms to Japan in exchange for valuable expertise and advice. His team brought the blueprints of the most advanced British carrier designs, protocols involving elements such as pilot training; the launch and recovery of aircraft; refueling and maintenance; and airborne operations. The British trained the young Japanese pilots in the latest Royal Navy aircraft, such as the Gloster Sparrowhawk fighter, along with torpedo bombers and dive bombers. They introduced

torpedo tactics to the Imperial Navy as well. Japanese engineers and designers experimented with their own ordnance and aircraft, several of which were patterned after British types, and perfected carrier operations and doctrine during the 1920s and 1930s.

Prior to the attack on Pearl Harbor, Lieutenant Commander Takeshi Naito, a naval attaché in Berlin, traveled to the port of Taranto, Italy, where the British had executed a successful attack against the Italian Fleet at anchor in November 1940. With the assistance of the Italian Navy, Naito assessed the dynamics of the Taranto raid and advised the Pearl Harbor planners on modifications to existing tactics. Eventually, wooden stabilizing fins were attached to Japanese aerial torpedoes, allowing them to run true in Pearl Harbor's shallow waters.

Dive bombers crowd a flight deck prior to Pearl Harbor

Type 91 Kai 2 torpedoes on the flight deck of the Imperial Japanese Navy aircraft carrier, Akagi. The carrier is at Hitokappu Bay in the Kuriles just prior to departing for the attack on Pearl Harbor

The battleship USS
Pennsylvania lies
behind the battered
destroyers, Cassin and
Downes, in dry dock at
Pearl Harbor

BOMBERS RAID MANILA

Journal NEW YORK **American**

AN AMERICAN PAPER FOR THE AMERICAN PEOPLE

B

No. 19,707—DAILY   MONDAY, DECEMBER 8, 1941   DAILY 3 Cents | SATURDAY 5 Cents | SUNDAY 10 Cents   5¢

In Two Sections—Section One

7TH SPORT WALL ST. CLOSING

U. S. DECLARES WAR ON JAPAN

---

times during the years between the world wars. However, bolstered by the British success, the staff of the Combined Fleet began, with renewed purpose in January 1941, to plan for just such a bold stroke. Lieutenant Commander Minoru Genda, one of the best known and most respected aviators in the Japanese armed forces, had observed American carriers operating in a unified, single strike force and attended war games in 1936, during which an offensive scenario against Pearl Harbor had ended in simulated disaster for the attacker. Still, Genda remained one of a relative few Japanese officers who believed it was possible for a carrier task force to successfully deliver a stunning blow against an enemy fleet at anchor.

As Japanese aircraft carrier strength reached sufficient levels to support a Pearl Harbor attack, Yamamoto instructed Admiral Takajiro Onishi, chief of staff of the Eleventh Air Fleet, to order Genda to evaluate the potential for success with, "…special attention to the feasibility of the operation, method of execution and the forces to be used." Yamamoto was reluctant to go to war with the US, however, he strongly believed that a substantial and successful first strike at the Pacific Fleet was the only option to bring such a conflict to a rapid and favorable conclusion for Japan.

"YAMAMOTO THREATENED TO RESIGN IF SENIOR COMMANDERS REFUSED TO SUPPORT THE ATTACK"

Yamamoto's assertion that Pearl Harbor should be Japan's target actually reversed traditional thinking at the highest command levels within the Imperial Navy. Although the army had been active on the Asian continent, naval doctrine had previously assumed a defensive posture. In the fall of 1940, Yamamoto's assertion became an ultimatum. He eventually threatened to resign if senior commanders within the Combined Fleet refused to support the proposal.

The blueprints for war

By the following August, the basic plan for the Pearl Harbor attack had been approved. The six aircraft carriers of the First Air Fleet were to be accompanied by two battleships, two heavy cruisers, a light cruiser, nine destroyers, three submarines, and eight tankers – a total of 31 vessels – sailing from their rendezvous

point at Hitokappu Bay in the Kurile Islands. The fleet was to sail on 26 November; take a northerly course, in order to avoid the busy Pacific trade routes and merchant shipping that plied the ocean; maintain strict radio silence; and launch its aircraft in two waves from a position 230 miles north of Oahu. The tentative date for the attack was designated as 7 December 1941. A cordon of fleet submarines was positioned around Oahu to provide early warning of American ship movements and attack any US Navy vessels that might be at sea near the harbor. Five midget submarines were to be launched from their mother submarines hours before the aerial attack, with the hope that they might infiltrate Pearl Harbor and launch torpedoes at anchored vessels of the Pacific Fleet.

Early in September, senior Japanese officers convened at the Naval War College in Tokyo and finalized the plans for the attack. One month later, senior pilots who would assume command of air groups were informed of the target against which they had been training so rigorously. They already had some idea of its nature, since the torpedo groups had worked to perfect their runs against capital ships anchored in shallow waters.

Combined Fleet Top Secret Operational Order No 1 was issued on 5 November, followed

A Japanese Mitsubishi Zero fighter roars off the flight deck of the aircraft carrier Akagi en route to Pearl Harbor

After a mission in the Solomon Islands, Aichi D3A Val dive bombers return to the aircraft carrier Shokaku

Photographed ten days after it crashed during the Pearl Harbor attack, the Zero of Petty Officer Shigenori Nishikaichi lies derelict

48 hours later by Order No 2, authorizing the fleet to weigh anchor at the end of the month and to execute the attack on Pearl Harbor.

When the fleet set sail, Admiral Kichisaburo Nomura and Special Envoy Saburo Kurusu were in Washington, DC, conducting last-ditch negotiations with Secretary of State Cordell Hull and President Franklin D Roosevelt. These negotiations were expected to fail, and when the impasse was reached, specific orders to launch the attack would be issued to Nagumo at sea. At the same time, the envoys, oblivious to the details of the Pearl Harbor attack, were instructed to deliver a message to the US government, officially terminating the negotiations. The government in Tokyo considered this diplomatic step essentially a declaration of war, timed for a half hour before the Japanese aircraft appeared in the sky above Pearl Harbor.

Lieutenant Commander Mitsuo Fuchida, leader of the air groups of the First Air Fleet, was assigned the task of allocating aircraft to specific targets, organizing the two waves of planes to coordinate their attacks and allotting fighter protection against any defending American planes that might make it into the sky to give battle. Fuchida assigned 185 aircraft to

the first wave. It consisted of 49 Nakajima B5N 'Kate' bombers carrying armor-piercing bombs, 40 Kates with aerial torpedoes, 51 Aichi D3A 'Val' dive bombers with general purpose bombs, and 45 superb Mitsubishi A6M Zero fighters to provide escort and strafe targets of opportunity.

While the Kates hit the warships anchored in Pearl Harbor, 25 Vals were designated to blast the primary American fighter base at Wheeler Field. 17 Vals were assigned to destroy Ford Island's patrol plane and fighter base and nine were to strike American bombers based at Hickam Field. The second wave included 54 Kates armed with 550 and 125-pound bombs to demolish installations and crater runways at the airfields, 80 Vals with 550-pound bombs to renew the attacks on the warships in the harbor and 36 marauding Zeroes.

Fuchida received an intelligence message from a Japanese spy on Oahu the day before the attack. It was tinged both with optimism that the element of surprise would be achieved and disappointment that the three American

aircraft carriers, Enterprise, Lexington and Saratoga were not present at the anchorage. It read, "No balloons, no torpedo defense nets deployed around battleships in Pearl Harbor. All battleships are in. No indications from enemy radio activity that ocean patrol flights being made in Hawaiian area. Lexington left harbor yesterday. Enterprise also thought to be operating at sea."

The Saratoga was steaming into the harbor at San Diego, California, when the Japanese attackers arrived above Pearl Harbor on 7 December. Although the aircraft carriers were absent, there was no turning back. The attack had to proceed as ordered and the Japanese rationalized that the remaining targets, particularly the US battleships, were high value enough to justify the risk being undertaken.

"Tora! Tora! Tora!"
As the sky was still dark over the deck of the Akagi, pitched in rough seas, a green lamp was waved in a circle and the first Zero fighter

"FOR SEVERAL HOURS, THE JAPANESE ATTACKERS WROUGHT DEVASTATION ON THEIR TARGETS BELOW"

roared down the flight deck into the air. Within 15 minutes, the entire first wave was airborne. At 7.40am, the north shore of Oahu came into view. Fuchida was exultant. He radioed "Tora! Tora! Tora!" to the anxious Nagumo, signifying that complete surprise had been achieved. For several hours, the attackers wrought devastation on their targets below.

Elsewhere in the Pacific, Japanese forces moved aggressively in concert with the Pearl Harbor attack, reaching for objectives that would minimize US interference with coming operations to seize the Dutch East Indies, secure vital resources such as oil and rubber for their war machine, and extend their defensive perimeter further into the expanse of the great ocean.

As the attack got underway in Hawaii, word was flashed to Midway Atoll at 6.30am local time on 7 December. The Marine garrison went on high alert and by dusk, the Japanese had arrived. Two Imperial Navy destroyers, the Akebono and Ushio, were sighted as they prepared to shell the installations on Midway.

War came to the atoll at 9.35pm, as Japanese 13cm shells crashed on Sand and Eastern Islands, the two spits of land that, within months, would become the

epicenter of World War II in the Pacific. As the destroyers cruised back and forth, the Marine guns responded with 7cm and 13cm rounds. Japanese shells set the large seaplane hangar ablaze. One enemy round scored a direct hit on the concrete structure that housed the Sand Island powerplant, smashing through an air intake and mortally wounding a young Marine officer, 1st Lieutenant George H Cannon, who refused to leave his post for medical treatment and later received a posthumous Medal of Honor.

The Midway battle lasted for about half an hour and Marine gunners claimed to have scored hits on at least one enemy destroyer, which was seen belching smoke and flame. When the Japanese finally withdrew, four Americans were dead and ten wounded. 36 Japanese bombers hit Wake Island on the morning of 8 December (across the International Date Line), destroying a dozen Grumman F4F Wildcat fighters on the ground. Meanwhile, Japanese troops landed at Kota Bharu on the coast of Malaya while the Pearl Harbor attack force was in the air. Within hours of the strike against Pearl, Japanese bombers hit Clark Field and other installations in the Philippines, catching American planes on the ground again.

Shocked and bloodied, the United States was suddenly at war. For a time, Japanese domination of the Pacific was virtually uncontested, but just as Yamamoto feared, a protracted conflict, one that Japan could not win, emerged. Even as Allied forces turned the tide and fought their way inexorably to Tokyo Bay and victory in 1945, the specter of Pearl Harbor haunted the Americans.

While conspiracy theories have surfaced in the three-quarters of a century since the 'Day of Infamy', these remain the topic of heated debate and conjecture. Some revisionist historians have reviewed all the proof they need to conclude that President Roosevelt and other high-ranking Allied civilian leaders and military officers – even British Prime Minister Winston Churchill – were aware that the attacks on Pearl Harbor and other locations were coming. However, the 'case' will probably never be closed.

On the tactical level, the Americans received several warnings of the Japanese air armada approaching Pearl Harbor on 7 December 1941 – an encounter with a midget submarine and a radar sighting at Opana above Kahuku Point on the north shore, for instance. An open question remains as to whether American commanders in Hawaii should have taken action to improve preparedness and should have been more responsive to the signs of imminent attack on that fateful Sunday morning.

A DAY OF INFAMY

Despite the success of the attack on Pearl Harbor, Admiral Yamamoto correctly surmised that it was incomplete

As soon as Lieutenant Commander Mitsuo Fuchida was back aboard the Akagi, the leader of the Pearl Harbor strike reported to Vice Admiral Chuichi Nagumo on the carrier's bridge. Fuchida is said to have begged his commander to launch another attack.

Nagumo declined. The risk was too great and so he ordered the First Air Fleet to retire. When news of the successful attack reached Tokyo, citizens took to the streets in celebration. The highest echelons of the military exuded optimism.

However, Admiral Isoroku Yamamoto, architect of the raid, brooded. The American carriers had not been destroyed. Retribution would soon come. He had once warned fellow officers, "If I am told to fight regardless of the consequences, I shall run wild for the first six months or a year but I have utterly no confidence for the second or third year."

Pearl Harbor had been a tremendous tactical victory. The US Pacific Fleet was crippled but Yamamoto's words proved prophetic. Machine shops, repair facilities and stockpiles of fuel and oil were untouched. The submarine base was operational. The Americans recovered rapidly and just six months after Pearl Harbor, four of the Japanese carriers that had executed the raid were sunk by American planes at the Battle of Midway.

Admiral Isoroku Yamamoto envisioned a bleak future for the Japanese nation in the wake of the Pearl Harbor attack

JAPAN ATTACKS

How the Imperial Japanese Navy launched one of history's most devastating raids

PICKED UP BY RADAR
At 7.02am, the Opana radar station picks up the first wave, however, it's mistaken for the flight of B17s.

FIRST ATTACK

49 HIGH-LEVEL BOMBERS
51 DIVE-BOMBERS
40 TORPEDO BOMBERS
43 FIGHTERS

THE FIRST WAVE OF ATTACKING AIRCRAFT
Launched at 6.10am, it takes the 183 attack aircraft just 15 minutes to get airborne and in formation.

WHEELER FIELD
Japanese fighter planes target Wheeler first and, about four minutes later, attack Pearl Harbor.

SECOND ATTACK

54 HIGH-LEVEL BOMBERS
78 DIVE-BOMBERS
36 FIGHTERS

THE SECOND WAVE
At 7.20am, the Japanese launch another 167 attack aircraft. This follow-up assault is designed to hit specific military targets.

HALEIWA FIELD
Nine Japanese aircraft are shot down by pilots from this airfield.

BELLOWS FIELD
Eight Zeros attack, shooting down two US fighters.

Opana Radar Station

Haleiwa field

Schofield barracks

Wheeler field

Keneohe Nas

Keneohe

Ewa field

Bellows field

PEARL HARBOR

USS SHAW EXPLODES
This destroyer is in dry dock for repairs, and is bombed towards the end of the raid, causing its magazines to erupt.

AICHI D3A 'VAL' DIVE BOMBER
Of the 441 aircraft in Japan's task force, 153 were 'Val' dive-bombers. Thought to be obsolete by the Allies, they were used to devastating effect at Pearl Harbor. With a 550-pound bomb strapped to its fuselage, the Val went on to sink more Allied warships than any other Axis aircraft during the entire conflict.

AI-256

BATTLESHIP ROW
What vessels survived the attack?

USS Pennsylvania
Damaged

In dry dock at the time, repeated Japanese attempts to torpedo the caisson it was held in failed. Damaged by bombs, 68 of its crew were killed or wounded.

USS Arizona
Sunk

Attacked by ten Kate torpedo planes during the first wave. One torpedo hit the ship's forward magazine resulting in a gigantic explosion. Of its 1,512 crew, just 335 survived.

USS Nevada
Seriously damaged

Despite being torpedoed, Nevada was able to escape Battleship Row during the attack. It was repeatedly targeted by dive-bombers from the second wave.

USS Oklahoma
Sunk

Hit by three torpedoes early in the raid. As it capsized, a further two torpedoes smashed into its listing hull, and its crew were machine-gunned while attempting to abandon ship.

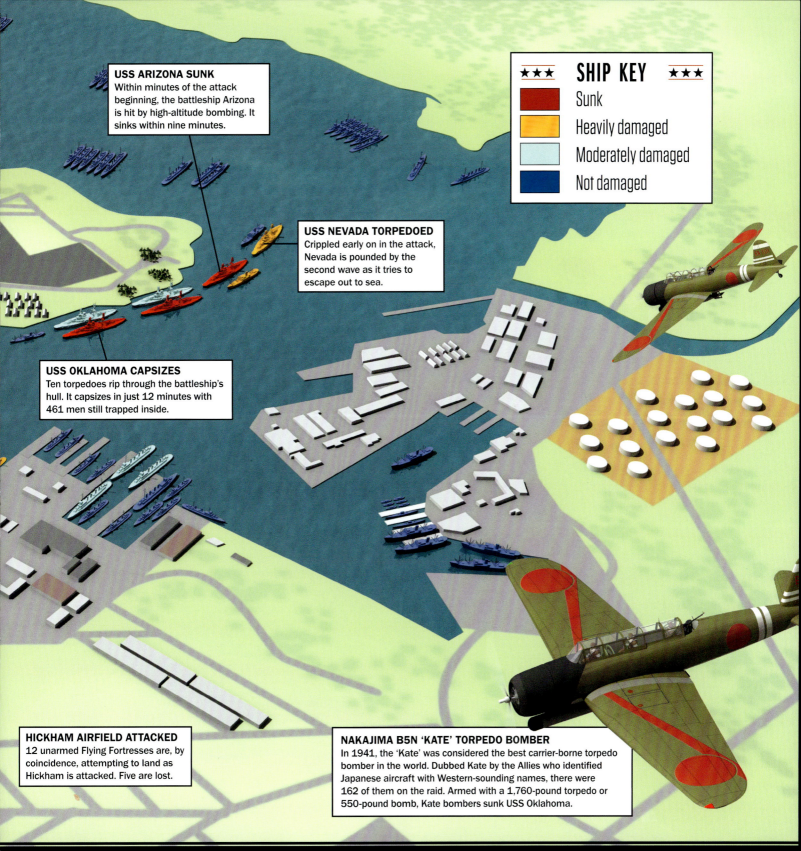

SHIP KEY ★★★ ★★★

- ■ Sunk
- ■ Heavily damaged
- ■ Moderately damaged
- ■ Not damaged

USS ARIZONA SUNK
Within minutes of the attack beginning, the battleship Arizona is hit by high-altitude bombing. It sinks within nine minutes.

USS NEVADA TORPEDOED
Crippled early on in the attack, Nevada is pounded by the second wave as it tries to escape out to sea.

USS OKLAHOMA CAPSIZES
Ten torpedoes rip through the battleship's hull. It capsizes in just 12 minutes with 461 men still trapped inside.

HICKHAM AIRFIELD ATTACKED
12 unarmed Flying Fortresses are, by coincidence, attempting to land as Hickham is attacked. Five are lost.

NAKAJIMA B5N 'KATE' TORPEDO BOMBER
In 1941, the 'Kate' was considered the best carrier-borne torpedo bomber in the world. Dubbed Kate by the Allies who identified Japanese aircraft with Western-sounding names, there were 162 of them on the raid. Armed with a 1,760-pound torpedo or 550-pound bomb, Kate bombers sunk USS Oklahoma.

USS Tennessee
Minor damage
Tennessee was hit by two armor-piercing bombs, which destroyed two gun turrets. Shrapnel from the first also killed the captain of USS West Virginia, which was moored next to it.

USS California
Sunk. Refloated and rebuilt by January 1944
All portholes and hatches on California had been left open causing flooding when it was hit by torpedoes. It took the ship three days to sink.

USS Maryland
Damaged
Hit by two armor-piercing bombs that exploded low on its hull, causing flooding. It stayed afloat, however, and its crew fought back. Two officers and two men were killed.

USS West Virginia
Sunk. Refloated and rebuilt by July 1944
Five torpedoes sunk West Virginia. When it was refloated, 66 bodies were recovered with evidence some had survived for 16 days.

THE FALL OF SINGAPORE

8 DECEMBER 1941 - 15 FEBRUARY 1942

British defenses in Malaya and Singapore proved unable
to stop the Japanese juggernaut, or even slow it down

WORDS DAVID SMITH

Image: Getty

At the same time as the Japanese struck against the United States at Pearl Harbor, they also moved against the British Empire in Malaya and Singapore. The resources of Malaya and the Dutch East Indies would be critical if the Japanese war machine was to be supplied.

Britain was far from oblivious to the threat posed by an increasingly aggressive Japan. Plans were in place that necessitated the forces in Malaya and Singapore to simply hold out until massive reinforcements could be sent. Originally, this was specified as 70 days, but as war broke out in Europe, and other theaters took precedence, it was extended to 180 days. Even though this time frame, a full six months, was more daunting, there was still reason to believe that the forces Britain had at its disposal could hold out against any attack. The Japanese takeover of Indochina, with the blessing of Vichy France, brought their armed forces within striking range of Malaya and on 4 December 1941, an invasion force set sail, bound for various landing spots in Thailand.

Britain had plans for a bold forward defensive strategy, codenamed Matador, which would see them take positions in Thailand to thwart any Japanese incursions, but the plan was not implemented. It was a disastrous decision. Over the course of a 70-day campaign, the Japanese would overrun greatly superior forces in Malaya and bring the British to their knees in Singapore. Winston Churchill would describe it as "the worst disaster and largest capitulation in British history".

Ominous opening

A major naval flotilla was planned to rush to the aid of Singapore, but in the end only two capital ships, HMS Prince of Wales and HMS Repulse, were sent, with a small destroyer escort. They were sunk, with great loss of life, on 10 December, marking an ominous opening to the campaign. More ominous still was the disastrous performance at the Battle of Jitra a day later. Britain had ample resources in Malaya, with around 88,000 men in total, hailing from Britain, India, and Australia, as well as local troops. There were no tanks in the defending force, however, and the Japanese would take full advantage. Although outnumbered in terms of infantry, their 160 light and medium tanks posed a problem that the British forces never got to grips with.

At Jitra, a single Japanese battalion, with tank support, scattered the 11th Indian Infantry Division. Fighting under appalling weather conditions, the poorly trained Indian troops proved incapable of dealing with the Japanese armor. The Japanese pushed ahead and on 7 January 1942, at the Slim River engagement, a reconstituted 11th Indian Infantry Division was again unable to hold its ground. Some 3,000 prisoners were taken by a Japanese force spearheaded by just 30 tanks.

Although buying time was the main goal of the British defenders, they proved unable

Above: Speed of movement was the key for the invading Japanese army, which covered 400 miles in 54 days

Left: General Percival (right) and the British contingent on their way to surrender Singapore to the Japanese

THE LIFE OF FORCE Z

Intended to reassert British power in the region, Force Z instead sailed into history for all the wrong reasons

HMS Prince of Wales was the second battleship in the King George V class, launched in 1939. Powerful and fast, she was armed with ten 14-inch guns and was a symbol of Britain's maritime power. She was also, however, to become a symbol of a bygone age, one in which battleships ruled the waves. Originally intended to be part of a major naval force, numbering seven capital ships, she was eventually sent to Singapore with just one notable companion, the elderly battlecruiser HMS Repulse. 'Force Z' was still a formation that demanded respect, but the world had changed. The day after Japan had displayed the potential of air power at Pearl Harbor, Force Z left Singapore to intercept the Japanese convoys bringing an invasion force to take Malaya.

By the end of the following day, wary of Japanese planes, Force Z turned back towards Singapore, but an erroneous report of a Japanese landing at Kuantan persuaded Admiral Sir Tom Phillips to investigate. It was a fateful decision. On the morning of 10 December, at 1100 hours, the first wave of Japanese planes appeared and attacked. Neither ship was particularly equipped to fend off a determined aerial attack, but the Repulse, built in 1916, was by far the weaker and was the first sunk. After just two hours of fighting, Prince of Wales followed her.

Not interested in the five destroyers that were escorting the capital ships, the Japanese returned to their bases, allowing the destroyers to pick up many of the survivors of the attack. Nevertheless, more than 800 men perished.

Repulse (bottom left) and Prince of Wales under attack from Japanese planes on 10 December 1941

Japanese soldiers march through Singapore following their victory

to slow the Japanese advance down. Time and again their tanks punched through British defenses, or were able to find side roads that allowed them to bypass defensive positions. By 18 January there were already murmurs of withdrawing to the island of Singapore, and the Japanese simply refused to allow the British time to gather their thoughts. Disaster struck again when the 45th Indian Brigade was completely wiped out as the relentless advance continued.

British humiliation

On 25 January, the British began to withdraw across the causeway at Johore Bahru. Around 3,280 feet long and 66 feet wide, it allowed for an orderly withdrawal in what many observers described as the best organized part of the entire campaign for the British. Once on Singapore, however, there was little hope of deliverance. Reinforcements were on their way, but were arriving piecemeal. Even if they had all arrived at once there were insufficient numbers to stop the Japanese offensive. On 31 January the withdrawal from Malaya was complete and the causeway was destroyed.

The British now had Hurricane fighters in their arsenal, but in too few numbers to make a difference and major air strikes on Singapore had been going on since mid-January. The majority of the RAF's planes

"JAPANESE LOSSES AMOUNTED TO A LITTLE LESS THAN 10,000, WHILE THEY TOOK AROUND 130,000 PRISONERS OF WAR. AMONG THEM WERE THE MEN OF THE BRITISH 18TH INFANTRY DIVISION"

had been forced to relocate to southern Sumatra to protect themselves from Japanese air strikes, and this heightened the sense of abandonment and helplessness of the garrison on Singapore. Around a million people were now on the island, doubling its pre-war population, and an adequate water supply became a major concern.

On 8 February, the Japanese made their first landing, pushing the 22nd Australian Infantry Brigade aside. A second landing followed on the night of 9-10 February. The 27th Australian Infantry Brigade offered stiffer resistance but was forced to retreat. With the Japanese now established on the island, the situation was dire. Counterattacks failed and with the city's water supply faltering, surrender became inevitable. On 14 February, as the British continued to fall back in the face of the advancing Japanese, the military hospital was overrun by Japanese soldiers who, ignoring attempts to surrender, massacred around 250 patients and staff. The following day, the 70-day campaign came to its end.

Japan's stunning success has been attributed largely to the woeful performance of the British forces and commanders, including General Arthur E Percival, but the Japanese general, Tomoyuki Yamashita, also took full advantage of the fighting spirit of his infantry. Believing, rightly, that his men had more will to fight, he repeatedly closed with and scattered his enemy.

Japanese losses amounted to a little less than 10,000, while they took around 130,000 prisoners. Among them were the men of the British 18th Infantry Division, the bulk of whom had only just landed as reinforcements. Not even able to get into the battle, they now faced three and a half years in captivity. The defeat was a blow to British prestige, but it also gave Japan the resources it needed to maintain its war effort. For the people of Singapore it was a disaster. The Japanese occupation was harsh and sometimes brutal, starting with the murder of between 5,000 and 50,000 Chinese nationals on the island. The British would not return to Singapore until September 1945.

CONQUERING 'THE GIBRALTAR OF THE EAST'

The fall of Singapore was completed by incompetent British-led withdrawals and Japanese tactics that were both cunning and brutal

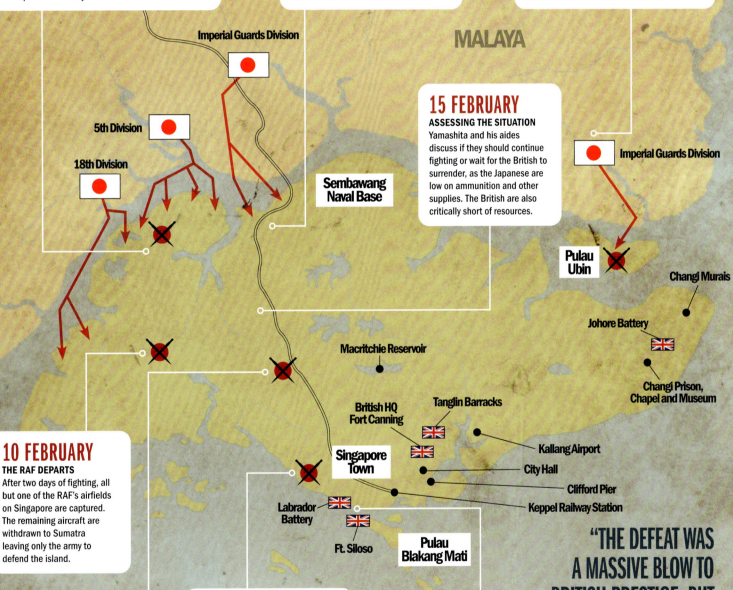

8-9 FEBRUARY
BATTLE OF SARIMBUN BEACH
Two Japanese divisions land in northwest Singapore with Australian machine gunners firing on the invaders. The 22nd Brigade takes the brunt of the attack from the Japanese and they are forced to withdraw.

11 FEBRUARY
THE JAPANESE ADVANCE
The Japanese 5th Division attacks British, Indian and Chinese troops along the Choa Chu Kang and Bukit Timah roads and forces them to retreat further inland.

7-8 FEBRUARY
A DECEPTIVE MANEUVER
The Imperial Japanese Guards Division carry out a feint to the northeast of the island while shelling increases. Percival does not change his thinly spread positions despite the feint.

15 FEBRUARY
ASSESSING THE SITUATION
Yamashita and his aides discuss if they should continue fighting or wait for the British to surrender, as the Japanese are low on ammunition and other supplies. The British are also critically short of resources.

10 FEBRUARY
THE RAF DEPARTS
After two days of fighting, all but one of the RAF's airfields on Singapore are captured. The remaining aircraft are withdrawn to Sumatra leaving only the army to defend the island.

15 FEBRUARY
THE BRITISH CAPITULATE
A British surrender party arrives at Yamashita's headquarters at the Ford Motor Factory. After fractious negotiations, terms of surrender are signed at 6.10pm and the guns fall silent at 8.30pm.

12-15 FEBRUARY
BATTLE OF PASIR PANJANG
The Malay Regiment fights bravely against a Japanese attack along the Pasir Panjang Ridge on Singapore's southwest coast. There are heavy casualties and fierce hand-to-hand fighting before the Malay troops are finally overwhelmed.

14 FEBRUARY
HOSPITAL ATROCITY
The Japanese capture the main British ammunition dump at Alexandra Barracks before entering the nearby military hospital. They murder hundreds of wounded patients and staff.

MALAYA

Imperial Guards Division

5th Division

18th Division

Sembawang Naval Base

Imperial Guards Division

Pulau Ubin

Changi Murais

Johore Battery

Changi Prison, Chapel and Museum

Macritchie Reservoir

British HQ Fort Canning

Tanglin Barracks

Kallang Airport

City Hall

Clifford Pier

Keppel Railway Station

Singapore Town

Labrador Battery

Ft. Siloso

Pulau Blakang Mati

"THE DEFEAT WAS A MASSIVE BLOW TO BRITISH PRESTIGE, BUT IT ALSO GAVE JAPAN THE RESOURCES IT NEEDED TO MAINTAIN ITS WAR EFFORT"

ALLIES TAKE CONTROL

The Yorktown at the moment it was struck by a Japanese aircraft-launched torpedo

MIDWAY

CENTRAL PACIFIC OCEAN 4 JUNE 1942

Despite an overwhelming advantage in numbers, the
Japanese offensive against Midway failed in the face
of superior American intelligence gathering

WORDS WILLIAM WELSH

Image: Alamy

Burning oil tanks hit by Japanese bombs on Sand Island in the Midway Atoll on 4 June

Dauntless dive bombers from the US aircraft carrier Enterprise spotted the Japanese fleet north of Midway Atoll at 10.05am on 4 June 1942. They closed on it and queued up in a single line at 19,000 feet for their attack. The air group commander barked instructions for the 33 dive bombers to attack the heavy carriers Kaga and Akagi, but in the confusion of battle most of the aircraft went after the 38,200-ton Kaga. 15 minutes later, the metal birds swooped down on their prey.

The flight deck of the mighty Kaga was packed with aircraft. Air crews were refueling Zero fighters and making last-minute adjustments to fully armed bombers that were minutes away from launching against the US carrier strike force. "Dive bombers!" shouted a lookout on the Kaga as the Dauntless aircraft began releasing their 500-pound bombs at 2,500

Right: Chuichi Nagumo was one of the Imperial Japanese Navy's (IJN's) most seasoned officers and hero of the Pearl Harbor attack

feet. "I saw this glint in the sun – it looked like a beautiful silver waterfall – these were the dive bombers coming down," said Lt Cdr John S 'Jimmy' Thach, a fighter pilot from the Yorktown who witnessed the attack.

The first bomb struck the Kaga starboard aft among the aircraft waiting to launch. The second and third exploded near the forward elevator, one of them penetrating to the hangar deck, where it set off secondary explosions among armed bombers waiting to be sent to the flight deck. The fourth bomb struck amidships on the port side.

The survivors abandoned ship. At dusk, a pair of internal explosions rocked the great vessel, and she rolled over and sank.

Before the day was over, the Imperial Japanese Navy's other three large carriers participating in the Battle of Midway suffered the same fate. The titanic battle for supremacy in the Pacific would only cost the US Navy one of its valuable carriers. In a single day, the Americans wrested the initiative in the Pacific Theater from the Japanese.

Two offensives

Following the initial clash between Japanese and United States aircraft carriers in the Coral Sea in May 1942, the Japanese sought to return to the offensive against the US. The Americans had landed a heavy psychological blow against the Japanese by the daring long-range bomber strike against Tokyo known as the Doolittle Raid in April 1942. The following month, Japanese and American aircraft carriers clashed for the first time in the Coral Sea. These two events spurred Admiral Isoroku Yamamoto to devise a comprehensive plan whereby the Japanese would retake the momentum from the Americans.

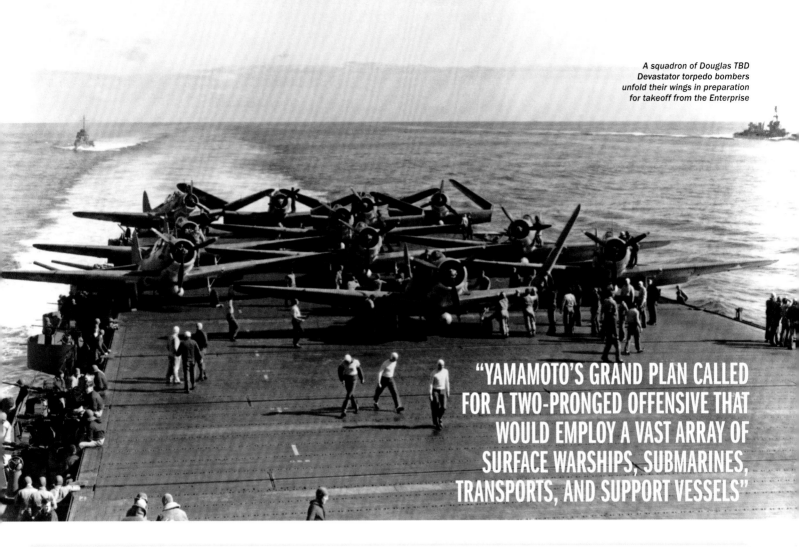

A squadron of Douglas TBD Devastator torpedo bombers unfold their wings in preparation for takeoff from the Enterprise

"YAMAMOTO'S GRAND PLAN CALLED FOR A TWO-PRONGED OFFENSIVE THAT WOULD EMPLOY A VAST ARRAY OF SURFACE WARSHIPS, SUBMARINES, TRANSPORTS, AND SUPPORT VESSELS"

Japanese Zero fighter aircraft on the deck of the heavy aircraft carrier Akagi in early 1942

Yamamoto wanted to extend the Japanese Empire's eastern perimeter into the Central Pacific to furnish a greater buffer for Japan's Home Islands. To do this, he drew up a plan for his Combined Fleet to capture Midway Atoll, an outlier of the Hawaiian Islands located 1,300 miles northwest of Pearl Harbor.

The objective of Yamamoto's offensive was to capture Midway in order to use its airstrip to project Japanese airpower deep into the Central Pacific Ocean. Yamamoto's grand plan called for a two-pronged offensive that would employ a vast array of surface warships, submarines, transports, and support vessels.

Operation Aleutian Islands (Operation AI) was a feint designed to draw one of the US carriers to the northern Pacific. To execute the operation, Rear Admiral Kakuji Kakuta's Second Carrier Strike Force had 40 attack aircraft on the light carriers the Ryujo and Junyo. Kakuta was to send his carrier aircraft on 3 June to bomb Dutch Harbor, the principal port in the Aleutians, while Japanese amphibious forces landed on Attu and Kiska Islands at the tip of the Aleutian Chain.

The main attack, known as Operation Midway Island (Operation MI), would go forward the following day. Yamamoto planned to devote the bulk of the Combined Fleet's forces to the operation. Vice Admiral Chuichi Nagumo, the hero of the attack on Pearl Harbor, would once again have the same four heavy carriers – Akagi, Kaga, Soryu, and Hiryu – that he had used in the surprise attack six months earlier.

On 4 June, Nagumo was to take up a position 300 miles northeast of Midway and launch aircraft from his First Carrier Striking Force to pulverize Midway's defenses in preparation for the amphibious landing. Nagumo's carrier force would have 261 aircraft as its offensive arm.

Other large forces would follow behind Nagumo's carrier group. Rear Admiral Raizo Tanaka's invasion force of 5,000 troops in a dozen transports would rendezvous off west of Midway with Vice Admiral Nobutake Kondo's Second Fleet, which would escort them to their objective. Bringing up the rear would be the First Fleet's Main Force under Yamamoto, which would deploy 300 miles west of Nagumo. Yamamoto would direct the various components of the operation from his flagship, the gigantic battleship Yamato.

The unsinkable carrier

Following the action in Coral Sea, US Pacific Fleet commander Admiral Chester Nimitz recalled Task Force 16, which was built around the carriers Hornet and Enterprise, to return to Pearl Harbor. Its veteran commander, Vice Admiral William Halsey, was seriously

BATTLE OF MIDWAY
4 JUNE 1942

0510, 5 June:
Horyu scuttled
0900: Sank

1920:
Soryu sinks

0500, 5 -june:
Akagi scuttled

1925:
Kaga sinks

B-17S

Hiryu Second Strike Force (B5N2s only)

Hiryu Strike Force (D3A1s only)

SBD+TBD+F4F

SBD+TBD+F4F

1331
1104
1045
1000
Hiryu
Kaga
Akagi
1025-30
Soryu
0730
B-26 +TBF
0755
SBD
0810-39
0928

2400
1700
1550
1445

TOMONAGA

SB2U-3

B-17

Search arc of Catalinas extend...

03 ASSAULT ON IJN CARRIERS
Japanese lookouts spotted American dive bombers at 10.20am over the carrier group. The Americans caught the Akagi, Kaga, and Soryu carriers at peak vulnerability; however, they did not see the Hiryu. The flight decks were crowded with the flight deck crews refueling A6M Zero fighters and preparing armed bombers for launch against the American carriers.

04 CARRIERS AFLAME
The American dive bombers in the first strike wave hit the Kaga with four bombs, the Soryu with three bombs, and the Akagi with two bombs. The dive bomber attack lasted only four minutes. The bombs touched off secondary explosions that transformed the decks of all three ships into infernos.

02 THE IJN ATTACKS
At 6.30am, Japanese dive bombers screamed down on Eastern Island to drop their single-bomb loads on the airfield, while level bombers dropped high-explosive ordnance on the infrastructure on Sand Island to the west. US anti-aircraft batteries shot down 11 Japanese aircraft.

01 MIDWAY ATOLL
US-held Midway Atoll consisted of Eastern Island, where an airstrip was located, and Sand Island, which housed a seaplane base, radar installations, and fuel dumps. Nimitz toured Midway in early May to inspect its defenses, and afterwards reinforced it with aircraft, troops, and heavy weapons from Pearl Harbor.

MIDWAY ISLAND

0600

N
W E
S

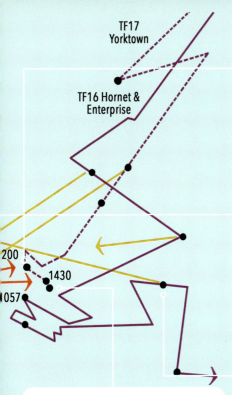

TF17 Yorktown

TF16 Hornet & Enterprise

200
1430
057

05 YORKTOWN ATTACKED

18 dive bombers escorted by six fighters from the Hiryu attacked the Yorktown at noon. Three bombs struck the deck of the carrier. One bomb struck the forward flight deck, another struck the aft flight deck and penetrated the funnel, and yet another hit the number one elevator on the aft deck.

06 TORPEDO STRIKE

A second strike wave from the Hiryu composed of ten Japanese torpedo bombers, escorted by six Zeros, approached the Yorktown at approximately 5pm. Of the five bombers that managed to launch their torpedoes, two hit their already stricken carrier. The torpedoes slammed into the port side of the Yorktown, damaging her fuel tanks and boilers.

07 HIRYU IS CRIPPLED

A second strike wave composed of dive bombers from the Enterprise and Hornet hit the Hiryu with four bombs at 5pm. Two bombs landed amidships, and two bombs struck the fore deck. The bombs penetrated to the hangar deck, where they set off secondary explosions that ruptured the hull plates below the water line and caused flooding.

08 YORKTOWN SINKS

Salvage crews worked tirelessly on the Yorktown, which was listing badly, in an effort to save her. But in the early afternoon of 6 June, Japanese submarine I-168 snuck up on the Yorktown and launched a spread of torpedoes. Two hit the Yorktown, causing her to sink on the following morning.

Areas under Japanese control by July 1942

→ Japanese Air Strikes A6M, B5N2, D3A1
→ Midway Land Based Air Army B-26, Navy TBF, Marine Corps SBD, SB2U-3
→ Midway Based Army B-17s
→ US Navy Carrier Air Strikes SBD, TBD, F4F

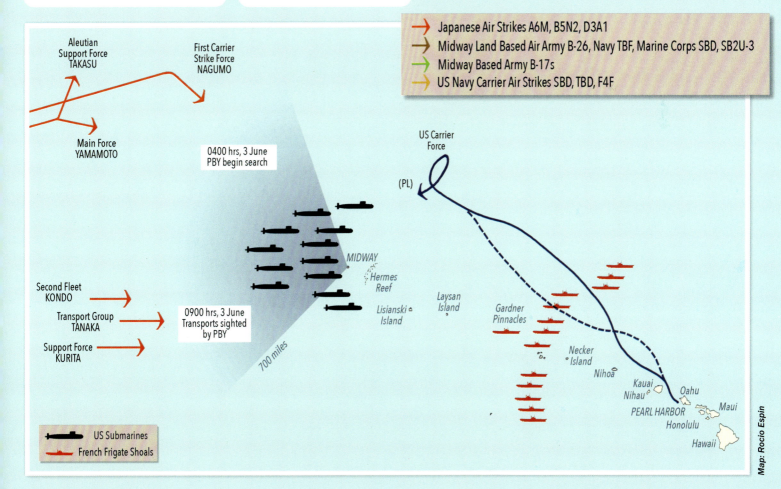

Aleutian Support Force TAKASU

First Carrier Strike Force NAGUMO

Main Force YAMAMOTO

0400 hrs, 3 June PBY begin search

Second Fleet KONDO

Transport Group TANAKA

0900 hrs, 3 June Transports sighted by PBY

Support Force KURITA

US Carrier Force

(PL)

700 miles

MIDWAY
Hermes Reef
Lisianski Island
Laysan Island
Gardner Pinnacles
Necker Island
Nihoa
Kauai
Nihau
Oahu
Maui
PEARL HARBOR
Honolulu
Hawaii

⊢⊣ US Submarines
━ French Frigate Shoals

ill, and Nimitz replaced him with neophyte Rear Admiral Raymond Spruance.

Overall command of the two task forces went to Rear Admiral Frank Fletcher, commander of Task Force 17, who had performed ably in the Coral Sea. The nucleus of Task Force 17 was the carrier Yorktown, which had sustained major damage in the same skirmish, and was in need of urgent repairs if she were to participate in Midway. She arrived in Pearl Harbor on 22 May to get patched up so that she could take part in the battle that was brewing. Meanwhile, Task Force 16 arrived in Pearl Harbor on 26 May for refueling and resupply.

Altogether, the two US task forces had a total of 233 carrier aircraft, which included 112 dive bombers, 42 torpedo bombers, and 79 fighters. In addition, the Americans possessed an assortment of 115 Navy and Marine aircraft, many of which were obsolete, on Midway Atoll.

US Navy Captain Cyril Simmard, the senior commander at Midway, had 3,650 troops of the Sixth Marine Defense Battalion and multiple anti-aircraft batteries with which to defend Midway against the expected amphibious attack.

The air group that Simmard commanded at Midway would function as an "unsinkable aircraft carrier" that would help balance the Japanese advantage in carriers. Both Yamamoto and Nimitz knew that whoever won the battle in the sky would control the island when the battle was over.

Yamamoto did not expect the US Pacific Fleet to be in a position to contest the invasion force. The Japanese mistakenly believed that both the Lexington and Yorktown had been destroyed in the Coral Sea. The Americans had indeed lost the Lexington at Coral Sea, but not the Yorktown. As for the other US carriers, the Enterprise, Hornet, and Saratoga, the Japanese had no idea where they were in the Pacific. The Saratoga was unavailable for Midway because it was undergoing extensive repairs in Puget Sound following a Japanese submarine attack in January 1942.

Intelligence failure

Although the Imperial Japanese Navy had destroyed the American battleships in its Pearl Harbor attack on 7 December 1941, it had failed to catch any of the American carriers in the harbor. Yamamoto believed that the American aircraft carriers would sortie from Pearl Harbor once the invasion was in full swing. At that point, Nagumo and Yamamoto would team up against the weaker US Pacific Fleet and destroy it in a decisive battle that would compel the United States to sue for peace.

To monitor the movements of the US Pacific Fleet, Yamamoto ordered Vice Admiral Teruhisa

"NAGUMO BELIEVED IT WAS IMPERATIVE TO COMPLETELY DESTROY THE AIRSTRIP SO THAT ENEMY AIRCRAFT COULD NOT LAUNCH REPEATED SORTIES AGAINST HIS CARRIERS"

Image: Alamy

Komatsu to deploy his fleet of ten submarines in an arc between Hawaii and Midway no later than 2 June to watch for the US aircraft carriers. The only way the Japanese would know how many they would be up against at Midway was from Komatsu's submarines and from scout planes launched by Nagumo's fleet once it had arrived north of Midway.

Through back-breaking effort, the US combat intelligence unit at Pearl Harbor gleaned that the Aleutians strike was nothing more than a diversion, and that the real objective was Midway. The intelligence data spurred Nimitz to put his two task forces into position northeast of Midway to ambush Nagumo's carrier strike force. Both US task forces included cruisers and destroyers with which to screen their carriers from attack by Japanese carrier aircraft and submarines.

During the last week of May, both sides sailed for the waters around Midway. Nagumo's carrier group departed from Japan on 27 May, and other elements followed over the next several days both from Japan and the Marianas Islands. Meanwhile, Task Force 16 sailed from Pearl Harbor on 28 May, and it was followed two days later by Task Force 17. Both task forces were in position 350 miles north of Midway before the Japanese submarines were in place between Oahu and Midway. The result was an intelligence failure

for the Imperial Japanese Navy that would leave Nagumo's carrier group vulnerable to a first strike by the American carriers.

While Nagumo's carrier group moved into position north of Midway, Admiral Kakuta sent strike aircraft from his two light carriers on 3 June to bomb Dutch Harbor. Nimitz sent a task force to counter the Japanese thrust in that sector, but he did not send any of his prized carriers. The feint failed to draw off a US carrier.

The Japanese carriers began launching 108 aircraft to bomb Midway at 4.30am on 4 June. Lieutenant Joichi Tomonaga led a strike group that comprised 36 each of Mitsubishi A6M Zeros, Aichi D3A1 dive bombers, and Nakajima B5N bombers. The Americans used easy-to-pronounce names to report sightings of Japanese aircraft. Thus, 'Val' and 'Kate' were the names appropriated for the Aichi D3A1 dive bomber and the Nakajima B5N bomber. The Kate bombers could be configured either for torpedo missions or for level bombing from high altitude. The Vals carried one 550-pound bomb, and the Kates

one 1,760-pound high-explosive bomb. For the first strike wave against Midway, the carriers Hiryu and Soryu launched their Kates, and the Akagi and Kaga unleashed their Vals.

Midway radar picked up the incoming hostile aircraft when they were 93 miles out. Air raid sirens wailed as the pilots of the Navy and Marine aircraft scrambled to get aloft in order to avoid near-certain destruction if the aircraft had remained on the ground. 25 minutes later, the airfield was empty. The motley group of US fighters and bombers flew north directly toward the incoming Japanese aircraft.

Sporadic dogfights between the incoming Japanese and outgoing American aircraft from Midway broke out 30 miles from the atoll. Japanese Zeros peeled off from the strike wave to engage the American aircraft, while the Japanese bombers continued on to Midway. Likewise, the US dive, torpedo, and level bombers from Midway continued flying north in search of the Japanese carriers.

After his strike group had bombed Midway at 6.30am, Tomonaga radioed Nagumo that

"THE RESULT WAS CATASTROPHIC, WITH NEARLY ALL OF THE AIRCRAFT BEING SHOT DOWN WITHOUT REGISTERING A SINGLE TORPEDO HIT"

Right: Despite the best efforts of its crew, the carrier Yorktown capsized and sunk on 7 June

another strike was needed to ensure maximum damage to the airstrip and other infrastructure.

Nagumo's dilemma

Earlier that morning, at 5.52am, PBY Catalina pilot Lieutenant Howard Ady reported sighting two Japanese carriers and reported their bearing, course, and speed. Upon hearing the report, Fletcher ordered Spruance to close with the Japanese carrier group and launch his bombers.

Nagumo had only a fraction of the number of search planes looking for the Americans as they had looking for him. At dawn, five Japanese warships launched a total of seven search aircraft. In contrast, the Americans had 33 PBY Catalinas based at Midway, and they had been searching since 30 May for the approaching Japanese warships. This gave the Americans a considerable advantage in aerial reconnaissance, and enabled them to spot the Japanese carriers early in the battle. Early sightings had enabled the Americans to send Boeing B-17 Flying Fortresses against the Japanese warships, but they missed their targets.

While the first wave of Japanese aircraft was assaulting Midway Atoll, Nagumo's air crews were arming a second wave of aircraft to strike the American carriers once they were located. In anticipation of a second strike wave against the American carriers,

Nagumo had his air crews arming 'Vals' with armor-piercing bombs and 'Kates' with torpedoes, both highly effective against ships.

Upon receiving Tomonaga's message calling for a second strike against Midway, Nagumo issued orders at 7.15am for the air crews to arm the Vals and Kates for a second strike against the atoll, rather than the unsighted carriers. Nagumo believed it was imperative to completely destroy the airstrip so that enemy aircraft could not launch repeated sorties against his carriers.

The Japanese air crews had to rush to arm the Vals on the hangar decks of the Hiryu and Soryu with high-explosives rather than armor-piercing bombs, and to take the torpedoes off the Kates on the Akagi and Kaga and replace them with high-explosive bombs. The crews needed to work at breakneck speed, because soon the carriers would have to recover the aircraft returning from Midway.

Nagumo received a report at 7.30am that dramatically altered the situation. The pilot of a Japanese floatplane from the cruiser Tone accompanying the First Carrier Fleet reported spotting warships of an enemy task force 240 miles northeast of Midway. 50 minutes later, he confirmed the presence of an enemy carrier in the task force.

The report from the Tone rattled Nagumo and his staff, as they had not expected the carriers

of the US Pacific Fleet to be so close to Midway that early in the battle. After learning of the presence of an American task force, Nagumo issued orders at 7.45am for the air crews to leave the torpedoes on any Kates they had not yet reconfigured with high-explosive bombs.

At 7am, the first strike wave of 121 aircraft took off from the Hornet and Enterprise. Air Group Commander Stanhope Ring led the Hornet's 60 aircraft, and Lieutenant Commander Wade McClusky led the Enterprise's 61 aircraft. As the US bombers and fighters raced toward the Japanese carriers, the US land-based dive and torpedo bombers from Midway were approaching Nagumo's carriers from the south.

Nagumo's fleet had assumed a box formation, with the screening warships protecting the carriers inside. Inside the box, the carriers zigzagged or sailed in wide circles to avoid being struck by enemy torpedoes. The strike aircraft from Midway arrived in small groups over the course of a 90-minute period. However, they failed to register hits, and were either shot down or warded off.

Fletcher, who retained a large number of the Yorktown's aircraft for a follow-up attack, ordered the Yorktown to launch 35 aircraft to join the first strike wave at 8.30am. Shortly after the Yorktown launched her planes, the Japanese carriers began recovering Tomonaga's

Midway Atoll contained an airfield essential to Japanese plans to expand into the Central Pacific

Survivors from Yorktown transfer between USS Portland (right) and USS Fulton (Left)

Images Alamy

aircraft. He ordered his fleet to turn east-northeast in preparation for a strike against the American carriers. The US strike aircraft from Midway had completed their attacks by 9.30am. Nagumo and his subordinates knew that more attacks were coming, and they rushed to get the Vals and Kates ready for the strike against the American carriers.

Nagumo's course change confounded the dive bomber formations looking for the Japanese carriers. Both Ring and McClusky arrived at the position where they expected the enemy fleet to be only to find open ocean below them. Ring failed to locate the enemy and landed to refuel at Midway. However, McClusky turned north at 9.35am in the hope of finding the enemy before having to abort his strike and return to the Enterprise. The torpedo bomber squadrons from the three American carriers had no trouble finding the Japanese carriers, though, and they began making slow glide approaches against the carriers at 9.20am.

Suicide mission

Each Devastator carried a 12-foot-long, 1,200-pound torpedo. As many as 50 Zeros pounced on the attacking planes, eight miles from the carriers. In what turned out to be tantamount to a suicide mission, all but six of the obsolete Devastators were shot down by Zeros and anti-aircraft guns on the warships. The flak was so intense that many of the torpedo bombers never made it close enough to their targets to launch their deadly cargo.

The result was catastrophic, with nearly all of the aircraft being shot down without registering a single torpedo hit. Their sacrifice was not in vain though, because they tied up shipboard anti-aircraft batteries and Zeros that might have been used against the incoming Dauntless dive bombers. Additionally, the torpedo bombers delayed the takeoff of the second wave of Japanese strike aircraft against the US carriers.

As McClusky led his 33 aircraft, Leslie was guiding 17 dive bombers from the Yorktown toward the Japanese carriers. McClusky's aircraft formed up at 19,000 feet for attack, while Leslie's formed up at 14,500 feet. Leslie approached the carriers from the southeast and McClusky advanced from the southwest.

Although McClusky intended for his 33 dive bombers to split into

"THE JAPANESE WERE THIRSTING FOR REVENGE, AND IT FELL TO THE HIRYU'S AIRCRAFT CREWS TO INFLICT DAMAGE ON THE AMERICANS"

two groups to attack the Akagi and Kaga, all but three went for the Kaga because of a communications mistake. Three of the pilots realized this error and diverted instead to the Akagi. As for Leslie, he led his dive bombers in an attack on the Soryu. All three carriers suffered heavy damage from the US Navy dive bombers. Nagumo was forced to transfer his flag from the burning Akagi to the cruiser Nagara.

The Japanese were thirsting for revenge, and it fell to the aircraft crews of the Hiryu to inflict damage on the Americans. The Hiryu began launching its aircraft at approximately 11am. Fletcher ordered an additional 15 Grumman F4F Wildcats to launch to join the 12 fighters already conducting combat air patrol. Because the Yorktown's radar picked up the attackers as they were inbound, the flight deck crew was able to send parked aircraft to the hangar deck. Although the Yorktown's anti-aircraft guns and fighters downed 13 Vals, the Japanese dive-bomber attack was a success. Three bombs exploded

on the flight deck of the Yorktown. The heavy damage compelled Fletcher to transfer his flag to the cruiser Astoria. Damage control crews succeeded in putting out the fires after which the flight deck crew was able to recover Leslie's dive bombers as they returned from their mission. In addition, they refueled the Wildcats in anticipation of a second strike.

When Rear Admiral Tamon Yamaguchi on the Hiryu learned from search aircraft after 1pm that three American carriers had attacked the carrier group, he ordered another strike. The Hiryu began launching torpedo bombers for a second strike against the American carriers at 1.30pm. Since the damage control crews on the Yorktown had put out the fires started by the first strike, the Japanese Kates attacking the Yorktown mistakenly believed they were attacking a second carrier.

Flaming flattops

An American search plane finally located the Hiryu at mid-afternoon, and less than an hour afterwards, 30 dive bombers took off from the Hornet and Enterprise against Nagumo's last functioning carrier. They destroyed it with four bombs.

As the sun set over the flaming flattops that were once the pride of Japan, the horror of what occurred spread through the Imperial Japanese Navy. Massive explosions ripped through the Kaga and Soryu, sinking within minutes of each other. Both sides lost large numbers of aircraft. The Americans lost 179 land-based and carrier aircraft, while the Japanese lost all 261 of their carrier aircraft, as well as 71 fighters that the carriers were ferrying for service on Midway once it was captured. Though the Japanese had other carriers, the four lost at Midway were the pride of the navy, and their absence was felt.

Four Japanese destroyers fired torpedoes at the Akagi at dawn on 5 June to sink her, and the Hiryu went down a few hours later. Yamamoto canceled Operation MI that same afternoon. Nimitz had outfought Yamamoto; in so doing, he torpedoed Yamamoto's dream of destroying the US Pacific Fleet and of forcing the Americans to sue for peace.

Admiral Chester Nimitz was highly successful in the Pacific Theater and masterminded the defeat of the IJN

*The Battle of Stalingrad
claimed the lives of
approximately 1.2
million people*

BATTLE OF STALINGRAD

SOVIET UNION 23 AUGUST 1942 – 2 FEBRUARY 1943

During the final months of this deadly struggle, an entire army would crumble and the fortunes of war would permanently turn against Nazi Germany

WORDS NIK CORNISH

Image: Alamy

It had not been one of the major objectives of the Axis's summer offensive of 1942, but by September that year Stalingrad had become the focal point of the Eastern Front, as its defenders simply refused to give up. This led to an increasing number of German troops being committed to its reduction. However, by 16 November 1942 what was to be the Sixth German Army's final, desperate attempt to push the battered remains of the city's defenders from their blood-soaked toeholds on the western bank of the Volga River, ended.

Stalingrad was a model garden and industrial city that ran for 25 miles along the western bank of the unbridged Volga River, which at some points reaches a width of 4,900 feet. At roughly five miles wide the city was long and narrow, and was home to some 400,000 people. Much of the population worked in the large factory district located in the northern part of the city. Here the Dzerzhinsky tractor factory, Red October steel works, Silikat factory, and the Barrikady artillery factory dominated the city's landscape.

South of the city center the area was overlooked by the 335-feet high ancient burial mound Mamayev Kurgan, control of which would allow one side or the other the perfect artillery position from which to dominate the city. Just to the south of the Mamayev Kurgan, near to the main ferry landing point, the Tsaritsa River ran along a narrow gorge into the Volga at 90 degrees. Beyond the city's suburbs the steppe stretched, undulating gently in all directions and rising gently to the west, where it met the Don River over 62 miles away.

Defending the rubble of central and northern Stalingrad were the men of the 62nd Army commanded by Lieutenant General Vasily Chuikov. To the south, a less industrialized area, was the 64th Army led by Major General Mikhail Shumilov. By mid-November the Soviet troops in the city were reduced to holding pockets of varying sizes, like islands adrift in a sea of rubble, often connected only by the Volga, across which all their meager supplies and reinforcements arrived. Yet, by some supreme act of desperation, bravery, and tenacity they held on, grinding down their attackers in conditions that resembled those of Verdun.

Facing them, the German Sixth Army, under Lieutenant General Friedrich Paulus, and part of Army Group B (a sub-division of AGS) commanded by Colonel General Max von Weichs, had pushed eastwards from the city's outskirts, coming to within 1,640 feet of the Volga. There they had stalled, trapped in a nightmare landscape of their own air and artillery attacks' creation. Dependent on a supply line that stretched across the steppe to the Don River bridgeheads, particularly the railway crossing at Kalach 45 miles away, Sixth Army was exhausted but still anticipated victory. But they were unaware of the extent of the Soviet forces concentrating on their flanks.

Soviet planning

Planning for an ambitious counteroffensive in the Stalingrad area had been underway since

POWS crossing the frozen waters of the Volga

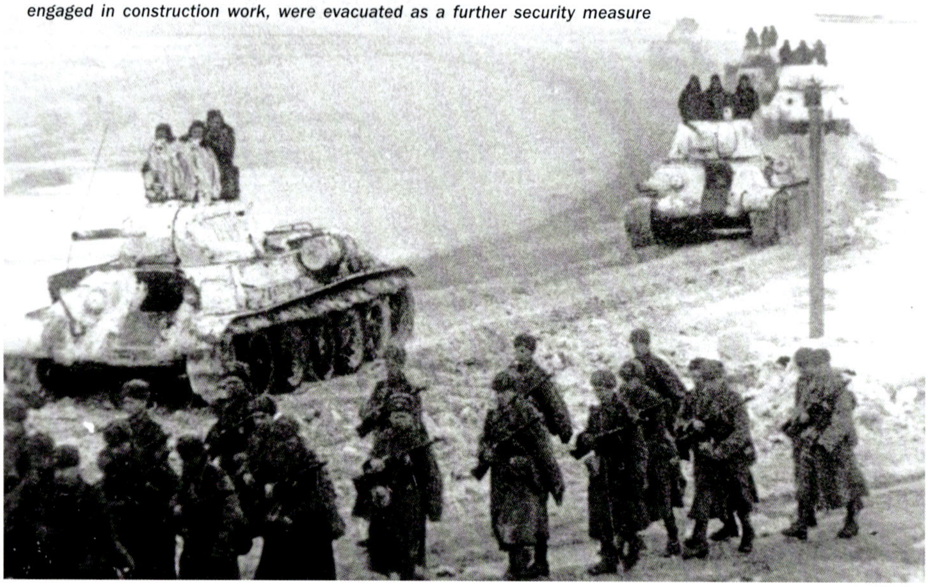

The assembly of men and machines for Operation Uranus was carefully undertaken. Movement into assembly areas took place mainly at night or during periods of bad weather. During October all civilians, other than those engaged in construction work, were evacuated as a further security measure

SIXTH ARMY POWS

Prisoners faced a bleak future as they were herded together

It had taken the Soviets some time to realize the numbers trapped in the Stalingrad pocket. Consequently there was a degree of confusion over the numbers actually captured. There is no doubt that many Axis troops were summarily executed during the fighting as a reaction to the conditions many Soviet troops had seen their own men kept in as POWs. Furthermore, of the large number of Hiwis, many attempted to melt into the chaos. A figure that is generally accepted for Axis POWs is 91,000.

As Paulus underwent interrogation and had his staff car confiscated, his hungry, exhausted, and sick men stumbled across the river they had bled to reach. Thousands died of malnutrition, frostbite, and mercy shots as they were herded eastwards to camps that they were often expected to build for themselves. As their former commanders bickered and took positions that either damned or supported their government, their men continued to die.

The POWs were divided by nationality, and the non-Germans were treated marginally better and placed in positions of power over their former allies. Inevitably there was dissent. Of the 45,000 who survived into the spring and summer, work was the only way to ensure some hope of a return home. Those with building skills were set to rebuild towns and cities ruined by the war or for party apparatchiks in Moscow, where their work was highly valued. In 1955 only 5,000 Stalingrad veterans returned to Germany.

"IN 1955, ONLY 5,000 STALINGRAD VETERANS RETURNED TO GERMANY"

The legacy of Stalingrad: Axis corpses await burial on the outskirts of the city

Above: Following the end of their November attacks the German troops in and around the city resigned themselves to the prospect of another winter in the USSR. Their preparations for a quiet, relatively cosy Christmas were to prove overly optimistic

Right: Across the lines outside of Stalingrad the Soviets had been building up two groups of armies. To the north was the Southwestern Front, to the south the Stalingrad Front. Don Front lay between them. Stalingrad's defenders, 62nd and 64th Armies were assigned to Stalingrad Front. Up to 700,000 men and 1,300 tanks now waited for orders

12 September. At a conference in Moscow, General of the Army Georgy Zhukov and Colonel General Aleksandr Vasilevsky suggested to Stalin that Sixth Army be encircled by thrusts through the left and right flanks that were defended by the Third and Fourth Romanian Armies respectively. Both Romanian forces were weak in armor and anti-tank weapons and were holding positions that were vulnerable and made poor use of the terrain. Armored forces were to break through the Romanians, drive across the steppe and then link up at Kalach. The distance to be covered by the northern arm was 80 miles, the southern 60 miles. Southwestern and Don Fronts (under commanders Lieutenant General Nikolai Vatutin and Lieutenant General Konstantin Rokossovsky respectively) were to comprise the northern thrust and Stalingrad Front would perform the southern thrust.

When the encirclement was complete, part of the force would face inwards to contain Sixth Army, and part outwards to prevent any relief effort that, it was anticipated, would come from the southwest. Stalin gave the plan his backing within 24 hours of its proposal. Code-

"THE ROMANIAN ARMOR RAN INTO THE T34S OF XXVI TANK CORPS AND NARROWLY ESCAPED COMPLETE DESTRUCTION"

named Operation Uranus, its start date was to be 9 November. In order to assemble the vast amount of men, weapons, and supplies needed, it was decided that Stalingrad's defenders would only be allowed a minimum of reinforcements: everything possible was to be sent to the flanks.

Intelligence discounted

The Romanian Third Army, aware of some sort of Soviet build-up, requested permission in late October to liquidate the Soviet bridgeheads over the Don River at Serafimovich and Kletskaya, but the request was refused. German intelligence was convinced that the major Soviet offensive of the winter would be directed at Army Group Center, which still threatened Moscow. Furthermore, Stalingrad itself appeared to be on the brink of capture and all Sixth Army's resources were focused on that objective. Romanian Fourth Army, to

the right, was equally concerned at Soviet movements and build-up, but these concerns were also dismissed.

To an extent the Soviets had contributed to this by a series of poorly prepared counterattacks made to the north of the city during October that had been easily repulsed, giving Sixth Army a false sense of security. Indeed, Hitler himself scoffed at the possibility of the Red Army carrying out anything approaching a major operation, as he regarded it as a spent force awaiting the coup de grace shortly to be delivered. However, Sixth Army's intelligence staff did warn Paulus of a Soviet build-up, but their concerns were felt to be overly pessimistic and were discounted. It was a classic case of underestimating the enemy.

Third Romanian Army declared that a Soviet attack was due on 7 to 8 November, 25 years after the Bolshevik Revolution. Although nothing happened, Luftwaffe reconnaissance flights

A Soviet 76mm infantry support gun prepares to fire. Pockets of resistance were left to be mopped up by follow-up units. Food and other supplies were sacrificed for fuel and ammunition

THE AIRLIFT

The efforts to create Hitler's promised sky bridge fell short

Supplying the men and machines in the Stalingrad pocket by air began on 23 November. Ju-52 transport planes flew into Pitomnik airfield (roughly 12 miles from central Stalingrad) mainly from Tatsinskaya to the west.

Despite the objections of local Luftwaffe commanders Hermann Göring would not explain to Hitler that the air bridge was unable to deliver the necessary tonnage of supplies. It was estimated that 300 tons per day would keep the garrison functioning, whereas 750 tons would enable it to perform at an operational capacity. This latter figure was revised down to 500 tons. The reality was somewhat different. Even when He-III and FW-200 bombers were pressed into service to supplement the Ju-52s the delivery of 300 tons was achieved only once.

Tatsinskaya was overrun by Soviet armor on 24 December. It was recaptured four days later. Flights were switched to airfields further west, extending the flight time. Up to 45,000 wounded were evacuated by air. Pitomnik fell on 17 January, and Gumrak became the main airstrip for six days, until it too was captured. The remaining airfield couldn't deal with transport planes. Supplies were parachuted in but most were lost in snow.

Above: *The Soviets placed battery after battery of anti-aircraft guns on the flight paths to Stalingrad. These took a heavy toll on the lumbering, fully laden aircraft both arriving and departing*

Above: *A wrecked Ju-52 at Tatsinskaya. Surprised by the attack, many aircraft took off but 72 (Luftwaffe figures) were destroyed on the ground. The Soviets claimed 300 destroyed including "a trainload of disassembled aircraft". Whichever figure is correct, it was a heavy blow to the airlift*

backed up the Romanians' concerns – the Soviets were increasing their forces to the north of the city. Hitler agreed to reinforce the Romanians with XXXXVIII Panzer Corps' 14th and 22nd Panzer divisions and First Romanian Armored Division. But these units were understrength and lacked both modern tanks and fuel. Nevertheless, it looked like a powerful force – at least at Hitler's HQ if not out on the steppe. When General Hermann Hoth, commanding Fourth Panzer Army – which included XXXXVIII Panzer Corps and VI Romanian Corps – voiced his concerns about the Soviet concentrations developing opposite VI Corps, he too was ignored. Hoth's five Romanian infantry divisions covered the line south from Stalingrad to Romanian Fourth Army's position. Again, to soothe his ally's nerves, Hitler sanctioned the issue of a small number of anti-tank guns and mines to Romanian Fourth Army.

Operation Uranus (North)

The build-up of Soviet forces for Operation Uranus took longer than anticipated, so Zhukov asked for a postponement of the attack and was granted ten days. On 18 November Chuikov was informed of the attack, and for his 62nd Army it came just in time, as the Volga was almost frozen to the point where it was too difficult for ships, but too weak for foot soldiers or vehicles to cross.

As the ice floes ground downstream to their rear, Stalingrad's defenders had been split into three groups – two small pockets and the main one, which ran from the Red October steel works to the southern suburbs. When the frontoviki (front line men) heard the gunfire to the north during the morning of 19 November they did not believe the rumored counteroffensive was underway. It was only when artillery fire was heard coming from the south 24 hours later that they let themselves believe it was true.

The first victim of Operation Uranus was Third Romanian Army. At 8.50am Fifth Tank Army (Southwestern Front) struck at the junction of the Romanians' left flank, where it abutted the Italian Eighth Army. To the Soviet right, First Guards Army was positioned to prevent any Italian counterattacks. Four hours of desperate fighting resulted in a Soviet breakthrough with support from the Red Air Force as the morning mist rose. Alerted to the Soviet attack, Paulus's HQ was nevertheless unaware of its seriousness until later in the day. By then Soviet tanks of IV Tank Corps supported by III Guards Cavalry Corps were through IV Romanian Corps defenses, supported to their right by Fifth Tank Army, which was reducing Romanian II Corps

In the city patrolling continued. A nicely posed shot of Germans moving cautiously through the Red October steel works provided the media at home with optimistic propaganda for civilian consumption

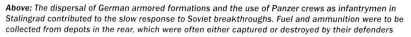

Above: *The dispersal of German armored formations and the use of Panzer crews as infantrymen in Stalingrad contributed to the slow response to Soviet breakthroughs. Fuel and ammunition were to be collected from depots in the rear, which were often either captured or destroyed by their defenders*

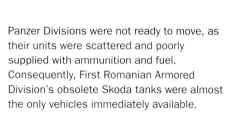

to a state of confusion. At Army Group B's headquarters, Weichs ordered Paulus to halt operations in Stalingrad, "with the objective of moving forces to cover the rear [left] flank of Sixth Army and secure lines of communication".

Convinced that Don Front's attack was the main threat, Weichs had ordered XXXXVIII Panzer Corps to drive to the Romanians' rescue. In effect Weichs was trying to assemble a mobile striking force to hold the Soviet armor, utilizing virtually all of Sixth Army's Panzer and motorized divisions. However, 16th and 22nd

Panzer Divisions were not ready to move, as their units were scattered and poorly supplied with ammunition and fuel. Consequently, First Romanian Armored Division's obsolete Skoda tanks were almost the only vehicles immediately available.

The Romanian armor ran into the T34s of XXVI Tank Corps and narrowly escaped complete destruction. Soviet armor and cavalry forces were under strict orders to avoid serious combat, their primary objective being to encircle Sixth Army, so they pushed ahead,

Above: Other bridges, such as that at Vertyachy, were still in German hands, and it was for these that the Axis forces west of Stalingrad headed. However, a shortage of horses meant that a lot of equipment had to be abandoned

Left: Men and officers celebrate the link-up of Stalingrad and Southwestern Fronts at Sovietsky Farm nine miles closer to Stalingrad on 23 November

Operation Uranus (South)

Sixth Army HQ was situated 12 miles north of Kalach – the proposed Soviet junction point – at Golubinsky, unaware that Soviet tanks were within 19 miles of their position. During the course of 21 November it was decided to relocate to the rail junction of Gumrak, just west of Stalingrad, where there was also an airfield. However, during this movement a message came through ordering Sixth Army to "stand firm in spite of danger of temporary encirclement", but was overlooked. Paulus's staff were not fully aware of the threat moving towards them from the southern pincer.

Stalingrad Front, under Colonel General Andrey Yeremenko, preceded its attack with a 45-minute bombardment on 20 November. As the gunfire died away the infantry rushed forward at 10.45am, supported by tanks of XIII Mechanized Corps. Soviet reports of the breakthrough suggested a mix of stolid Romanian defense and abject surrender, while nearby German observers noted that "masses of Soviet tanks… in quantities never seen before" were pouring across the snow into Fourth Romanian Army's positions.

The Soviet breakthrough came speedily: after only two hours Romanian VI Corps was approaching near collapse. The timely intervention of German 29th Motorized Infantry Division stabilized the situation briefly, but it was ordered to withdraw in order to protect Sixth Army's southern flank, leaving the battered Romanians to their own devices. By this point, virtually no organized defense lay between Stalingrad Front's armor and Kalach: only the problem of refueling the Soviet T34s could slow their rapid progress.

The bridge at Kalach crossed the Don River roughly 47 miles from Stalingrad, but its garrison only discovered they were under threat on 21 November and remained unaware that XIII Mechanized Corps was within 30 miles of their position. The units in and around Kalach consisted of some Luftwaffe anti-aircraft guns, a variety of supply and support troops plus some field police, and laborers of the Organization Todt. Most of the flak pieces were positioned on the higher western bank overlooking the bridge and the village of Kalach on the eastern bank, where an ad hoc battlegroup was forming.

The Soviet XXVI Tank Corps approaching from the northwest was in a hurry to close the trap and allocated several captured German vehicles to an armored group that, after three hours of confused fighting, captured the bridge intact and liberated the village. Although the

leaving disorganized groups of Romanian defenders to be dealt with by the supporting infantry. The German infantry divisions north of Stalingrad were now forced to realign themselves westwards to cover their flanks and rear. German 376th Infantry Division was closest to the Romanians and began to bend to its left, as did the German 44th Infantry Division but, due to fuel shortages, this was a problematic maneuver and equipment had to be abandoned. During the next 24 hours these formations and 384th Infantry Division

pulled back to the southwest and the Don. South of these units, 14th Panzer Division was attempting to determine the direction of the Soviet thrust while 22nd Panzer Division was falling back in the face of I Tank Corps.

To further complicate Army Group B's difficulties was the fronts their flanking divisions were trying to hold. In the case of Romanian Third Army this was 12 to 15 miles. To the south, Romanian Fourth Army's right flank was patrolled by Eighth Cavalry Division, which was attempting to monitor a 93-mile line.

Soviets claimed 1,500 POWs, other accounts noted that German troops managed to drive away and head for Stalingrad, having destroyed supply and repair facilities. The following day troops of the southern pincer, IV Mechanized Corps, arrived at Kalach. Stalingrad was, at least tenuously, surrounded.

As the Germans approached the Don bridges, queues began forming to make the crossing. Priority was given to Germans, and many Romanians were pushed aside with the butt of a feldgendarme's machine pistol. Rumors of Soviet attacks only fueled the increasing sense of confusion that was slipping inexorably towards chaos. Once across the river there seems to have been little sense of anything but a pervasive desire to reach the haven they believed Stalingrad to be. The question on every man's lips was summed up in one diary entry: "Will we get through to the big pocket?"

Elsewhere other pockets of resistance, such as that of the Romanians commanded by General Mihail Lascar from the remains of V Army Corps, were crumbling under Soviet pressure. Stalingrad, the 'big pocket', seemed to offer security, order and the chance to survive, whereas the snow-blown steppe was a frozen, featureless wasteland where Soviet cavalry roamed at will scooping up stragglers. The men of the German army in the east, almost to a man, believed the Red Army rarely bothered to keep POWs alive. By 26 November the only organized groups of German troops left on the west bank of the Don were 16th Panzer Division and elements of 44th Infantry division. They crossed the Luchinsky bridge that evening, blowing it after the last man had crossed.

The Soviets now began to develop their inner and outer rings of enclosure as Paulus and his staff struggled to bring some sort of order to Sixth Army. On 23 November, in what Hitler called 'Fortress Stalingrad', Paulus was to carry out his order to "adopt hedgehog [all-round] defense, present Volga line and northern front to be held at all costs [as] supplies coming by air". Furthermore the Führer created a new command, Army Group Don, under the command of Field Marshal Erich von Manstein, on 20 November to restore the situation in southern Russia, despite his other concerns, such as the Anglo-American invasion of North Africa and the occupation of Vichy France.

Within the fluid 124-mile perimeter that enclosed Fortress Stalingrad were some 22 divisions, numbering roughly 240,000 men – including much of Romanian 20th Infantry Division, a group of Italians looking for building materials, and the entire Croatian 369th Reinforced Infantry Regiment fighting in the factory district. There were also up to 50,000

"ON 18 NOVEMBER CHUIKOV WAS INFORMED OF THE ATTACK, AND FOR HIS 62ND ARMY IT CAME JUST IN TIME AS THE VOLGA WAS ALMOST FROZEN TO THE POINT WHERE IT WAS TOO DIFFICULT FOR SHIPS BUT TOO WEAK FOR FOOT SOLDIERS OR VEHICLES TO CROSS"

Soviet soldiers closed in on the surrounded Sixth Army but found that the Germans had reorganized themselves into a dangerous defensive force

Russian volunteers working for or fighting alongside the Germans. Known as Hiwis (short for Hilfswilliger or voluntary assistant) they were often POWs collaborating to avoid a dire fate or anti-Soviet groups such as the local Kalmyks and Don Cossacks. These men and women would be a particular target for the NKVD, who were tasked with rooting out all collaborators. Surrounding them as the inner cordon were seven Soviet armies that included both the Don and Stalingrad Fronts, along with

21st Army from Southwestern Front and 62nd Army in the city itself.

The external cordon followed the Chir, Don, and Aksay rivers for 200 miles. Fourth Panzer Army had managed to hold onto a bridgehead across the Chir at Kotelnikovo to the southwest, while 16th Motorized Infantry Division covered the empty, inhospitable Kalmyk Steppe between Army Group Don and Army Group A far away to the south in the Caucasus. This latter formation was now in danger of isolation – very

little covered its lines of communications to the west through Rostov, and it was naked before the Red Army. The obvious question now was what should Sixth Army do? Should it try to break out, or stand firm and trust Hitler's promise of an air bridge?

Operation Winter Storm

As the Red Army organized itself around the city, established supply lines, and caught its breath, Manstein frantically prepared what was proclaimed to be a relief mission for Sixth Army. However, the matter of a breakout provoked controversy from the moment of encirclement. Manstein was allocated three infantry divisions and three Panzer divisions, only one of which was immediately available. Hitler was only prepared to sanction a thrust to Stalingrad that would enable its resupply and ensure that the city would not fall, but reserved the right to allow a breakout. However, Manstein lacked the resources to accomplish this and re-establish the front to cover Army Group A in the Caucasus. Nor had the Soviets called a halt to their offensive as the continuation of Operation Uranus, Operation Saturn, was timed to start on 10 December.

Saturn was a far more ambitious envelopment offensive that was to break the Italian Eighth

As the Soviets advanced into the city they were amazed at how many civilians emerged from hiding to greet them. These people were not so lucky. It is likely they were killed by the Germans for their warm clothing

"STALINGRAD, THE 'BIG POCKET', SEEMED TO OFFER SECURITY, ORDER, AND THE CHANCE TO SURVIVE"

Assault guns move up to their start lines for Operation Winter Storm, which began on 12 December

"AS THE SENIOR OFFICERS WERE DRIVEN OFF TO A RELATIVELY CIVILIZED CONFINEMENT, THE LOWER RANKS SHUFFLED TOWARDS THE VOLGA RIVER AND A VERITABLE DEATH MARCH TO THE EAST"

Soviet infantry attack the outskirts of a village during Operation Winter Storm. This offensive caused the postponement of Operation Ring

Army, which was positioned to the left of Romanian Fourth Army's former position north of Stalingrad, and then push on to Rostov, thus isolating Army Group A. In preparation for the operation, Vasilevsky instructed Don and Stalingrad Fronts to squeeze Sixth Army's perimeter and link up at Gumrak. Fighting began during the first week of December but rapidly ground to a halt in the face of a fierce, well-organized defense, which demonstrated that Moscow had underestimated the power and size of Sixth Army. The Soviets were convinced they had trapped a mere 100,000 men with little combat capability. Consequently, Stalin ordered Rokossovsky to draw up a plan for a more considered offensive against the Stalingrad pocket, code-named Operation Ring.

As Manstein's forces gathered at Kotelnikov bridgehead, Vasilevsky attempted a spoiling attack, which failed but obliged Manstein to alter his line of attack. Now it would take a longer route across terrain that involved crossing the Aksay and Myshkova rivers. The attack caused the Soviet forces of the inner perimeter to concentrate on preventing any breakout. It also led to Operation 'Little' Saturn that would defeat Manstein's thrust. Operation Saturn proper was reduced and was now intended to simply break into the rear of Army Group Don via the Italian position.

Its start date was to be 16 December. As Manstein's armor reached the Myshkova – the second river it faced – Soviet Sixth and First Guards Armies tore into the Italian positions, which caved in after 48 hours of hard fighting. Simultaneously XXXXVIII Panzer Corps' line west of the Don along the Chir River began to crumble. To crown everything, Stalingrad Front counterattacked along the Myshkova River, pushing Army Group Don's armor back to its start line over the course of the next three days. On 28 December a much shaken Hitler agreed to pull Army Group A out of the Caucasus and ordered Manstein to establish a defense line 150 miles west of Stalingrad.

Paulus and Sixth Army were on their own. With the Volga frozen, Chuikov's 62nd Army was supplied with relative ease as their enemy slaughtered horses and stared at the skies for the very few aircraft and parachutes that appeared. Christmas celebrations were muted as the morale of Sixth Army gradually eroded, worn down by lack of food and little hope of relief. The Soviets husbanded their resources in preparation for Operation Ring.

Operation Ring

The start date for Ring was 6 January but was delayed by four days. The whole operation was to be carried out by Don Front with holding attacks to be mounted by 62nd and 64th Armies. The pocket was to be sliced up with an initial attack to cut off the 'nose' that poked westwards from the city.

The attack began at 9am. 62nd Army's assault groups took the Mamayev Kurgan and the Red October factory, while out on the steppe three Soviet armies hammered the perimeter lines, destroying 44th and 376th infantry and 29th Motorized Divisions, whose troops scattered towards the built-up areas to the east. Pausing briefly to regroup, the next phase of Rokossovsky's attack reduced Sixth Army by a further five divisions and forced Paulus to move his HQ into the cellars of the Univermag department store in the city center.

When on 26 January men of Don Front met up with troops of Chuikov's command, the pocket was split into two, north and south. Five days later Paulus was promoted to Field Marshall to stiffen his will to fight on, but to no avail. At 7.45am on 31 January the southern pocket and Paulus announced their intention to surrender. The northern pocket continued to fight on under the leadership of Major General Karl Strecker, who surrendered on 2 February.

As the senior officers were driven off to a relatively civilized confinement, the lower ranks shuffled towards the Volga River and a veritable death march to the east.

SECOND BATTLE OF EL ALAMEIN

Montgomery's Eighth Army takes on Rommel's Axis coalition
in this huge desert clash to decide the course of World War II

WORDS TOM GARNER

Two Commonwealth soldiers capture a German on 25 October during a sandstorm. British imperial troops formed a significant part of the Eighth Army

Image: Getty

For most of 1942, the North African campaign had not gone well for the Allies. Since the fall of France in 1940, Britain had borne the brunt of the fighting against both Nazi Germany and Fascist Italy, but two years later, the struggle in the desert had witnessed dramatic changes in fortunes on both sides.

With the Axis dominating the northern half of the Mediterranean Sea, Britain's imperial possessions in the Middle East came under direct threat. Chief among their concerns was the security of the Suez Canal. If Axis forces took it, then Britain's communication and supply routes to its empire in India and the Far East would be cut off. Without the canal, it was widely believed that Britain could not carry on fighting the war.

Both sides knew this, and therefore the deserts of North Africa became an intense fighting ground that ebbed and flowed depending on the combatants' fighting ability, logistical constraints and the strategic priorities of political leaders. At first things went well for the British. They were initially faced with the Italians who attacked Egypt from their colony of Libya, but were easily swept back. Next, however, they faced the Afrika Korps

of the Wehrmacht sent by Adolf Hitler in support of his Italian allies. The Korps was led by the formidable Field Marshal Erwin Rommel – a highly experienced general, tank commander, decorated World War I veteran, and a key player during the Battle of France. His use of surprise tactics and continued momentum to push the Allies out of Libya, despite often being outnumbered, soon earned him the nickname the 'Desert Fox'.

By 1942, the British Eighth Army was withdrawing to the Egyptian frontier. The Allied fortress of Tobruk fell on 21 June with more than 30,000 British and Commonwealth soldiers taken prisoner. This was the largest number of Allied prisoners taken since the fall of Singapore earlier in the year. This meant the situation had become perilous for the British.

However, one of Rommel's weaknesses was that he often suffered from a shortage of supplies, particularly fuel for his panzers and other armored vehicles. This was largely because the Royal Navy and RAF in the Mediterranean and the Atlantic harassed the German supply routes. This handicap was temporarily eased by the fall of Tobruk, as Rommel captured lots of supplies from the British. This enabled him to advance much further into Egypt.

Building defenses

There was now a real threat that Egypt could fall to the Axis forces and the entire North African campaign would be lost. By this time, the USA had entered the war but not yet arrived in sufficient numbers to tip the balance in the Allies' favor. It was up to the Eighth Army to reorganize and throw Rommel back.

The British commander, Lieutenant General Claude Auchinleck, constructed a new defense line from the minor railway station at El Alamein. The line stretched more than 30 miles from the coast to the Qattara Depression in the south. The Depression was important, as its terrain was full of features that were impossible for motorized vehicles to pass through, such as salt lakes and very fine powdered sand. Additionally, the El Alamein defenses were effectively fenced off at the Depression by high cliffs, which made it impossible for Rommel to outflank the British. For the Eighth Army, the Alamein line became the last defense – if Axis forces broke through, Auchinleck intended to hold the Germans on the Suez Canal and even in Palestine if necessary.

What became known as the First Battle of El Alamein started on 1 July when Rommel attacked the British line. This offensive

Scots Guards move forward under the cover of a smoke screen and protected by tanks

During Bertram, tanks were made to look like trucks and trucks were made to look like tanks

A Matilda II tank disguised as a lorry

OPERATION BERTRAM

How Monty's army of illusionists fooled the Germans and secured victory

When Winston Churchill announced the victory of El Alamein to the House of Commons, he stated: "By a marvelous system of camouflage, complete tactical surprise was achieved in the desert." What he was referring to was an ingenious part of Montgomery's battle plan: Operation Bertram.

Bertram was the largest visual deception campaign of the war. It was an elaborate maneuver of real and fake military equipment undertaken by the Camouflage Unit. Formed in 1940, the group consisted of civilian soldiers who were usually artists, sculptors, filmmakers, theater designers, and set painters. It even included the famous magician Jasper Maskelyne. The fake army was largely made out of string, canvas, straw, and wood.

Disguised tanks were codenamed 'Sunshields' and disguised guns were known as 'Cannibals'. 722 Sunshields, 360 Cannibals and many more dummy tanks and transport vehicles were constructed in six weeks before the battle started. The tactics for Bertram involved hundreds of tanks and artillery pieces being moved overnight into combat positions hidden under canvas covers that disguised them as harmless lorries. Decoys were left behind where the real tanks and guns had been. The dummy army was placed largely in the south of the El Alamein line in the weeks before the battle started. There was even a fake water pipeline, with gradual construction that crept southwards. The idea was to fool the German reconnaissance into reporting a large build-up of forces in the south while in reality the attack would be further north.

On the eve of the battle, the unit performed the biggest conjuring trick in history by making 600 tanks 'disappear' and then reappear 50 miles to the north disguised as trucks. After the battle, the captured General von Thoma, Rommel's second-in-command, confirmed to Montgomery that the Axis leaders were fooled by Bertram, expecting the attack to come from the south. They had been completely taken aback by the northern offensive. The deception had worked.

Above: Jasper Maskelyne was a famous magician serving in the Camouflage Unit

"BERTRAM WAS THE LARGEST VISUAL DECEPTION CAMPAIGN OF THE WAR. IT WAS AN ELABORATE MANEUVER OF REAL AND FAKE MILITARY EQUIPMENT UNDERTAKEN BY THE CAMOUFLAGE UNIT"

Images: Alamy; Wiki / War Office photograph WO201-2841

SECOND BATTLE OF
EL ALAMEIN
23 OCTOBER – 11 NOVEMBER 1942

Railway

Miteiriya Ridge

El Alamein

Devil's Garden Minefield

Ruweisat Ridge

01 **OPERATION LIGHTFOOT**
The battle begins on the night of 23-24 October with an Allied offensive consisting of a powerful artillery bombardment. Afterwards, British infantry units open paths in the minefield to allow the armored divisions to pass through.

02 **THE ALLIES GET STUCK**
Around 4am on 24 October, dust clouds, hidden mines and fierce Italian resistance slow down the Allied tanks in the minefield. By dawn, many of the minefields have not been cleared, disrupting Montgomery's battle plans.

Munassib Depression

Qattara Depression

05 FIGHTING AT KIDNEY AND SNIPE
On 26 October, there is fierce fighting at the Snipe, an area of Axis resistance southwest of a feature called the Kidney. The Rifle Brigade bravely holds its ground against Rommel's tank regiments. Eventually both sides withdraw from the Snipe in error, believing the other to be near victory.

04 ROMMEL TAKES CHARGE
Rommel returns to North Africa after a medical absence. He immediately orders a counterattack on 26 October in the north battle sector. The Australians take the brunt of the assault. In the south, the British fail to take advantage of Rommel's diverted panzers and are stalled by anti-tank fire.

03 THE 'CRUMBLING'
Between 24 and 25 October, Montgomery pushes forward to scatter Axis forces using heavy bombardment and breaking up their divisions. Panzers attack the 51st Highland Division but are halted. The Desert Air Force makes more than 1,000 sorties. However, brutal infantry and tank battles plus continuing problems with mines slow the Allies' progress.

06 THE TIDE SLOWLY TURNS
Rommel loses the initiative when a panzer attack fails to break the Allies. The Australian Ninth Division attacks north of the Snipe to drive the Axis from the coast. The heavy fighting here convinces Montgomery that Rommel expects him to fight in the north. Consequently, the Allies attack further south.

08 ROMMEL RETREATS
Realizing the battle is lost, Rommel retreats west under severe bombardment leaving the Italians to hold the line while the Afrika Korps withdraws. The Italians fight bravely but many are killed or taken prisoner. The Egyptian border area is secured for the Allies and Rommel retreats into Libya.

07 OPERATION SUPERCHARGE 1-2 NOVEMBER
Rommel's fuel supply becomes critically low. Montgomery now launches Operation Supercharge, another aerial and artillery offensive designed to take the Axis base at Tel el Aqqaqir, three miles northwest of the Kidney. The British Ninth Armored Division is heavily mauled but inflicts great damage among the German tanks.

© Rocío Espín

The Axis forces engaged at El Alamein lost 30 per cent of its starting strength

Erwin Rommel with his officers. By October 1942, the 'Desert Fox' had pushed the Allies across North Africa and far into Egypt

"NOW THAT HE WAS IN COMMAND, MONTGOMERY FELT IT WAS IMPERATIVE TO HAVE THE MAXIMUM NUMBER OF TROOPS AND EQUIPMENT BEFORE TAKING ON ROMMEL"

was repulsed thanks to the Desert Air Force and a timely sandstorm, so Rommel made further assaults against the line throughout the month, all unsuccessful.

At the same time, the British could not drive Rommel back. The result was a stalemate. This first battle prevented Rommel from advancing further into Egypt, but it was only a temporary measure. El Alamein was 150 miles from Cairo and, more alarmingly, only 66 miles from the vital port of Alexandria. The sense of emergency was becoming acute.

In particular, Winston Churchill was becoming highly impatient with his generals – the British Army had not won a major land battle since the war began and he was becoming increasingly frustrated with the situation in North Africa. He remarked after the fall of Tobruk: "Defeat is one thing, disgrace is another," and he was still not satisfied after the First Battle of El Alamein had checked the Axis advance. Even Rommel remarked to captured British soldiers at Tobruk: "Gentlemen, you have fought like lions and been led by donkeys."

Churchill needed to prove to his new American allies that the British were a force to be reckoned with on the battlefield. With that in mind, he removed Auchinleck, despite his early success at El Alamein, and installed Lieutenant General William Gott as commander of Eighth Army. However, before he could take up his post, Gott was shot down and killed in a plane crash. He was then replaced by Lieutenant General Bernard Montgomery.

Monty's moment comes

Montgomery was not Churchill's first choice to command the Eighth Army – he had a reputation for being difficult to work with. Churchill later remarked about his famous general: "In defeat unbeatable, in victory unbearable." However, Montgomery was extremely confident and immediately set

Though they fought bravely, tens of thousands of Italian soldiers were taken prisoner during and after the battle

about reorganizing the army and improving morale. When he was appointed, he found his troops "brave but baffled" after two years of grueling stalemate and defeat. He now made it clear there would be no retreat from the El Alamein line, declaring to his men: "I want to impress on everyone that the bad times are over."

His strategy was relatively simple: to repulse Rommel's next attack and then go on the offensive. Part of his new strategy was to make himself visible to his troops and encourage them. He concluded that: "It seemed to me that the men needed not only a master but a mascot. I deliberately set about fulfilling this requirement." To this end, Montgomery visited every unit possible, explained the situation to them and adopted the black beret of the Royal Tank Regiment – this had the dual effect

of making him instantly recognizable and like one of the ordinary soldiers. Consequently, he became a popular commander, and his troops nicknamed him 'Monty'.

Now that he was in command, Montgomery felt it was imperative to have the maximum number of troops and equipment before taking on Rommel. This was at odds with Churchill, who wanted a quick attack before the end of September at the latest, but Montgomery remained insistent. Meanwhile, Rommel was having logistical problems. He was very short of fuel, largely thanks to the British attacking a German fleet of six tankers and ammunition ships. Four of the ships were sunk and two did not reach the Afrika Korps on time. This meant that Rommel was lacking the resources to reach the Suez Canal and would be forced to rely on capturing British

fuel dumps. Montgomery took this opportunity to bait Rommel into attempting to take the Alam Halfa ridge beyond the El Alamein line in September. Rommel obliged, and was eventually forced to withdraw after encountering problems with minefields and attacks from the air, as well as tanks from the ridge itself.

By now the Desert Fox was dangerously low on fuel. Axis ports on the Egyptian and Libyan coasts were under constant Allied air attacks and many German supplies had to come all the way from Tripoli more than 994 miles away. The stress of the campaign was making Rommel ill, and he left to recuperate in Germany on 23 September, leaving strict instructions to strengthen the minefields that covered his positions.

The mines that the Germans laid would become a considerable problem to the Allies

The Allies were equipped with more than 1,000 tanks ahead of the battle

The Allied victory at El Alamein was one of the most decisive turning points in World War II

– approximately three million mines were placed directly in front of the El Alamein line, as well as large entanglements of barbed wire. Montgomery could have no hope of outflanking what became known as the 'Devil's Garden' and made preparations for a full-frontal assault over the next month.

Opening shots

By late October, the Eighth Army numbered nearly 200,000 men, including great numbers of soldiers from India, New Zealand, South Africa and, most significantly, Australia. The forthcoming battle was arguably to be the last great pitched fight of the British Empire. In addition to the imperial divisions, there were Free French, Polish and Greek brigades on the Allied side. Montgomery was also well equipped, with more than 1,000 tanks, 900 artillery pieces and 1,400 anti-tank guns.

The Axis forces looked small by comparison. They had about 116,000 German and Italian soldiers, 540 tanks, 500 artillery pieces and 490 anti-tank guns. Montgomery had good reason to feel confident, and made a rousing speech to his men: "Every soldier must know, before he goes into battle, how the little battle he is to fight fits into the larger picture, and how the success of his fighting will influence the battle as a whole." This raised the Eighth Army's morale to a level not seen for a long time. Nevertheless, the coming clash would be no walk in the park, and the Axis forces would show they were a dangerous foe.

On the night of 23-24 October, the Second Battle of El Alamein began with a huge Allied artillery barrage that lasted for more than five hours, first with a general heavy bombardment and then a more systematic shelling of targets. This first phase of the battle was codenamed 'Operation Lightfoot', and its intention was to distract Rommel's troops while Allied infantry and engineers of XXX Corps worked their way through the minefield. They were attempting to create two channels for the British armored divisions to advance through. It was a painstaking, hazardous process that involved clearing five miles of mines, but was necessary as it meant that many of the mines would not be tripped by the walking troops – hence the name Operation Lightfoot.

At about 4am on 24 October, the armored X Corps began to enter the middle of the minefield. However, they became hampered by traffic jams, dust clouds created by their own vehicle tracks and many remaining mines. The forward infantry were also under a determined attack by the Ariete, Brescia, and Folgore Italian brigades. Many of the British tanks suffered punishing losses from anti-tank guns and none of the Allies' original objectives were met.

Ignoring the setbacks, Montgomery held his nerve and commenced the next stage of his attack. After surveying the situation at dawn on 24 October, he ordered the minefield paths to be fully cleared before starting the 'Crumbling' of the Axis defenses, which involved a continued heavy bombardment that was designed to break up the enemy divisions. At the same time, the Desert Air Force made more than 1,000 sorties against the Axis forces. A unit of Panzer tanks tried to attack the 51st Highland Division of infantry but were halted. The Afrika Korps also suffered the loss of Commander Georg Stumme when he died of a heart attack en route to assessing the battlefield situation and had to be replaced by General Wilhelm von Thoma.

The Allies were also suffering, as there had been little progress made throughout 24-25 October against intense tank battles and continuing problems with mines, which were still disabling armored units. In the heat of this deadlock, Rommel returned to North Africa and assessed the situation. Thanks to Montgomery's 'Crumbling', the Axis had taken heavy losses, with some Italian units taking 50 per cent casualties. In general, his troops were under strain and short on equipment, and the entire army had only a few days of fuel left. He concluded that the only option was to immediately counterattack while he still could, so struck north with Panzer and Italian divisions and forced an Australian battalion back.

By now much of the general fighting was taking place around a hilly feature called the 'Kidney', positioned at the far edge of the Axis minefield. If it could be successfully overrun, then the Allies would be able to start a general advance. Rommel diverted many of his tanks north of the Kidney for the counterattack, but the British were unable to take advantage of this diversion and were stalled by anti-tank fire. Luckily for the Allies, that day the RAF sunk two German oil tankers at Tobruk, removing the last chance to refuel the Afrika Korps. This incident would hinder Rommel's chances of success.

'Operation Supercharge'

On 27 October, fierce fighting began southwest

"HE CONCLUDED THAT THE ONLY OPTION WAS TO IMMEDIATELY COUNTERATTACK WHILE HE STILL COULD"

A German artillery piece captured by Allied troops

of the Kidney in an area of resistance called the 'Snipe'. The British Rifle Brigade had captured the area and brought up 13 anti-tank guns to defend the position, so Rommel threw the 21st Panzer Division at it.

Despite being nearly overrun, the riflemen held their ground, destroying many German and Italian tanks in the process. Eventually the panzers withdrew, but the British were also withdrawn without being replaced, leaving the Snipe unoccupied.

Despite this, and the continuing ferocity of the fighting, the tide was now beginning to slowly turn in the Allies' favor. Between 28 October and 1 November, Montgomery's superiority in men and equipment began to pay dividends. For instance, two panzer divisions combined to make a determined attack on 28 October but were eventually driven back by sustained fire.

Rommel had by now lost the initiative, and from this point would continually be on the back foot in Africa. Montgomery ordered his units in the Snipe area to go on the defensive while he launched an attack further north. The Australian Ninth Division was ordered to attack German positions near the coastal area in order to force them southwest. They reached some of their objectives, but encountered great resistance as Rommel threw in a large part of his army to block them.

In the end, the Australian operation was called off, but its actions were of great tactical use to Montgomery. He had observed that Rommel was committing reserves against the Australians, thereby indicating that he anticipated an Eighth Army offensive in the north. It was decided to launch the new offensive further south. Monty ordered the Australians to relaunch their attack, to distract Rommel while the rest of the Eighth Army regrouped. When the Australians restarted their assault, the Axis counterattack resulted in bloody, hand-to-hand fighting, draining Rommel's resources further. On 2 November, Montgomery launched 'Operation Supercharge'.

Supercharge's aim was to force the enemy out of the minefield and into open ground, destroy its armor, whittle down its fuel supplies even further and take Rommel's defense base at Tel el Aqqaqir, which was three miles northwest of the Kidney.

If anything, the Allied aerial, armored and artillery firepower were more intense than during Operation Lightfoot. Tel el Aqqaqir was bombed from the air for seven hours before four hours of artillery fire. Afterwards, led by New Zealand infantry, Allied tanks advanced toward the German positions and received a hammering from Axis anti-tank guns and panzers. The Ninth Armored Division suffered particularly, losing 75 per cent of their tanks. At the same time, Axis counterattacks failed when the First Armored Division joined the remains of the Ninth Armored Division and the Afrika Korps were reduced to 35 tanks by the end of 2

November. This fighting became known as the 'Hammering of the Panzers'. On the same day, the Allies finally took the Snipe, and Montgomery made preparations for the final push.

The Desert Fox withdraws

Rommel concluded that the battle was lost and decided to save what he could of his army, despite receiving an order to fight to the end from Hitler. He began a gradual withdrawal, with the Italians doing most of the fighting. On 4 November, the Allies broke out into open desert and punched a hole in Rommel's lines that was 12 miles long. The Desert Fox was left with no choice but to order a retreat west. The Italians fought bravely under the circumstances, with the 40th Bologna Regiment not surrendering until they were virtually out of ammunition. Along the hole in the Axis lines, the Allies were attacked by Italian troops. At the same time the vast majority were taken prisoner with some Italian divisions being wiped out entirely.

The Allies pursued Rommel's retreating force for days, attempting to encircle and trap it particularly at Mersa Matruh and Sidi Barrani. These attempts failed, but by 11 November, all Axis troops had been chased out of Egypt. At

A British soldier gives a 'V for victory' sign to German prisoners captured at El Alamein

this point Montgomery halted his infantry, only allowing some armored and artillery units to carry on the pursuit in Libya. He wanted to regroup and reinforce his supplies before pushing further forward. Rommel lived to fight another day, but the Afrika Korps was now a hunted army.

The Second Battle of El Alamein was over. At a cost of 13,500 Allied casualties, Montgomery had won a decisive victory that changed the course of the Western War. Rommel's force had suffered badly, losing approximately 37,000 troops, totaling 30 per cent of all Axis forces engaged – they were losses he could ill afford. His army on the Libyan-Egyptian border now only consisted of 5,000 men, 20 tanks and 50 guns. A combined Anglo-American force had also landed at Morocco on 8 November and had Montgomery followed up his pursuit, the Afrika Korps might have been neutralized by the end of 1942.

However, this is not to denigrate the achievement of El Alamein. For the first time since the war began, the British Army had won a decisive battle against the Axis forces, restoring its martial reputation in the process. Montgomery turned into an overnight hero and would spend the rest of the war at the highest echelons of Allied command, much to the discomfort of some American commanders.

In many ways the true significance of El Alamein was psychological. It is true that the reality was a hard-fought success. The main factors that ensured

victory were Montgomery's superior manpower, intelligence, and equipment supplies combined with Rommel's numerical inferiority and woeful fuel situation. Had Rommel been better supplied, the final outcome might have been quite different. Some of the most significant actions took place away from the battlefield, such as Rommel's initial absence and the sinking of crucial German oil tankers by the RAF.

Nonetheless, British morale was boosted to a level yet unseen and Churchill ordered church bells to be rung across the country in celebration – many for the first time since 1939. El Alamein also proved to the occasionally skeptical Americans that British and imperial troops were more than capable of defeating Axis armies. By coincidence, the battle was the last time the British fought a large engagement without US co-operation.

For the remainder of 1942, the Afrika Korps was relentlessly chased across Libya, Algeria, and Tunisia until they were eventually driven out of North Africa in 1943. This allowed the Allies to invade Sicily and Italy, and provided essential strategic security for preparations to invade France in 1944.

Once the war was over, El Alamein came to be seen as one of the most decisive turning points in the conflict. As Churchill once famously said: "Before Alamein we never had a victory. After Alamein we never had a defeat."

Bernard Montgomery watches his tanks move during the battle. 'Monty' reinvigorated the Eighth Army and reorganized its fighting capability

Images: Alamy, Getty, Topfoto

KURSK

THE KURSK SALIENT, SOVIET UNION 5-13 JULY 1943

As the German invasion of the Soviet Union stalled, two mechanized heavyweights came face to face in the largest clash of armor the world has ever seen

WORDS WILL LAWRENCE

Soviet soldiers wait as a T-34 crosses a trench

"THE GERMAN HIGH COMMAND WAS USING SIMILAR TACTICS TO THOSE EMPLOYED BY MONTGOMERY AT EL ALAMEIN"

The last major German offensive on the Eastern Front, 1943's Operation Citadel saw Hitler launch a huge attack on the Kursk salient, or bulge. It was a move that he believed would provide a victory so bright it would "shine like a beacon around the world." This was a battle of the elite, with both German and Soviet armies near their apex in terms of skill and weaponry, hardened by two years of unrelenting warfare.

The Germans, though depleted in manpower, were, for the first time since the invasion of the Soviet Union in 1941, fielding qualitative superiority in terms of armor with the formidable Tiger I tanks and new Panthers. These outstripped the Soviet T-34 Model 43s, which had in the intervening years, with their sloped armor and 76.2mm gun, proved masters of the battlefield.

The Red Army, meanwhile, was a very different beast from that which had faced the German invasion during Operation Barbarossa two years earlier. At the beginning of 1943, more than 16 million men were under arms, supported by a vast number of artillery pieces. Stalin claimed that "artillery is the god of war", and by 1943, the Red Army boasted the largest and most effective artillery divisions in the world. It also had somewhere approaching 10,000 tanks.

Clash of the titans

At Kursk, these two heavily mechanized forces came together in an enclosed theater of operations, like two mighty pugilists meeting for a final championship bout. The result was a watershed. "Stalingrad was the end of the beginning," said Winston Churchill, "but the Battle of Kursk was the beginning of the end."

The German plan was to launch a double envelopment against the Kursk salient using Army Group Center in the north, specifically Colonel-General Model's Ninth Army, while Army Group South battered the southern section with Army Detachment Kempf and Colonel-General Hoth's formidable Fourth Panzer Army. This was an awe-inspiring demonstration of German strength, with 2,700 tanks and assault guns taking to the field.

For Stalin and his senior commanders, Marshals Zhukov and Vasilevsky, the plan was to launch a massive offensive by first wearing down the mobile German forces in a battle-slog around the Kursk sector. They would use three Fronts (the Soviet equivalent of an Army Group) – Central Front, Voronezh Front, and the reserve Steppe Front – to grind down German mechanized forces and thereby leave their territories vulnerable to huge counter-offensives.

German heavy armor crosses a Soviet defensive ditch near Belgorod

In his bid to snare the German armor, Stalin ordered the transformation of the region into what historian and Kursk expert Dennis E Showalter believes to be "the most formidable large-scale defensive system in the history of warfare": a triple-ringed matrix absorbing almost one million men, 20,000 guns and mortars, 300 rocket launchers, and 3,300 tanks. Russian engineers uncoiled more than 500 miles of barbed wire and lay almost 650,000 mines. The Germans' only chance, says Showalter, was the might of the steel-headed sledgehammer they eventually swung in July.

Operation Citadel

That blow came on 5 July, after several days of preliminaries involving the German and Soviet air forces and the roar of countless heavy guns. Tank armadas were suddenly on the move, with the Germans committing squadrons of 100 and in some cases 200 machines or more, with a score of Tiger Is and Ferdinand assault guns in the vanguard. Groups of 50 or so medium tanks came next and then floods of infantry, protected by this armored screen, moved in behind.

These German armored wedges were known as 'Panzerkeil' and, according to the late historian Alan Clark, amount to a rejection of the traditional principles of the panzer army. In fact, the German high command was using similar tactics to those employed by Montgomery at El Alamein, with the difference here that the defenders' armor was at numerical parity with the attackers', or greater, and their defensive organization meant that many of their tanks were held in reserve. This proved decisive during the mighty clash at Prokhorovka.

As 5 July unfolded, Colonel-General Model in the north committed more than 500 armored vehicles from his Ninth Army to the attack in a series of staggered bursts, but so violent was the Soviet resistance that about half of these were out of action by the day's end. Part of the problem stemmed from the committing of both battalions of the Porsche-built Ferdinands to the attack. These formidable machines, also known as 'elephants', were designed for tank-busting and the destruction of large anti-tank guns. Their 200mm-thick armor provided them with ample protection from static gun positions. Their enormous 88mm cannons, meanwhile, picked off Russian T-34s before they even had the chance to come within range.

However, the Ferdinands became separated from the lighter tanks and infantry they needed for close-range support. With their static hulls and lack of machine guns, they proved sitting ducks for Soviet infantry units, who boarded them while they were on the move and squirted flamethrowers over the engine ventilation slats.

THE BATTLE OF PROKHOROVKA
12 JULY 1943

01 **The SS tank March**
SS divisions Leibstandarte and Totenkopf move first in their Panzerkeil wedge formation, with Tigers to the fore and lighter Panzer IIIs and IVs moving in behind. The Russians respond with an artillery barrage before moving their own armor into battle.

03 **The iron fists clash**
Both Leibstandarte and Totenkopf
are drawn into close-quarters combat,
and confusion reigns. Individual tank
battles are the order of the day and
hundreds of tanks are disabled by direct
hits to the weaker side armor. It is said
that some burning T-34s ram their
German adversaries.

04 **Soviet flank attacks**
Several corps from the Fifth
Guards Army engage Totenkopf's left
flank. Though seen as a tank battle,
infantry units fight ferociously at
Prokhorovka, with Russian anti-tank rifles
in particular used to maximum effect.
Preventing Totenkopf from commanding
the position north of Prokhorovka is vital
to halting the German advance.

02 **The Soviet armor engages**
The Soviet Fifth Guards Tank
Army moves out to counter the German
advance as quickly as possible, bidding
to get into close combat and therefore
minimize the efficacy of the Germans'
longer-range guns. The Luftwaffe
continues its support, outfighting the
Soviets in the air.

05 **The southern edge**
South of Prokhorovka, a tough
corps from the Fifth Guards Tank Army
engages the SS Das Reich division,
forcing the Germans to adopt a mostly
defensive position on the right flank.
The Soviets are keen to ensure that
potential support arriving in the form of
the approaching III Panzer Corps does
not reach the field.

Ed Crooks

123

A Russian communiqué claimed that on the first day of battle, 586 German panzers were destroyed or disabled

The Ferdinands, however, ploughed through the first line of Soviet defenses, allowing the infantry to follow them into the breach, but more than half these beasts of war were lost.

The morning of 5 July also saw the Fourth Panzer Army launch its main offensive thrust in the south, moving along a 30-mile front. According to Kursk expert Mark Healey, 700 tanks and assault guns smashed their huge metal fist into the face of the Soviet Sixth Guards Army on the Voronezh Front, but the Russian defenses were so tightly entrenched that the German attack stalled. Eventually, the Luftwaffe's aerial superiority began to take effect and the Fourth Panzer managed to split the Sixth Guards Army in two.

The fighting in both the north and south of the salient was ferocious, and within 12 hours both sides were feeding the fires that raged across the battle for Kursk. Swathes of ground-attack aircraft strafed the battlefields. The armor continued to mass and move "on a scale unlike anything seen elsewhere in the war," according to the historian John Erickson.

The Soviet tank armies responded to the German assault by moving up into their primary defensive positions and somewhere approaching 7,000 tanks were steadily drawn into this immense clash of steel, leaving an ever-growing number of dying hulls smoking on the battlefields.

The second day of Citadel, 6 July, was heavily overcast and rain hampered both sides throughout. Along the northern sections of the Kursk salient, the Soviets launched a dawn counterattack with General Rokossovsky's Central Front enjoying temporary success, until a force of 250 panzers with infantry moving in its wake halted them in their tracks. Throughout the day, Central Front and the Ninth Army were locked in perpetual struggle.

The German offensive rolled on, with Model aiming for the village of Olkhovatka as a prime strategic objective. This high ground provided control over the eastern, southern and western section of his field of operations. The Soviets had already identified this region as strategically vital, and in the weeks running up to Citadel's launch, had transformed it into one of the strongest sections of the defensive belt. The German Panzerkeil, with the Tigers to the fore, thrust ahead, and by noon on 6 July the Germans had no fewer than 1,000 tanks committed to a six-mile front between the villages of Soborovka and Ponyri.

Soviet resistance

The Russian defenses again proved too strong. Time and time again, Model's Panzer Corps ran into trouble. Unperturbed, he tried again on 7 and 8 July, redeploying huge swathes of aircraft in a bid to penetrate the Soviet resistance. The Soviets were just too well dug in, however, and the German attack ground to a halt once more. "The wrack of shattered panzers marking Ninth Army's advance," writes Healey, bear "mute testament to the fact that the momentum of Model's offensive was already beginning to decay."

Meanwhile, along the southern stretch of the Kursk salient, the second day of Citadel's operations looked promising for the Germans. The elite section of Hoth's Fourth Panzer Army, II SS Panzer Corps, had already bitten into the first line of Soviet defense and looked set to devour the second line on the morning of 6 July.

General Vatutin, commanding the Voronezh Front, suggested an immediate counterattack, but was swiftly deflected by a senior officer who highlighted the destruction caused by the Tigers' and Panthers' large turret guns with their far superior range. Digging in their T-34s and preparing a wall of defensive fire would serve them better, he argued.

Still, with help from the Luftwaffe, the German armor rammed through the Russian defense and by the end of 6 July, the SS Panzer Corps was wreaking havoc amid the second Soviet defensive line. The following day was cold and the two sides fought in the descending mist, with the Germans pushing steadily on towards the small town of Oboyan, which defended Kursk from the south.

Early in the morning on 7 July, 400 panzers supported by armored infantry and airpower crashed onto the First Tank Army of the Voronezh Front, which wavered under the onslaught. By 10 July, members of Hoth's XLVIII Panzer Corps seized Hill 244.8, which stood as the most northerly point taken by the Germans in their bid to reach Kursk. SS Panzer Corps, meanwhile, fought a path through the Soviet defensive line and regrouped to direct a major assault against Prokhorovka, which, if successful, looked set to smash Soviet resistance in the south.

"THEY PROVED SITTING DUCKS FOR SOVIET INFANTRY UNITS, WHO BOARDED THEM WHILE THEY WERE ON THE MOVE AND SQUIRTED FLAMETHROWERS OVER THE ENGINE VENTILATION SLATS"

Soviet soldiers fire on Germans during the Battle of Kursk

"PROKHOROVKA OFFERED A HEAD-ON, STAND-UP GRAPPLE BETWEEN THE ELITE TROOPS OF THE WORLD'S BEST ARMIES UNDER CONDITIONS THAT LEFT NO ROOM FOR FANCY MANEUVERS"

Back on the northern face of the salient, Model continued his bid to take the village of Ponyri and fierce hand-to-hand fighting erupted, earning Ponyri the name of 'Stalingrad of the Kursk'. The two sides fought to a bitter standstill. On the night of 10 July, Model committed his last reserves to the fray, and although by 12 July his divisions held most of the village, the Russian defense was too robust and the Ninth Army couldn't effect a full breakthrough. When the Germans received intelligence suggesting a major Soviet offensive was set to launch against the Orel bulge, Army Group Center pulled sections of the Ninth Army away from the action and Model's attack halted.

Come the night of 11 July, and although the Germans were eroding the Soviet position in the south, Stalin and his generals couldn't fail to feel confident. Model's position, hemmed in at Ponyri, left them free to move their armored reserve, the Fifth Guards Tank Army of the Steppe Front, against Hoth's divisions in the salient's southern section.

With Stalin realizing that a final battle was set to unfold, the Fifth Guards Tank Army was placed under the command of General Vatutin on the Voronezh Front, a move that led to what is widely regarded as Kursk's defining moment, the mighty tank battle at Prokhorovka.

"All the elements of myth were at hand," Showalter says of this imminent clash of armor. "Prokhorovka offered a head-on, stand-up grapple between the elite troops of the world's best armies on a three-mile front under conditions that left no room for fancy maneuvers or for air and artillery to make much difference."

The German II SS Panzer Corps, incorporating the panzer grenadier divisions 'Leibstandarte', 'Das Reich', and 'Totenkopf', was pitted against the Fifth Guards Tank Army. These elite troops met as both went on the attack, "an encounter battle in the literal sense, suggesting predators in rut." Other Soviet units also took to the field, including divisions of the Fifth Guards Army, as well as sections of the First Tank Army and Sixth Guards Army.

Colonel-General Hoth of the German Fourth Panzer Army, his armor having penetrated the Russian defensive line, was keen to push on before "a defensive scab could form over the thin membrane exposed in the remaining Russian defenses," as Kursk historian Lloyd Clark writes.

At the same time, divisions from the III Panzer Corps, part of Army Detachment Kempf, were moving northward to join II SS Panzer Corps, provoking the Soviets to engage Hoth's forces post-haste. Aware that the German Tigers and Panthers had a longer range than their T-34s, the Soviets bid to move into close combat.

They grossly overestimated the quality of German tanks on this battlefield, according to Clark, who claims that the Germans fielded no Panthers or Ferdinands at Prokhorovka, and that II SS Panzer Corps had just 15 Tigers – ten with Totenkopf, four with Leibstandarte, and just a solitary giant with Das Reich. Other historians disagree.

Battle of Prokhorovka

Whatever the truth, Leibstandarte, Das Reich, and Totenkopf moved in to attack and the great Battle of Prokhorovka began beneath leaden skies, warm and humid, which unleashed rain and peels of thunder as the day wore on. The Germans fielded approximately 600 tanks and assault guns, the Russians 900. Hostilities erupted early on 12 July and the inferno blazed all day. The Luftwaffe flew sorties overhead, and the Germans maintained air superiority throughout the battle, though this counted for little in the end.

SS divisions Leibstandarte and Totenkopf moved first in wedge formation, their Tigers in the vanguard, stopping to unload their mighty 88mm shells before moving onward. At about 0830, the Soviet lines unleashed a 15-minute artillery barrage before the Fifth Guards Tank Army rolled towards the tide of panzers, bidding to get into close-quarters combat.

Before long, scores of tanks were churning up the battlefield in individual engagements. Up close, the tanks' thinner side armor was more easily penetrated. Thick smoke from the blazing hulls drifted across the battlefield, making gunnery all the more troublesome. The SS Panzer Corps maintained the pressure throughout the day and the Germans tried desperately to bring III Panzer Corps from Army Detachment Kempf into play. If these machines could enter the battle, it may well have turned the advantage firmly in the Germans' favor. III Panzer, however, couldn't break through in time and the SS had to fight for Prokhorovka with no further ground support.

Historians talk of a last surge by Leibstandarte and Das Reich aimed at breaking the Soviet lines on the battlefield's western edge, but Fifth Guards Tank Army's Lieutenant-General Rotmistrov engaged his final reserves and the tanks clashed head-on once more, darkening the sky with smoke and dust. The fierce fighting continued well into the night but the Soviets had done their job – they had stopped the German advance.

It is estimated that more than half of the Fifth Guards Tank Army's machines were destroyed. "The Waffen SS won a tactical victory on 12 July," writes Showalter. "Prokhorovka was not a Tiger graveyard but a T-34 junkyard. Operationally, however, the palm rests with the Red Army." Prokhorovka bled the German military machine dry. About 300 panzers lay abandoned on the battlefield, and though some may have been salvaged, the field remained in Soviet hands.

Between 13-15 July, SS Panzer Corps continued to make sorties against the Russian defenses but in reality it was all over. Hitler called off Operation Citadel on 13 July as the Russians launched a massive offensive, Operation Kutuzov, aimed at Army Group Center along the Orel salient. The Battle of Kursk ceded the initiative to the Red Army, which then rolled on towards Berlin. For Hitler and the Wehrmacht, defeat was edging ever closer.

This memorial on the site of the Battle of Prokhorovka commemorates the clash

Images: Alamy, Getty

BATTLE OF MONTE CASSINO

ITALY 11 JANUARY – 18 MAY 1944

A small Italian town held the key to the advance on Rome, and
the Germans were not about to give it up without a fight

WORDS DAVID SMITH

A British Bofors 40mm anti-aircraft
gun amid the ruins of Cassino

130

Following the collapse of the German position in North Africa, in May 1943, the Allies were faced with a dilemma. An invasion of France was not yet a realistic proposition, but the fight had to be taken to continental Europe somehow.

A compromise was reached between the British and Americans: Italy would offer a convenient route into Europe, being just a short hop across the Mediterranean. There was an idea that Italy was in some way the 'soft underbelly' of Hitler's Europe and that notion was not outlandish while the country was held by Italian troops.

The initial landing at Sicily was badly managed and around 100,000 German and Italian troops escaped. However, the fall of Mussolini's regime in July led the Italians to open negotiations with the Allies. A race ensued, one that the Allies mishandled. While they dithered, the Germans poured more troops into Italy. The stage was set for some of the hardest fighting of the entire war.

The German strategy was to force the Allies to fight for every inch, while staging organized withdrawals to a series of defensive lines. The most formidable of these, the Gustav Line, was to be held with even greater determination.

The most obvious route to Rome was along Route 6, the Via Casilina, which cut through the narrow Liri valley. To break through into the valley, however, the Allies had to get past two formidable 'gateposts', Monte Maio and Monte Cassino. Cassino would be the scene of fighting that some compared to the worst experienced in World War I. Four separate attempts,

German troops turn the ruined town into a defensive strongpoint

The battered town under another bombardment during the repeated Allied assaults

spanning 129 days, would be made to wrest the strategic town from the Germans' control.

Bloody battles

On the night of 11-12 January 1944, the first battle opened. Men of the French Expeditionary Corps (Moroccans and Algerians under Marshal Alphonse Juin) attacked to the north and made good progress. Juin, in fact, was convinced after six days of fighting that if he was reinforced he could break through into the Liri valley and unpick the entire Gustav Line.

General Mark Clark, commanding the US Fifth Army, was unimpressed and instead pressed on with his original plan. British X Corps units crossed the Carigliano River close to the coast, but were met by a fierce counterattack as soon as they reached the opposite bank. The German 94th Division, reinforced by tanks, held firm and were helped when further British crossings were foiled by bad weather and a swollen river.

Clark then chose to press ahead with the third phase of his attack, unleashing the US 36th Division across the Gari River, but this was a disaster, with half of the men who managed to get over the river killed, wounded or captured.

Still, the First Battle of Monte Cassino lurched on. Partly to distract from the major Allied landings at Anzio on 22 January, Clark probed further north with the men of Juin's FEC and the US 34th Division. Little impact was made on the German defenses (although men of the 34th Division came agonizingly close to the walls of the ancient monastery atop Monte Cassino) and the first battle fizzled out.

The landings at Anzio were a complete success and ought to have undermined the entire Gustav Line, but the commander of US VI Corps, General John P Lucas, was overly cautious and frittered away his advantage, eventually getting bogged down as German forces responded to his surprise arrival. A great opportunity had been lost, and Cassino would need to be attacked again.

More troops had been made available, with the shifting over of three divisions from the British Eighth Army. The 2nd New Zealand, 78th British, and 4th Indian Divisions were grouped into II NZ Corps, under the command of General Bernard Freyberg. These men would fight the Second Battle of Monte Cassino.

German fallschirmjäger (paratroop) units offered tough opposition to the Allied forces

The sixth-century monastery is flattened by Allied bombers on 15 February

It would kick off with one of the most controversial episodes of the campaign. The monastery on top of the hill was considered of vital cultural importance and the Germans assured the Allies that they had not and would not occupy it. Clark took them at their word, but Freyberg was unconvinced. Feeling sure the Germans would have placed units in the monastery, he insisted that it be destroyed by aerial bombardment, on 15 February, prior to his assault. The Germans, in fact, had been telling the truth, but after the monastery had been flattened by waves of heavy bombers (at a cost of around a hundred civilian lives), they no longer felt obliged to respect what was now a pile of rubble. The ruins of the monastery became a formidable defensive position and the German General Fridolin von Senger summed up the situation when he commented: "The bombing had the opposite effect to what was intended. Now we would occupy the abbey without scruple, especially as ruins are better for defense than intact buildings."

Marshal Juin, commander of the FEC, still had hopes of breaking through into the Liri valley and asked for II NZ Corps to join with his forces, but Clark again demurred. The

subsequent attack of the mixed New Zealand-Indian-British corps faltered and then failed as it proved impossible to bring its full weight to bear on the German defenses. The Second Battle of Monte Cassino was another failure.

By now it was clear that a more concerted effort was needed to crack the German position. The decision was taken to bring in yet more men and await better weather in May, enabling the Allies to make better use of tanks. To fill the pause, however, and to ensure the Germans kept their attention on the Gustav Line while plans for Operation Overlord were completed, a third assault was improvised.

Operation Dickens, which spawned the Third Battle of Monte Cassino, was therefore little more than a placeholder. Starting on 15 March, it again opened with a massive aerial bombardment, this time hitting the entire town. General Freyberg had once more insisted on

this display of aerial power, but the 600 Allied bombers failed to achieve much of anything.

A three-hour artillery bombardment after the bombing presented the Germans with yet more defensible piles of rubble, and although they were living through hellish conditions, their morale remained unbroken. Taking cover in cellars, which sometimes became tombs, the Germans were mostly able to scramble out of their improvised shelters in time to meet their advancing foe.

When Allied tanks attempted to roll into Cassino, once the guns had fallen silent, they found progress agonizingly slow because the roads were all blocked. A single German Panzer IV, well sited and under cover, knocked out one Sherman tank after another as they attempted to pick their way through the debris. Bulldozers were called up to clear the way, but they came under heavy fire

"OPERATION DIADEM PROMISED TO FINALLY END THE STALEMATE. THIS WAS TO BE ON A COMPLETELY DIFFERENT SCALE TO THE FIRST THREE BATTLES WITH 108 BATTALIONS AND 2,000 TANKS"

The shattered remnants of the monastery after repeated Allied bombardment

LOST IN TRANSLATION

A misunderstood radio intercept may have sealed the fate of Cassino's ancient monastery

The destruction of the monastery at Monte Cassino was widely condemned at the time, and new evidence suggests it may have been the product of a simple misunderstanding. There was no appetite for destroying such an important building, but under the pressure and harsh realities of war, where men's lives had to be balanced against the value of a building, difficult decisions were made.

There was suspicion that even if the Germans did not have fighting units in the building, they at least had artillery spotters. The commanding elevation of the monastery made it a prime location for spotters, and German artillery fire was extremely accurate.

General Bernard Freyberg worked hard to convince General Mark Clark to bomb the ancient building, and he was clearly persuasive, but a badly translated intercept may have factored in to the final decision. A German paratroop officer was heard to ask: "Ist Abt in Kloster?" This was taken to mean, "Is the battalion in the abbey?", with 'Abt' being interpreted as an abbreviation for 'Abteilung'. Instead, the officer had been inquiring on the whereabouts of the Abbot. It is possible this provided enough of a pretext to justify the bombing of the monastery, but there is debate over how such flimsy evidence could have turned the tide of the argument.

Clark himself believed the decision was wrong and freely criticized it after the war, calling it a "tactical military mistake of the first magnitude", while conveniently forgetting that the final decision had been his.

An American anti-tank gun, pictured during the fighting around Cassino

themselves and when the rains returned the battle became a brutal slogging match.

Fourth and final assault

The town was gradually occupied, however, tank attacks then failed badly due to poor planning. Advancing without infantry support, the tanks were massacred and the assault called off. Operation Diadem promised to end the stalemate. This was to be on a different scale to the first three battles, with 108 battalions and 2,000 tanks attacking on a 20-mile front. As if the Allied forces were not already cosmopolitan enough, a corps of Polish troops arrived and was given the task of taking the monastery, the symbol of the entire struggle.

At 11pm on the night of 11 May, 1,600 artillery pieces opened fire for 40 minutes before the massive assault began. Men of the 8th Indian Division found their crossing of the Rapido River to be a deadly undertaking. The canvas boats employed had been stored for extended periods and had been weakened by insect infestation. Many men drowned as their riddled boats sank during the crossing.

The weight of the attack, however, was irresistible. By 16 May, British tanks had found their way to the Via Casilina beyond Cassino and the German position was no longer tenable. German troops began to pull out under cover of darkness that night and on 18 May, II Polish Corps took possession of the devastated monastery on top of Monte Cassino.

The four battles had exacted a terrible price on the Allies. Not only had they been held up in their advance on Rome, but they had also taken around 50,000 casualties. German losses were less than half that, and they had managed to once more withdraw in good order.

On 25 May, US VI Corps finally broke out from its Anzio beachhead and linked up with Clark's Fifth Army. Faced with the choice of bottling up the retreating Germans or grabbing the headlines by liberating the Eternal City, Clark chose glory and rushed into Rome.

The Germans were able to fall back to yet more defensive positions, in the formidable Gothic Line north of Florence. They would not finally surrender until 2 May 1945.

OPERATION OVERLORD

NORTHERN FRANCE 6 JUNE – 30 AUGUST 1944

The establishment of the second front in Western Europe
hastened the end of Nazi Germany and World War II in Europe

WORDS MIKE HASKEW

American soldiers crouch behind the gunwales of a landing craft as they approach Omaha Beach on D-Day

dolf Hitler boasted that the Atlantic Wall, a string of fortifications stretching from the North Sea to the French frontier with Spain, was impregnable. Nevertheless, Allied commanders knew that the establishment of a second front in Western Europe was a prerequisite to the final defeat of Nazi Germany in World War II.

Since the summer of 1941, Soviet Premier Joseph Stalin had clamored for a second front. His Red Army had borne the brunt of the ground war against the Nazis. However, the United States and Great Britain were not militarily prepared to launch such an endeavor until mid-1944. Dubbed Operation Overlord, the long-awaited invasion occurred on D-Day, 6 June, along an 50-mile stretch of coastline in French Normandy.

When finally unleashed after a weather delay, Operation Overlord involved more than 150,000 troops, nearly 7,000 ships and 4,100 aircraft. In the early morning, Allied soldiers stormed ashore on five invasion beaches. From east to west, the British Third Division assaulted Sword Beach, the 50th Division Gold Beach, the Canadian Third Division Juno Beach, and elements of the American First and 29th Divisions Omaha and the Fourth Division Utah beaches respectively.

American General Dwight D Eisenhower led the senior Allied command structure, while his immediate subordinates were British. Air Chief Marshal Sir Arthur Tedder was deputy supreme commander; Admiral Bertram Ramsay led the seaborne effort; Air Chief Marshal Trafford Leigh-Mallory the air; and General Bernard Law Montgomery the ground forces. American General Omar N Bradley commanded the US First Army under Montgomery, and General Miles Dempsey led the British Second Army.

The Allies knew that Operation Overlord was fraught with risk. The assault troops had to force a lodgment on the Norman coast and not only defend against certain German counterattacks from elements of Army Group B under the resourceful Field Marshal Erwin Rommel, but also somehow rapidly expand the beachhead inland. The naval forces would be subject to attack from enemy submarines and air assets in the relative confinement of the English Channel.

Still, the riskiest proposition of Overlord was the predawn insertion of three airborne divisions, parachuting or gliding into the countryside to secure the flanks of the landings, holding vital bridges and causeway exits, disrupting communications, and standing fast until relieved with a linkup of advancing troops off the beaches. The American 82nd and 101st

Airborne Divisions came down widely dispersed in the west, while the British Sixth Airborne's glider landings occurred on the eastern flank. Casualties were expected to run high, but Eisenhower deemed the operation worthwhile. In the end, the airborne forces performed with great distinction.

The invasion begins

At about 11.30pm on 5 June, the invasion armada set sail for Normandy. Soon after, transport aircraft took to the sky carrying the airborne contingent. It was hoped that naval bombardment and frequent air raids against German defensive positions and infrastructure had paved the way for a successful landing and a push inland that would secure vital objectives and close gaps between the beaches swiftly.

At first light, Allied troops stormed ashore in Normandy. On Sword Beach, the British fought their way inland to capture the German defensive position at La Breche and reached the outskirts of Ouistreham. At Gold, the British seized Port-en-Bessin, 3.7 miles inland. Heavy seas hampered the landing of reinforcements and the movement of supporting tanks, and though their beachhead was secure, the British failed to take the transport and communications center of Caen, a primary D-Day objective.

American troops accompany M4 Sherman medium tanks through the ravaged French village of Coutances during Operation Cobra

BOYS OF POINTE DU HOC

US Army Rangers scaled cliffs on D-Day to attack German gun emplacements that threatened the invasion beaches

Among the daring exploits of D-Day, a detachment of 225 US Army Rangers of the Second Battalion scaled the cliffs at Pointe du Hoc, west of Omaha Beach. Their objective was a German battery believed to house six 155mm howitzers capable of delivering devastating fire against either Omaha or Utah Beach.

Led by Lieutenant Colonel James Rudder, the Rangers were to silence the guns after climbing the promontory while under enemy fire. On paper, it looked like a suicide run. But the Rangers were equal to the task. They planned to use grappling hooks on ropes fired toward the summit and then work their way hand over hand to the top. They also borrowed ladders from the London Fire Brigade for the task.

Once in position, the Rangers found that most of their ropes were soaked. With the added weight the catapults failed to reach the desired height. Undeterred, the Rangers won the crest and drove the Germans off only to discover that the guns had been removed. Five of them were later located in an apple orchard and destroyed with thermite grenades.

The Rangers stood their ground, fighting off several counterattacks until relieved on 8 June. Of those engaged, only 90 remained unscathed.

After the capture of Pointe du Hoc, German prisoners march into captivity near the command post of Lieutenant Colonel James Rudder

The scale of the Normandy landings was immense, as seen in this aerial shot from 6 June

A COMMUNIQUÉ NEVER SENT

Although he had faith in the success of Operation Overlord, General Dwight Eisenhower was required to prepare for the worst

The weather was horrific but thousands of soldiers were poised to assault Hitler's Fortress Europe. While rain pelted and wind howled, General Dwight D Eisenhower assembled senior commanders at Southwick House in Portsmouth, England, early on 5 June 1944 to seek advice. Weather forecasts indicated a window for the D-Day operation, already postponed by 24 hours, to launch the next day.

Security concerns were rising. Such an immense operation could not remain secret indefinitely. The troops were ready. Another postponement would sap combat efficiency. The next favorable conditions were two weeks away. Field Marshal Bernard Montgomery

piped, "I would say go!" Others nodded, and Eisenhower pronounced, "OK, we'll go!"

Failure was unthinkable, but Eisenhower prepared a statement shouldering command responsibility: "Our landings in the Cherbourg-Havre area have failed to gain a satisfactory foothold and I have withdrawn the troops. My decision to attack at this time and place was based upon the best information available. The troops, the air and the navy did all that bravery and devotion to duty could do. If any blame or fault attaches to the attempt it is mine alone." Ultimately, the decision to order Overlord was Eisenhower's. The message stayed in his pocket and was given to a staff officer as a souvenir.

General Dwight D Eisenhower, supreme Allied commander, poses with senior Allied officers during planning for Operation Overlord

At Juno, the Canadians faced intense opposition and fought for two hours to dislodge defenders along the shoreline. Eventually, the Canadians linked up with the British from Gold Beach, but a gap still remained between Gold and Sword. The Allies were actually aided by the ineptitude of the German response. The bulk of their armored divisions were held in reserve to be released only on Hitler's personal order. Therefore, the German 21st Panzer Division mounted the only substantial counterattack of the day, driving between Sword and Gold beaches all the way to the coast. However, there were no reinforcements to exploit the gain and the Germans were compelled to withdraw.

The American landings at Utah Beach went fortuitously awry. The Fourth Division actually came ashore in the wrong place, but assistant division commander General Theodore Roosevelt Jr proclaimed, "We'll start the war from here!" Within just a few hours, the Americans were plunging ahead against unexpectedly light resistance.

Though many of the enemy troops that garrisoned the Atlantic Wall defenses were static units or conscripts from occupied countries, the 352nd Infantry Division was an experienced formation that took full advantage of the cliffs at Omaha Beach and made the broad expanse of the shoreline at low tide a killing ground.

Omaha was the most horrific battle of D-Day. Many US soldiers of the first wave were shot as soon as the ramps of their landing craft were lowered. Others were weighed down by combat packs and drowned. Rough seas swamped amphibious tanks meant to add firepower to the assault. The situation was in such doubt at mid-morning that General Bradley contemplated withdrawing the troops from the beach and diverting reinforcements to quieter sectors.

Then, the resilience of the GIs prevailed as junior and noncommissioned officers got up from the makeshift shelter of beach obstacles to take on German strongpoints one by one. Finally, in the afternoon the situation at Omaha stabilized. But the beachhead was precarious and a nine-mile gap existed between the Americans at Omaha and the Canadians at Juno. The distance was even greater to a linkup with the Fourth Division at Utah.

Despite the difficulties encountered on D-Day at the cost of 2,500 dead and another 7,500 wounded, the Allied forces solidified their foothold in Normandy. Looking beyond the beaches, though, weeks of tough fighting lay ahead. Operation Overlord, the Normandy campaign, proceeded – painfully at times.

Montgomery hammered away at Caen, but the Germans held the city and the dominating high ground of Hill 112 for more than a month.

Churchill addresses US paratroopers in May 1944, ahead of Operation Overlord

"MANY US SOLDIERS OF THE FIRST WAVE ON OMAHA WERE SHOT AS SOON AS THE RAMPS OF THEIR LANDING CRAFT WERE LOWERED"

Still, the British commander contended that his design was to draw the bulk of the German armored divisions, finally released by Hitler, upon himself to enable the Americans on his right flank to advance.

Breaking out

The Americans were challenged by the terrain as centuries-old hedgerows made a patchwork of the Norman countryside, turning meadows into free-fire zones and country lanes into deathtraps. Progress was slow as some formations turned toward the Cotentin Peninsula and the deepwater port of Cherbourg, while others maintained the advance against the town of Saint Lo and other objectives that would unhinge the German resistance.

While the British finally secured Caen in mid-July, the Americans launched an all-out effort to break free of the hedgerows. Bradley's plan, called Operation Cobra, involved the saturation bombing of German positions along the front lines followed by a swift assault of American armor and infantry that would lead the spearheads into open country.

On 25 July, Cobra was unleashed. The defending Germans were stunned, and one division – the Panzer Lehr – ceased to function due to the ferocity of the bombing. During the next 48 hours, American forces advanced 17 miles. Simultaneously, renewed British efforts combined to unhinge the German defenses in Normandy. A foolhardy counterattack ordered by Hitler served only to further weaken the German forces, depleting their armored contingent significantly.

With the enemy in retreat a golden opportunity to bag the entire German Seventh Army and other formations presented itself. A giant Allied pincer movement converged on the area of Falaise. By mid-August Allied forces had thrown a bridgehead across the River Seine while Montgomery fixed the bulk of the German armor to the north and the Canadian First Army swung toward the enemy right flank. Meanwhile, the newly activated Third Army under General George S Patton Jr dashed across France, threatening to outflank the Germans in the south.

Although fanatical German resistance held the shoulders of the 'Falaise Pocket' open and allowed about 40,000 enemy soldiers to escape, Allied air and artillery turned the area into a meatgrinder. More than 10,000 Germans were killed and 50,000 captured. Eisenhower visited the battleground and remarked that he could not step in any direction without touching the body of a dead enemy soldier.

By late August, the Allies had destroyed organized German resistance in Normandy, vaulted the Seine, secured the Cotentin Peninsula, and raced across Brittany deep into the interior of France. On 25 August, Paris was liberated. Operation Overlord and the Normandy campaign were over. The Allies sustained over 200,000 casualties while the Germans lost over 200,000 soldiers who were either killed, wounded, or captured.

More grievous losses were sustained during months of fighting, but in April 1945 US soldiers linked up with the Soviet Red Army, advancing west, at the German town of Torgau on the Elbe River. Within days, the Third Reich was no more.

OPERATION MARKET GARDEN

THE NETHERLANDS 17-25 SEPTEMBER 1944

For over 75 years the underlying reasons for the failure at Arnhem have gone largely unremarked upon, despite being in plain sight

WORDS WILLIAM F BUCKINGHAM

The Battle of Normandy effectively ended on 21 August 1944 with the closing of the Falaise Gap, 76 days after Allied troops first set foot on the D-Day landing beaches. The battle cost the Germans up to 20,000 dead and more than 50,000 prisoners, along with almost all their heavy equipment and vehicles, and an estimated tide of 20,000 survivors fled eastward as far as southern Holland, where the local civilians dubbed Tuesday 5 September 'Dolle Dinsdag' or 'Mad Tuesday'.

The Allied pursuit began on 28 August with British tanks reaching Arras on 1 September, Brussels was liberated two days later and by 6 September the advance was approaching the Dutch border in the face of stiffening German resistance. In an effort to maintain the momentum Allied Supreme Commander General Dwight D Eisenhower authorized Operation Market Garden, which was intended to bypass the Westwall fixed defenses guarding the German frontier and open a route into the North German Plain and thus the heart of the Third Reich.

Operation Market was the largest airborne operation in history and involved landing 40,000 men from three Allied Airborne Divisions along a 60-mile corridor running north from the Belgian border to the Dutch city of Arnhem on the Lower Rhine, tasked to seize and hold 17 bridges across eight separate waterways starting at the Wilhelmina Canal just north of Eindhoven. The operation began on 17 September 1944 with the US 101st Airborne Division assigned to secure the southern third of the corridor, the center portion including the city of Nijmegen was the responsibility of the US 82nd Airborne Division, and the furthest third was allotted to the British 1st Airborne Division.

The ground component of the Operation, codenamed Garden, tasked British 30 Corps – spearheaded by the Guards Armored Division – to break through the coalescing German defense on the Belgian border and advance rapidly up the Airborne Corridor, relieving each crossing in turn. All this was scheduled to take 48 hours. In the event the two US Airborne divisions secured all their allotted objectives, although the first bridge across the Wilhelmina Canal was destroyed, prompting a 36-hour delay compounded by the tardy performance of 30 Corps, while the road and rail bridges across the River Waal at Nijmegen were not secured until the evening of 20 September, 24 hours behind schedule.

Matters went most awry at Arnhem, however, despite a near flawless delivery. The 1st Airborne Division's plan was to despatch the 1st Airborne Reconnaissance Squadron and the 1st Parachute Brigade to secure the objectives in Arnhem. The bulk of the first lift would remain at the landing area until the second lift arrived the following day, after which the entire division would also move into Arnhem.

In the event only a small part of the 1st Parachute Brigade managed to slip through to the north end of the Arnhem road bridge, where they held the objective for 80 rather than 48 hours before being overwhelmed after an epic siege. The remainder of the 1st Parachute Brigade fought itself to destruction trying to reach the bridge before being driven back to the main body of the 1st Airborne Division, which was blocked and surrounded at Oosterbeek, midway between the landing area and Arnhem.

After another epic six-day siege that reduced Oosterbeek to rubble and the failure of three attempts to push reinforcements across the Lower Rhine, around 2,500 survivors were evacuated in small boats on the night of 25-26 September 1944. The evacuation effectively marked the end of Operation Market Garden.

Popular reasons for the failure

The search for reasons for the 1st Airborne Division's failure at Arnhem began as soon as Market Garden ended, and several recurring favorites have emerged over the years. These include: landing the division in daylight, spreading the division landing across three lifts on successive days, and the seven-mile-or-so distance between the landing area and Arnhem. All of these were mandated by external factors, however, and they did not impact adversely on events at Arnhem.

First, because Market was launched in a no-moon period, a daylight insertion was unavoidable because paratroopers and glider pilots alike required a degree of natural light to judge depth and distance

British paratroops of the 1st Airborne Division in their aircraft en route to Arnhem

At the time, Market was the largest airborne operation in history

An Allied paratrooper makes an uncomfortable landing

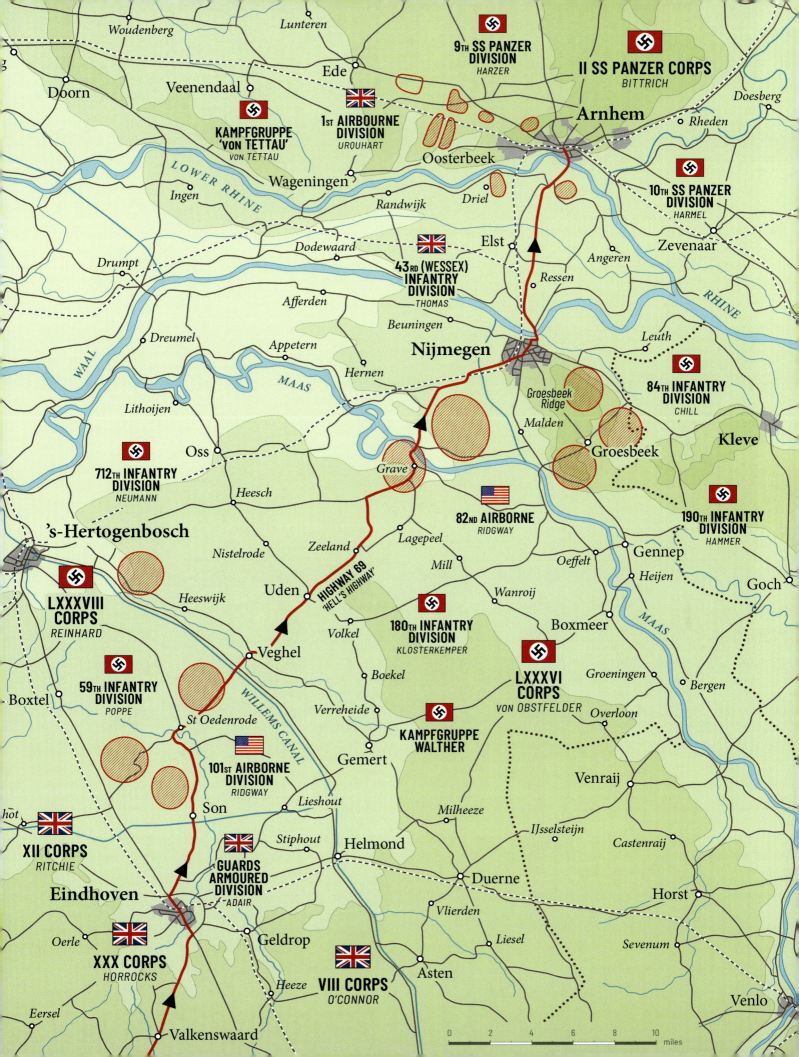

for landing. It should also be noted that the Market first lift was widely hailed as the most successful to date by experienced commanders from all three Airborne Divisions.

Second, the 1st Airborne was not alone in being delivered in multiple lifts spread over several days simply because there were insufficient transport aircraft available to deliver three complete Airborne divisions simultaneously. The shortening autumn days ruled out flying more than one lift per day because it would involve taking off or returning in darkness, and while RAF aircrew were trained in night flying and navigation techniques, their USAAF counterparts largely were not and also lacked trained navigators and ground crew.

Third, the landing area was selected because it was the closest site to Arnhem suitable for large-scale glider landings, as contemporary maps show. While the area at the south end of the Arnhem road bridge could have been used as a parachute landing zone, the planners considered it too soft and riven with deep, wide drainage ditches for safe use by heavily laden gliders. Furthermore, the distance between the landing area and the objectives in Arnhem was not the handicap it is often painted. The 2nd Parachute Battalion reached the Arnhem road bridge in just over four hours, fighting several

small actions en route and while shepherding a number of personnel and vehicles from the brigade column and a variety of support units. This shows covering the seven miles was perfectly feasible providing the attackers moved with sufficient speed and application.

The myth of enemy action

Enemy action is another often repeated reason for the failure, usually relying on two specific examples. SS Battalion Krafft, an approximately 400-strong replacement training unit billeted near Oosterbeek, is routinely credited with single-handedly holding back the 1st Parachute Brigade's advance to Arnhem until after dark on 17 September, largely due to a highly embellished and self-serving report by its commander, Hauptsturmführer Sepp Krafft.

The reality was rather more prosaic. Krafft serendipitously deployed his unit along the eastern side of what was to be the 1st Airborne Division's main landing area to avoid Allied preparatory bombing, but its impact was far less than popularly claimed, amounting to a handful of relatively minor clashes. One element was wiped out by the 2nd Parachute Battalion after straying onto the landing area, another spent several hours inconclusively skirmishing with a British unit defending the landing area and a third

caught two of the 1st Airborne Reconnaissance Squadron's Jeeps as they belatedly began their move from the landing area to the Arnhem bridge.

The most significant clashes were with the 3rd Parachute Battalion on the outskirts of Oosterbeek, consisting of a brief hit-and-run ambush in the late afternoon followed by an inconclusive two-hour fight with the tail end of the 3rd Battalion column at dusk that ended when the SS element withdrew. None of this materially impacted the 1st Parachute Brigade's advance toward Arnhem, however, and any connected consequences were attributable to other factors.

The second popular myth with reference to enemy action is the recurring idea that the 1st Airborne Division landed atop two fully functioning panzer divisions. While II SS Panzerkorps, consisting of 9th and 10th SS Panzer Divisions, had been in the vicinity of Arnhem since 8 September, the fighting in Normandy and the retreat across northern France and Belgium had reduced them to a fraction of a single division in total, with a relative handful of vehicles and heavy equipment, the bulk of which were despatched south to Belgium to block the Allied ground advance on 13 September, four days before Market commenced.

By 17 September, 10th SS Panzer Division had been ordered to refit in place in Holland at three locations up to 30 miles east and north of Arnhem, while 9th SS Panzer Division had been ordered to hand over its surviving heavy equipment to its running mate and the bulk of its personnel had already been despatched to Germany by rail to be re-equipped by the time Market began. The remainder, mainly service and supply personnel denuded of almost all heavy equipment and motor transport, were scattered across locations north and east of Arnhem between 16 and 35 miles from the landing area.

It is therefore clear that neither of II SS Panzerkorps' badly depleted formations were close to being under the 1st Airborne Division's landing and more importantly, none of 9th SS Panzer Division's elements were located between the landing area and Arnhem. They were therefore unable to seriously interfere with the 1st Parachute Brigade's advance into Arnhem in the first vital ten to 12 hours following

the landing, when the British formation's battle for its objectives was won and lost.

Apart from the riverside loophole that permitted the 2nd Parachute Battalion to slip through to the Arnhem road bridge, German reactions and deployments were exemplary, however. II SS Panzerkorps HQ issued warning orders less than an hour after receiving reports of the landing, 9th SS Panzer Division's denuded units were on the way to the scene of the action within three hours and within four hours Feldmarschall Walther Model had issued orders that framed the subsequent successful German conduct of the battle.

Unwarranted arrogance and poor discipline?

All this suggests that the reasons for the 1st Airborne Division's failure at Arnhem were a little closer to home, and at first glance the

problems appear to be with the division's attitude as a whole. Although the glider and parachute operations carried out by two of its constituent brigades in Sicily were effectively fiascos, the 1st Airborne Division returned from the Mediterranean in November 1943 with an overwhelming sense of its experience and capabilities; tendencies noted not least by the division's new commander Major-General Robert Urquhart, who observed a reluctance to accept the necessity of any additional training.

Similarly, Lieutenant-Colonel Mark Henniker from the division's Royal Engineer contingent referred to many surrounding themselves with a mystique that was not entirely justified by experience, while Major Philip Tower RA, who joined the division after its return to the UK, recognized the quality of his new Airborne comrades but felt they overestimated their abilities, and noted an unwillingness to

"URQUHART'S LACK OF AIRBORNE EXPERIENCE WAS CLEARLY APPARENT IN HIS PLANNING FOR ARNHEM, WHICH ELICITED DISBELIEF AMONG SENIOR US AIRBORNE COMMANDERS"

acknowledge that any worthwhile experience was to be had outside the Airborne fold. This is illustrated by an incident when umpires ruled against a particularly poorly co-ordinated attack by a 1st Airborne Division unit during Exercise Mush in April 1944, after which a company commander protested loudly that "you can't do this to us, we are the original Red Devils!"

The attitude manifested itself as indiscipline in the lower ranks, particularly within the 1st Parachute Brigade. Lieutenant-Colonel John Frost, who commanded the 2nd Parachute Battalion at Arnhem bridge, referred to low level disciplinary problems across the whole brigade from "hard cases" disinclined to obey regulations, along with widespread absenteeism which interfered with training and disrupted unit cohesion, while the commander of the 3rd Parachute Battalion was relieved after his battalion was unable to march on a test exercise.

The epicenter of indiscipline was the 1st Parachute Battalion where one commander was posted away after tightening discipline with the aid of a Guards RSM, which the troops considered to be "treating battle-hardened men like children" and his replacement was not popular either. The feeling was mutual. Lieutenant-Colonel Kenneth Darling later recalled, "Frankly, I was horrified by 1 Para, they thought they knew all the answers, which they did not, and their discipline was not what I expected." The upshot was a mutiny on 30 March 1944 when the battalion refused to

draw parachutes for a jump which led to Darling being replaced by Lieutenant-Colonel David Dobie, who led the 1st Battalion into Arnhem. In some instances the indiscipline spilled over into outright criminality. For example, on 12 February 1944 the local fire brigade had to be summoned after a smoke marker was ignited outside the Battalion Orderly Room, and just over a month later the safe in the battalion's NAAFI canteen was broken into and the funds stolen.

The obvious conclusion to draw from all this was that unwarranted arrogance and poor discipline were the reasons for the 1st Airborne Division's failure. However, events in Holland clearly show this was not the case. With regard to the 1st Parachute Brigade, the 2nd Parachute Battalion reached the Arnhem road bridge in just over four hours accompanied by the brigade column and other elements totaling approximately 740 men.

This force held the north end of the bridge for three and a half days, losing 81 dead and approximately 280 wounded in the process, almost 50 per cent of the force. They were only overwhelmed after running out of ammunition and food, and being literally blasted out of mostly burning buildings by artillery and tanks.

The 1st Parachute Battalion spent 11 hours trying to reach its objective north of Arnhem, losing 11 dead and over a hundred wounded, before moving immediately to reinforce Frost at the road bridge. It then joined the 3rd Parachute Battalion in repeated unsuccessful attempts to

break through the German blocking line in the western outskirts of Arnhem, during which both units fought themselves virtually to destruction. By midday on Tuesday 19 September the 1st Parachute Battalion had been reduced to around 200 men from the 548 who had jumped in two days earlier, while the 588-strong 3rd Parachute Battalion had been reduced to just 60.

Neither was this level of raw courage and application unique to the 1st Parachute Brigade, as the fight in the outskirts of Arnhem took a similar toll of battalions from the 1st Airlanding Brigade and 4th Parachute Brigade and was then replicated across the entire gamut of the 1st Airborne Division's units in the subsequent six-day siege of Oosterbeek. This all strongly suggests that the 1st Parachute Brigade's indiscipline was largely a case of good field soldiers making poor garrison soldiers, and that there was little wrong with the 1st Airborne Division up to the battalion level or equivalent, arrogance notwithstanding.

Poor planning and leadership

In fact, the root of the 1st Airborne Division's failure was higher up the chain of command, and at the very top. A Regular officer commissioned in 1920, Major-General Robert Elliot Urquhart assumed command of the 1st Airborne Division on 10 January 1944, having risen from the rank of major to major-general in the course of war service in a variety of staff positions, including a 13-month stint on the staff of the 51st Highland Division in North Africa. This was followed by his sole operational command appointment, four months commanding 231 Infantry Brigade in Sicily and southern Italy; he never commanded or served with an airborne unit prior to assuming command of the 1st Airborne Division.

Lieutenant-General Lewis H Brereton (left) commander of the First Allied Airborne Army, shakes hands with Major-General Urquhart

Among the criticisms of the operation is the tasking of airborne troops in regular infantry roles

His relatively rapid progress and elevation to the latter command over better-qualified candidates was due to the intervention of Field-Marshal Bernard Law Montgomery. Urquhart had been a Montgomery protégé since coming to the latter's notice when serving on the 3rd Infantry Division staff in October 1940, and he was given command of the 1st Airborne Division after Montgomery raised the idea with the commander of British 1st Airborne Corps, Major-General Frederick Browning. To be fair there is no evidence Urquhart sought the appointment and he created a good impression at his new command, but circumstances conspired to prevent him properly grasping the operational implications, restrictions and realities of his new role.

In the five months before D-Day, Urquhart attended numerous conferences and planning meetings in or near London over a hundred miles from his HQ in Lincolnshire and after the invasion he was fully involved in preparing for a total of 15 canceled operations. This was a punishing schedule and was likely a cause of the severe bout of malaria that hospitalized him for almost a month in April 1944. Urquhart's lack of airborne experience was clearly apparent in his planning for Arnhem, which elicited disbelief among senior US Airborne commanders. For example, Brigadier-General James Gavin, commanding the 82nd Airborne Division and the most experienced of all Allied airborne commanders, later likened Urquhart's scheme to a peacetime exercise.

Urquhart gave assembling his division in its entirety as much attention as accomplishing its mission, and his assumption that the Germans would permit it to sit in place for 24 hours before moving into Arnhem was fanciful, as the fact that the bulk of the 1st Airborne Division covered less than half the distance to Arnhem before being blocked and surrounded shows. Urquhart's thinking appears to have been rooted in conventional ground operation rather than what was required for an airborne insertion 60 miles behind enemy lines, and thus suggests a fundamental misunderstanding of the realities of airborne operations.

Urquhart compounded his unrealistic planning with a series of poor decisions after Market was launched, to the extent it can be argued he did not make a single correct decision in his first two days on the ground in Holland. He failed to clarify the division command succession until boarding the glider for Arnhem, a basic precaution and a vital one in airborne operations, given the routine risks inherent in aerial delivery even without enemy action. In the event his chief of staff was obliged to mitigate the consequences with diplomacy in the midst of the battle when Urquhart abruptly left his HQ shortly after landing in response to an erroneous rumor that the 1st Airborne Reconnaissance Squadron had failed to arrive in Holland.

Instead of checking the veracity of the rumor, Urquhart summoned the Squadron Commander, Major Freddie Gough, to Division HQ by radio before racing off in a Jeep to inform Brigadier Lathbury and the 1st Parachute Brigade in person. The kneejerk summons separated Gough from his command for the remainder of the battle and effectively ended the squadron's coup-de-main mission.

More seriously, it can be argued that at this point Urquhart effectively abdicated command of the 1st Airborne Division as he disappeared with no explanation or contact arrangements and then deliberately severed radio contact with his HQ, which was never re-established. His arrival at the 3rd Parachute Battalion at dusk was instrumental in that unit abandoning its move to Arnhem and halting in Oosterbeek for the night. Urquhart then chose to remain with the 3rd Battalion, still out of contact with his HQ and the rest of the division, and thus unable to exert any influence on the developing battle, until the late afternoon of 18 September. He then made an ill-advised attempt to regain his HQ accompanied by Brigadier Gerald Lathbury that ended with Lathbury being badly wounded and captured and Urquhart trapped in an attic for 12 hours, before finally regaining his HQ at 7.25am on 19 September, after a 40-hour absence. By that time the initial window of opportunity had gone and the Arnhem portion of Operation Market had effectively failed.

That is not to say that Urquhart was a bad or incompetent commander. He did a more than adequate job of rallying his division and establishing a defensible perimeter at Oosterbeek while in contact with the enemy, and then orchestrated the defense of that perimeter under ever increasing German pressure. When it became clear this was unsustainable and permission was granted to withdraw across the river, Urquhart planned and implemented an evacuation inspired by the retreat from Gallipoli during the First World War codenamed Operation Berlin, which succeeded in lifting over 2,000 men across the Lower Rhine on the night of 25-26 September. All that came after the airborne assault at Arnhem had morphed into a conventional defensive infantry battle, however, and the evidence strongly suggests that Urquhart did not fully grasp the realities of airborne operations.

That lack of understanding contributed significantly to the failure of the 1st Airborne Division at Arnhem and, by extension, to the failure of Operation Market Garden.

The Arnhem portion of Market might still have succeeded in spite of Urquhart's errors had the 1st Parachute Brigade managed to seize and hold the objectives in the city. This was not to be, however, as the brigade commander was only marginally more experienced himself. Brigadier Gerald Lathbury was commissioned in 1926 and his war service consisted of a number of separate staff appointments at the War Office, interspersed with eight months overseeing the raising of the 3rd Parachute Battalion and four months performing the same role with the 3rd Parachute Brigade.

He assumed command of the 1st Parachute Brigade on 25 April 1943 and led its operation to seize the Primasole Bridge in Sicily three months later. The operation was a fiasco as the brigade was scattered up to 20 miles from its objective, the ground force took 48 rather than 12 hours to arrive, and Lathbury was wounded in the back and legs during the fighting. These circumstances have concealed the unsuitability of Lathbury's plan, however, which employed six widely separated landing zones before dispersing the brigade over three separate locations spread across more than five square miles. This ruled out mutual support and breached the military maxim on maintaining focus on the primary aim. In fairness, there was not a great deal of airborne experience to draw upon in 1943, but Lathbury went on to commit exactly the same errors at Arnhem where again circumstances conspired to conceal the fact.

Lathbury's Arnhem plan was a slight reworking of an earlier scheme codenamed Comet and envisaged sending the armed Jeeps of the 1st Airborne Reconnaissance Squadron ahead to seize the Arnhem bridge followed by the brigade's three battalions moving along three parallel and widely spaced routes. The 1st Parachute Battalion was allotted the northern route codenamed Leopard, the 3rd Parachute Battalion was assigned the center Tiger route, and the 2nd Parachute Battalion was allocated the southern Lion route along the Lower Rhine. This dispersed the brigade's combat power, ruled out mutual support, and obliged each battalion to fight in isolation and the plan thus resembled a peacetime training exercise, an impression reinforced by the objectives selected. These isolated a third of the brigade on high ground north of Arnhem, dispersed a third across the pontoon bridge, the Arnhem rail bridge and the German HQ in the center of Arnhem with the remaining third holding the Arnhem road bridge.

Given that most of these tasks required a full battalion at minimum, the plan was a classic case of trying to do too much with too little, and virtually guaranteed that the 1st Parachute Brigade's sub-units would be isolated, overwhelmed, and defeated in detail.

Once on the ground in Holland, Lathbury exacerbated the flaws in his plan by micromanaging his subordinate commanders to a degree that interfered with their ability to carry out their assigned missions. This began by needlessly holding the battalions at the landing area for over an hour before releasing them despite the time-sensitive nature of the operation, and then motoring between the widely dispersed battalion routes urging the commanders to greater haste.

By early evening Lathbury was running the 3rd Parachute Battalion over the head of its commander near Oosterbeek. He ordered an unnecessary counterattack against elements of Bataillon Krafft that fired on the tail of the battalion column as it was moving away from the attackers and then compounded this by ordering the 3rd Battalion to halt in Oosterbeek for the night, presumably to protect Major-General Urquhart after he turned up unescorted at dusk. Lathbury then refused a radio appeal for assistance from his brigade major at the Arnhem road bridge, on the grounds that his men were tired.

Thereafter he effectively abdicated command by accompanying an equally passive Urquhart in remaining with the 3rd Parachute Battalion until he was wounded and captured while attempting to regain his HQ on 18 September. All this does not necessarily mean Lathbury was a bad or incompetent officer. His inadequate planning was attributable to inexperience and lack of higher guidance. His micromanaging was presumably due to his formation's disciplinary problems, and abandoning his mission to protect his superior was likely the result of his conditioning as a Regular officer. Nonetheless, it is perhaps instructive to note that the elements of the 1st Parachute Brigade that reached the Arnhem road bridge or fought themselves to destruction trying to reach it did so without the benefit of Lathbury's direct involvement.

It can therefore be seen that there was more to the failure of the 1st Airborne Division at Arnhem than popular assumptions about landing areas, drop arrangements, and enemy action, and that the underlying reasons were poor planning and leadership at the brigade and division level. Given the exemplary courage and tenacity exhibited by the men of the 1st Airborne Division in Holland, it is interesting to speculate on how the Arnhem portion of Operation Market might have turned out with more experienced hands at the helm.

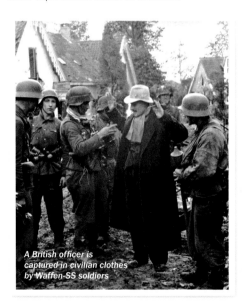

A British officer is captured in civilian clothes by Waffen-SS soldiers

American troops attempt to free trapped GIs from the wreckage of a crash-landed Waco glider

THE END NEARS

The light carrier USS
Princeton was hit by a single
Japanese bomb and sunk in
the Battle of the Sibuyan Sea

BATTLE OF
LEYTE GULF

LEYTE GULF 23-26 OCTOBER 1944

The US and Imperial Japanese navies squared off in a series of
engagements that came to comprise one of history's largest naval battles

WORDS MARC DESANTIS

On 20 October 1944, after a heavy naval bombardment, Supreme Allied Commander, Southwest Pacific Area, General Douglas MacArthur commenced landing 200,000 US troops on the island of Leyte with the goal of liberating the Philippines from Japanese occupation. Offshore in Leyte Gulf lay Vice Admiral Thomas Kinkaid's US Seventh Fleet covering the amphibious invasion force and delivering the ammunition, food and supplies necessary to sustain the troops heading inland.

The days before the landings saw major American carrier-plane airstrikes on Formosa and the Ryukyu Islands, and hundreds of Japanese aircraft fell victim to American fliers. Coupled with the devastating losses from the Battle of the Philippine Sea that June, the Japanese Combined Fleet would be largely without air cover for the upcoming battle.

In response to the American landings at Leyte, the Japanese high command initiated its Sho-Go 1 plan with the intention of destroying the US invasion fleet. This could not be achieved by Japan's very limited air power, so a Japanese surface fleet would have to do. Before the Japanese counter could begin, it would first be necessary for the US Third Fleet under Admiral William 'Bull' Halsey to be lured away from its position to the north-east of the Philippines so that it could not interfere with the Combined Fleet's attack on the US amphibious fleet in Leyte Gulf.

Sho-Go 1 was a complicated battle plan, in keeping with most Japanese naval operations of the war. It called for a 17-ship Northern Force departing from Japanese home waters under Vice-Admiral Jisaburo Ozawa and consisting of one fleet carrier and three light carriers, which were largely empty of airplanes, two battleships, and 11 lesser warships to lure Halsey away. A powerful Center Group under Vice-Admiral Takeo Kurita comprising five battleships, ten heavy cruisers, two light cruisers and 15 destroyers, sailing from Borneo, would traverse the middle of the Philippines through

"COUPLED WITH THE DEVASTATING LOSSES FROM THE BATTLE OF THE PHILIPPINE SEA, THE JAPANESE COMBINED FLEET WOULD BE LARGELY WITHOUT AIR COVER FOR THE UPCOMING BATTLE"

BATTLE OF LEYTE GULF
23-26 OCTOBER 1944

The unexpected appearance of Kurita's Center Group, including the 70,000-ton Yamato, stunned the Americans off Samar

03 NORTHERN FORCE DECOY
24 OCTOBER 1944
Word reaches Halsey of Ozawa's Northern Force and he decides to give chase, just as the Japanese hoped he would. Halsey takes all of his warships with him, leaving nothing behind to guard the San Bernardino Strait and the approaches to the invasion beaches in Leyte Gulf.

07 KURITA RETREATS
25 OCTOBER 1944
Shaken by the frenzied resistance of the American escort carriers and destroyers off Samar, and mistakenly thinking he is facing the main US fleet, Kurita breaks contact and his Center Group retreats back up the San Bernardino Strait.

01 THE JAPANESE PLAN
Kurita's Center Group makes for the San Bernardino Strait heading for Leyte Gulf, while Nishimura takes his fleet to the Surigao Strait, destination Leyte Gulf, where the US amphibious fleet lies offshore supporting the invasion forces. Ozawa's Northern Force steams south, intent upon luring away Halsey's Third Fleet.

02 BATTLE OF THE SIBUYAN SEA
24 OCTOBER 1944
On 23 October, US submarines Darter and Dace launch torpedoes against the ships of Kurita's Center Group, sinking two Japanese cruisers. They also notify Halsey of Kurita's position. The next day, carrier planes from Halsey's Third Fleet attack Kurita's ships, sinking the battleship Musashi. Halsey now mistakenly believes Kurita's fleet is a spent, impotent force.

Babuyan Islands

Laoag

Tuguegarao City

Baguio

Dagupan

San Jose

Tarlac

Cabanatuan

Angeles

San Fernando

Olongapo

Manila

Mariveles

San Pablo

Daeto

Lucena

Batangas

Naga

Iriga

Legaspi

South China Sea

Mindoro

CENTRAL FORCE (KURITA)

Calamian Islands

Sibuyan Sea

Roxas

Visayan Sea

Catbalogan

Samar

Tacloban

Cuyo Islands

Cadiz

Ormoco

Leyte Gulf OLD

Iloilo

Bacolod

San Carlos

Leyte

SHIMA'S FORCE

Negros

Cebu

Kabankalan

Su

Puerto Princesa

Cagayan

Tagbilaran

Palowan

Dumaguete

Mindanao Sea

Sulu Sea

SOUTHERN FORCE (NISHIMURA)

Dipolog

Gingoog

Cagayan

Iligan

B

TG 38.3
Oct 24

TG 38.2
Oct 24

22:40 24

Oct 24

22:00 25
San Bernadino Strait
0:00 25

04:0

12:00 24

12:00 24

24:00 24

24:00 24

12:00 24

Oct 24

06 BATTLE OF CAPE ENGAÑO
25 OCTOBER 1944

Halsey's carrier pilots catch Ozawa's Northern Force and sink three of its carriers during the Battle of Cape Engaño. A fourth is sunk by American cruisers. In the meantime, Halsey receives an encoded message about the plight of Seventh Fleet's escort carriers. He sends his battleships south to their aid but they arrive too late to be of any help.

06:30 25

3rd FLEET
(HALSEY)

08 VICTORY
The Japanese fleets retire to recover from their hammering. Despite miscommunication that left the invasion fleet exposed, Leyte Gulf is a dramatic victory for the US Navy. It sinks 26 Japanese warships for the loss of seven of its own.

Philippine Sea

04 BATTLE OFF SAMAR
25 OCTOBER 1944

Kurita's Center Group, including the super battleship Yamato, is much more powerful than Halsey supposed, and it rushes down the now-unguarded San Bernardino Strait. The only ships between them and the amphibious ships are several small escort carriers and their protective destroyers of Taffy 3. In a chaotic action off Samar, the Americans counterattack desperately as immense Japanese naval cannons blast at them. The battleships of Seventh Fleet are in the far off Surigao Strait and Halsey's Third Fleet is still pursuing Ozawa. Taffy 3 are on their own.

TG 3

Oct

GUE

09:20 25
:00 25

7th FLEET
(KINKAID)

05 BATTLE OF THE SURIGAO STRAIT
25 OCTOBER 1944

In the early morning of 25 October, Nishimura's Southern Force has engaged the battleships, cruisers and destroyers of Kinkaid's Seventh Fleet in the Surigao Strait. In the last battleship action ever fought, the Japanese battleships Fuso and Yamashiro are sunk. Shima's flotilla, coming up behind Nishimura's ships, retreats back the way it had come.

0 ———————— 100 Km

---

the San Bernardino Strait before making its way southward to the Leyte landing sites.

Lastly, the Southern Force, under Vice-Admiral Shoji Nishimura, consisting of two battleships, one heavy cruiser and four destroyers, would also sail from Borneo and be joined by another squadron from the Ryukyu Islands of two heavy cruisers, one light cruiser, and seven destroyers under Vice-Admiral Kiyohide Shima. These groups, especially the Center Group, which contained the 70,000-ton super battleships Yamato and Musashi, were supposed to fall upon the US invasion fleet at Leyte Gulf on 25 October and wipe it out with their big guns.

Oddly, neither the US nor Japanese fleets had overall commanders for their forces for the battle. The result was that there were instances of miscommunications and misunderstandings that had serious impacts on the course of the battle.

Battle of Palawan Passage

The Americans struck first when, early in the morning of 23 October, a pair of submarines, USS Darter and USS Dace, intercepted Kurita's Center Group off Palawan Island and torpedoed three Japanese cruisers, sinking two and badly damaging a third. Darter ran aground during the fight and the crew was rescued by Dace. Kurita's position was now known. Halsey's Third Fleet had its core striking power in fast carriers of Task Force 38 plus several battleships.

TF 38 comprised three smaller task groups, each built around several aircraft carriers, while a fourth was away at the fleet anchorage at Ulithi Atoll, rearming and refueling.

From his flagship, USS New Jersey, Halsey directed his three carrier task groups against Kurita's Center Group. He also became aware of the approach of Nishimura's vanguard group of the Southern Force, and that it was ultimately headed for Leyte Gulf, through the Surigao Strait. He presumed that Kinkaid's Seventh Fleet had more than enough firepower to fend off Nishimura, but he could not confer directly with Kinkaid. MacArthur, Kinkaid's superior, had forbidden any direct contact between the two fleets so messages took a long time. Halsey also recalled the fourth task group from its voyage to Ulithi.

On 24 October, in the Battle of the Sibuyan Sea, Halsey's carrier planes struck Kurita's Center Group ships, which had no fighter protection. Most of the US's attention was given to the super battleship Musashi, which was sunk after being hit with 17 bombs and 19 torpedoes. Kurita ordered a retreat away from San Bernardino Strait.

American losses were minimal. However, Third Fleet's pilots provided overly rosy reports of their attacks when they returned to their carriers and Halsey, accepting them at face value, came to the conclusion that Kurita was no longer a major threat. When a report of Ozawa's Northern Force location

Wildcat fighters prepare to launch from USS Kitkun Bay during the Battle of Samar on 25 October 1944

General Douglas MacArthur (left) comes ashore at the start of the Leyte invasion

came, he decided to take the whole of Task Force 38, comprising the carrier units of Third Fleet, plus all of his battleships, north to demolish it. He thought that Seventh Fleet had enough firepower left to defend itself and the invasion beaches but this was predicated on the belief that Kurita's Center Group had been hurt much worse than it had been. Crucially, Kinkaid never received clear notification that Halsey was taking his whole fleet away and continued to believe that some of it was guarding the San Bernardino Strait.

With the strongest elements of the US Navy now steaming north, Kurita turned his own fleet around and through the San Bernardino Strait. His Center Group emerged early on 25 October to discover Seventh Fleet's Task Force 77.4 between it and the invasion fleet's transports. Task Force 77.4, under the command of Rear Admiral Thomas Sprague, was composed of three units – Taffy 1, Taffy 2, and Taffy 3. Each was built around a clutch of escort carriers and some destroyers. Kinkaid's Seventh Fleet had been organized to provide air cover to the American troops ashore, not fight a major engagement against the Imperial Japanese Combined Fleet but that is what they had to do.

The outgunned and thoroughly surprised US Navy men of Taffy 3, under Rear Admiral

"OLDENDORF'S FLEET WAS CENTERED ON SIX OLD BATTLESHIPS THAT HAD BEEN REPAIRED AND SENT BACK TO WAR"

Clifton Sprague, mounted a desperate defense, attacking the Japanese with their own carrier planes, dropping whatever bombs had been already loaded on them for close air support missions ashore and then strafing the enemy warships with the machine guns of their obsolescent Wildcat fighters. They were joined by their companion destroyers, which mounted near-suicidal attacks against the bigger Japanese ships. Taffy 1 and 2 were still far away but immediately sent help. For the time being, Taffy 3 was all alone.

The ferocity of the US response, with destroyers charging in to trade fire with Japanese battleships coupled with the fog of war, convinced Kurita that he was facing the whole of Third Fleet, not a mere invasion fleet covering force. After losing three cruisers, he ordered a retreat. American losses were heavy but the fleet had been spared annihilation.

In the meantime, Third Fleet was still chasing Ozawa's Northern Force and, unfortunately, the rest of the Seventh Fleet was too far away. That same day, in the early morning

darkness of 25 October, Nishimura's Southern Force had come up the Surigao Strait with Shima's group forming a distant rearguard to be met by the bombardment ships of Seventh Fleet under Rear Admiral Jesse Oldendorf.

Final clashes

Oldendorf's fleet was centered on six old battleships that had been repaired and sent back to war. They'd been providing fire support for the invasion forces but now they dueled with the Japanese. Nishimura's vanguard was built around the battleships Yamashiro and Fuso. A torpedo attack by American destroyers badly damaged Fuso, which later exploded. Yamashiro was struck by torpedoes, too, and then had to contend with the eruption of fire from Oldendorf's battleships and cruisers. Aided by fire control radar, an avalanche of heavy shells plunged into Nishimura's ships. Yamashiro was sunk before dawn, and the heavy cruiser Mogami was lost later that day. Shima, far to the rear, seeing the catastrophe that had befallen Nishimura's

USS Claxton provides covering fire as smoke rises from USS Abner Read following a kamikaze attack

force, turned his own rearguard flotilla around and headed back out of Surigao Strait. The fight was history's last between battleships.

Having sought out Ozawa and at last found him, Halsey's Third Fleet carrier planes conducted strikes against the Northern Force on 25 October. Lacking airpower, the Japanese were mauled by the US Navy fliers. In this, the Battle of Cape Engaño, three Japanese carriers were sunk and a fourth was heavily damaged.

In the midst of the battle, Halsey received an encoded message from his commander demanding to know where he was. The escort carriers and destroyers of Taffy 3 at this moment were being pulverized and Third Fleet's battleships, which should have been protecting the invasion armada, were nowhere to be found. With a wounded Northern Force ripe for destruction, Halsey was forced to turn his battleships around and head back south to help the embattled Seventh Fleet – but by the time they arrived, the fight was over.

It was an inglorious end for Halsey to the Battle of Leyte Gulf, which was a huge American victory. All told, 216 US Navy ships and two Australian warships crushed a fleet of 64 Japanese vessels. By the end of the skirmish, 26 Japanese ships had been destroyed and only seven American ones.

US Coast Guard troops prepare to unload tanks during the Battle of Leyte Gulf

BATTLE OF THE BULGE

THE ARDENNES 16 DECEMBER 1944 – 25 JANUARY 1945

Thanks to TV series such as *Band Of Brothers* many assume that the 101st Airborne defended Bastogne alone during the Battle of the Bulge. In fact the US 10th Armored Division got there before them by eight crucial hours. Their motto was 'Terrify and Destroy' and their nickname was The Tiger Division

WORDS MARTIN KING

Vanguard of Kampfgruppe Peiper around eight miles before Malmedy, December 1944

On 16 December 1944 at 5.30am in a salient just east of the Belgian/German frontier, dispersed wide along an area known as the Schnee Eifel, green troops of the 106th Golden Lion Division were rudely awakened from their winter sojourn by spectral red, green, amber, and white thunder flashes irradiating the misty predawn sky. Moments later they heard the terrifying whine of 'Screamin meemies', Nazi 'Nebelwerfers' simultaneously belching out multiple mortar shells accompanied by booming artillery that collectively gouged and fractured the frigid earth where they stood. John Schaffner, a scout with 589th Field Artillery Battalion said, "Many rounds exploded real close and showered dirt and tree limbs about, I got down as low as I could and would have crawled into my helmet if my buttons hadn't gotten in the way." Shortly after these vulnerable American troops heard the menacing throaty rumble of approaching Tiger and Panther tanks.

"I was in a chateau in Sierck, France, I was told by a runner to return to HQ," said Clair Bennett, F Company, 90th Cavalry Reconnaissance Squadron (Mechanized). "As we were moving out, we found out that the Germans were attacking Belgium."

"ALTHOUGH HEAVILY OUTNUMBERED, THEY TENACIOUSLY REFUSED TO CONCEDE A SINGLE INCH OF GROUND AND INFLICTED TERRIBLE CASUALTIES ON THE GERMANS"

That same day, the US 12th Army Group commander General Omar Bradley began to acknowledge fragmentary reports concerning enemy activity in the Ardennes. This didn't deter him from attending his planned conference with Eisenhower at the Hôtel Trianon Palace in Versailles. The conference was attended by Air Chief Marshal Sir Arthur Tedder and Generals Walter Bedell Smith, Harold R Bull (his chief G-3, part of the American military intelligence operations), and Assistant Chief of Staff for Intelligence, British Major General Kenneth Strong. The proceedings were suddenly interrupted when an American deputy G-2 entered the conference room and delivered a message to Strong, who promptly got to his feet and officiously disclosed the subject matter. "Gentlemen, your attention please. This morning the enemy counterattacked at five separate points along Middleton's VIII Corps boundary in the 1st Army sector."

The statement was received with hushed exchanges as all officers present began to absorb the news. Bradley displayed his usual incredulity and broke the silence, "Ike, this is nothing more than a spoiling attack intended to draw Patton's troops out of the Saar." Eisenhower shook his head in disagreement, "This is no spoiling attack, Brad." Then Eisenhower made what was quite possibly one of his most coherent decisions of the whole war when he issued orders to dispatch the 10th and 7th Armored Divisions to the Ardennes with all haste. 7th Armored would go to the German-speaking Belgian town of St Vith and the 10th Armored were earmarked to get up to Bastogne.

Throughout the ensuing discussion Bradley remained in denial concerning the nature and purpose of the German attack, despite the fact that the US 1st Army's G-2 had already transmitted a captured copy of German Field Marshal von Rundstedt's 'Order of the Day'

THE 10TH ARMORED DIVISION

Activated at Fort Benning, Georgia. 15 July 1942. The 10th Armored Division was assigned to Patton's 3rd Army on arriving at Cherbourg on 23 September 1944

While the US 10th Armored Division's Combat Command A were ordered to join the 4th Infantry Division at Echternach in Luxembourg to stem the attack of Brandenberger's 7th Panzer Army, Combat Command B was dispatched to Bastogne. They were the first of Patton's 3rd Army units to reach there on 18 December 1944 and would precede the arrival of the 101st Airborne by about eight hours.

"When we arrived in Bastogne it was quite quiet and there were no civilians around," said Earl van Gorp, D Company, 3rd Tank Battalion. The civilians who hadn't managed to escape the city had taken to their cellars in anticipation of the approaching German offensive.

The 10th Armored Division nicknamed 'The Tiger Division' had arrived in Europe that September and had actively participated in Patton's punitive battles around Metz. When the three CCB teams arrived in Bastogne they were sent out to block three primary approach roads against overwhelming numbers of attacking German forces of Manteuffel's 5th Panzer Army. During those first integral 48 hours, although heavily outnumbered, they tenaciously refused to concede a single inch of ground and inflicted terrible casualties on the Germans. When the city became surrounded, survivors from Team Desobry and Team Cherry became Bastogne's 'fire brigade', a mobile reserve ready to strike where and when they were needed. Their fight didn't end when Patton's 4th Armored Division entered Bastogne on the afternoon of 26 December. The CCB would provide additional armored support and assist in deterring successive attempts by the Germans to take Bastogne until 18 January 1945.

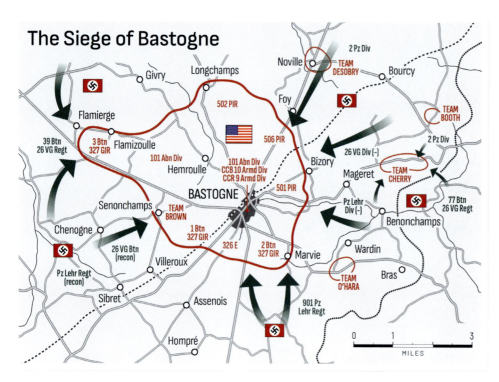

The Siege of Bastogne

"THE CRISP DAWN AIR WAS SOON IMBIBED WITH CHOKING BLACK EXHAUST FUMES AS A PLETHORA OF OLIVE DRAB PAINTED MILITARY ENGINES SHUDDERED AND GROANED LETHARGICALLY TO LIFE"

to SHAEF. This document plainly illustrated the German objectives. The following day Eisenhower committed his strategic reserve, the 82nd and 101st Airborne Divisions, to head north to the Ardennes. Precisely which division would go where would be determined while the paratroopers were en route. Poorly prepared and unsuitably attired, they would endure a freezing 13-hour ride in the backs of open tank transporters.

Bastogne is the main city in the Belgian province of Luxembourg that rests on an elevated plateau in the heart of the Belgian Ardennes. On a clear day it provides a commanding view of the surrounding area. Being centrally located, and where seven roads converged, it became a key strategic objective for both sides during this epic battle.

Middleton's moves

On 16 December, the VIII Corps Commander, 55-year-old Major General Troy Middleton's HQ was located at the former Belgian army barracks on the northeast perimeter of Bastogne where it had been established since early September 1944. VIII Corps were lucky to have him. Sporting glasses as thick as jam jar bottoms and pugnacious features, Middleton

was destined to be the right man in the right place at the right time. He had an impeccable combat record and was widely regarded as one of the most competent battlefield tacticians in the US Army during WWII. According to reports reaching his desk on that fateful day, the Germans were slicing through American lines like a hot knife through butter along an 89-mile front stretching from Aachen in the north all the way down to Luxembourg in the south. He had to act and act fast.

The Ardennes market town of Bastogne was garlanded with Christmas decorations in anticipation of the approaching festive season. As news filtered through to the resident garrison of men from the 28th Division Pennsylvania National Guard, the city became a hive of activity. Still licking their wounds after losing four-fifths of their number in the Battle of Hürtgen Forest, the 28th prepared to move out east to meet their adversaries.

At his HQ, in the northern Luxembourg town of Wiltz, D-Day hero General 'Dutch' Cota attempted to relay information to Middleton, who now faced the arduous task of formulating a cohesive plan to preserve and maintain his wafer-thin defenses against this increasingly threatening tirade of Nazi troops and armor.

He instinctively knew that he needed to slow or stem the advance and buy time for the 1st and 3rd Armies to get into the line.

While the 9th Armored Division's CCR (Combat Command Reserve) covered the left flank of the 4th Infantry Division in Luxembourg, the 28th Infantry Division straddled the Our River and attempted to hold the center ground. Just to the north of their position was the inexperienced 106th Infantry Division covering an area that extended almost 26 miles right up to the VIII Corps boundary with V Corps. Despite being unaware of the magnitude of the German attack, Middleton managed to organize his thin defenses in such a way that they would inevitably stagger and frustrate the enemy advance. When Manteuffel said after the war that German momentum began to dissipate in some sectors in those first crucial 24 hours, this can largely be attributed to Middleton's efforts.

Sending in the Tiger Division

Up until 16 December SHAEF had considered the Ardennes as the quiet sector where very little had transpired up until that juncture. On the Luxembourg/Germany frontier, the 28th's 110th Regiment was covering over 11 miles in the center of the division sector. Like the 106th Infantry Division in the northern sector they were strung out far too thin to offer any concerted resistance. As overwhelming waves of German troops and armor struck out west in an attempt to reach the River Meuse, the American line gradually began to disintegrate. They were being attacked by General Hasso von Manteuffel's 5th Panzer Army, which was the least provisioned but the best led of all three German armies that had launched at 5.30am with the vain objective of eliminating all Allied resistance and re-taking the port city of Antwerp.

During that first day of the assault five German divisions swarmed across the Our River that snaked along the Luxembourg/German border roughly 25 miles east of Bastogne. Two Panzer corps on Manteuffel's left flank soon devastated the thin lines of the 28th Division. On 16 December German forces on the Wiltz-Bastogne road had progressed rapidly and by late afternoon they were close to the city. The first German bomb to hit Bastogne impacted just outside the Church of Saint Peter around midday.

The 10th Armored Division war room ticker clicked into life at 3.30am on 17 December as movement orders began to arrive. At that time the division was in the northern French town of Rémeling recuperating after heavy fighting around Metz. On receiving the news, commanding officer of Combat Command B,

Tanks and infantrymen of the 82nd Airborne Division push through the snow in Belgium, December 1944

54-year-old Colonel William L Roberts, wasted no time in assembling his officers for an urgent briefing. The bespectacled Roberts had a sallow complexion and a demeanor more reminiscent of a funeral director than an army commander. He was known as a dour, feisty individual who never shied away from a fight. One of his subordinates, young Major William R Desobry, known as Des to his friends, furrowed his brow as Roberts explained the urgency of the situation developing further north in the Ardennes region. Desobry's face and gaunt features made him appear considerably older than his 26 years. Lieutenant Colonel Henry T Cherry and 'Smiling' Lt Col James O'Hara were also present. Cherry was known to be a strict disciplinarian who didn't lend his military acumen to spontaneous improvisation and preferred doing things by the book. The eldest of the three 'Team' commanders, he admired General Patton greatly and to some extent attempted to emulate him. O'Hara smiled. Even when the November rains had inundated the battlefields and the fighting had intensified around Metz, O'Hara had always sported a wide toothy grin that accentuated the roundness of his ruddy complexion. While some of his fellow officers found his smile reassuring and inspiring, others regarded it as downright disturbing.

"Move at a moment's notice"

"Hell, Colonel, we're Patton's 3rd Army but when we get up there we'll be 1st Army," moaned Desobry while shaking his head. Roberts peered above his glasses, "I don't think that will be a primary concern when you meet the enemy, Des." The colonel wasn't entirely sure what to make of the recent reports, but an uncomfortable feeling in his lower abdomen indicated that if his instincts were right all was not well. He rose to his feet and addressed all three officers, "Get the men ready to move at a moment's notice." With a dismissive wave he concluded the meeting and sat down again to peruse the maps laid out on his desk. Later on that same bitterly cold morning as the first hesitant rays of daylight began to illuminate the horizon of 10th Armored Division's camp, reveille was accompanied by rousing calls to action. Within minutes frenzied activity erupted across the whole encampment.

Stubble-faced GIs with heavy-lidded eyes began laboriously loading up supplies of arms and ammunition onto various forms of transport in preparation for an imminent move north to Bastogne. The crisp dawn air was soon imbibed with choking black exhaust fumes as a plethora of olive drab painted military engines shuddered and groaned lethargically to life. M3 halftracks, M4 Sherman

A German machine-gunner marches through the Ardennes during the Battle of the Bulge

HEROES OF BASTOGNE
The Battle of the Bulge called upon many acts of heroism

PT. JOHN SCHAFFNER.
SCOUT 589TH FAB, 106TH INFANTRY DIVISION
Two regiments of the 106th Infantry Division, around 6,800 surrendered. Schaffner was one of the lucky ones. His unit managed to escape and fight on.

COLONEL WILLIAM LYNN ROBERTS
COMMANDER CCB, 10TH ARMORED DIVISION
On 20 December, Middleton told Roberts, "Your work has been quite satisfactory." From that point on CCB were attached to the 101st Airborne Division.

LIEUTENANT 'SMILING' JAMES O'HARA.
TEAM O'HARA
Lieutenant James O'Hara was awarded the Silver Star for conspicuous gallantry and intrepidity while serving with the 10th Armored Division during World War II.

CLAIR BENNETT, F COMPANY, 90TH CAVALRY
RECONNAISSANCE SQUADRON (MECHANIZED)
The 90th endured a hard fight out at Longvilly but by 28 December the 1st and 2nd platoons had been assigned as mobile reserve for Team Cherry.

MAJOR WILLIAM DESOBRY. 'TEAM DESOBRY'
After the Battle of the Bulge, Desobry went on to become a two-star major general and served during the Vietnam War. He retired in 1975.

MAJOR WILLIS D 'CRIT' CRITTENBERGER JR,
HQ BATTERY 420TH AFAB
Crittenberger Jr was promoted to lieutenant colonel on Christmas Eve 1944 by General Patton, who also awarded him a Legion of Merit.

LIEUTENANT GENERAL TROY HOUSTON
MIDDLETON AND GENERAL EISENHOWER
Both General Patton and General Bradley requested Troy Middleton's assistance. His abilities as a military tactician were in great demand at SHAEF.

LIEUTENANT COLONEL HENRY THOMAS CHERRY,
JR. 'TEAM CHERRY'
Cherry was a West Point graduate who did things by the book. Widely regarded as an excellent tank tactician, he died in 1953 while serving as a US Army colonel.

PHILIP WILLIAM 'PHIL' BURGE C COMPANY,
55TH ARMORED ENGINEER BATTALION
Phil became the secretary of the 10th Armored Division Association and returned to Bastogne many times before he passed away 9 March 2018.

tanks, M10 and M18 tank destroyers began carving deep furrows through the hoar frost as they formed up the column to begin the ride north. By 1.20pm on 17 December, in compliance with orders, Combat Command B, 10th Armored Division was making its first tentative steps toward Bastogne. Something big was happening up there.

Three teams, one aim

Major Willis D 'Crit' Crittenberger, HQ battery, 420th Armored Field Artillery Battalion, said, "We heard about the Bulge because we always tuned our halftrack radios to the BBC. Around 2.00am we got a warning order from Division HQ saying they were getting ready to go north. Then at 8.00am we got our orders to be part of CCB and go to Bastogne. On the 17th we drove 60 miles up to Luxembourg and stayed overnight."

Robert's Combat Command B (CCB), numbering just 2,700 men, would be divided into three teams each named after their appointed commander. On the late afternoon of 18 December, CCB arrived in Bastogne and Roberts promptly reported to Middleton, who issued specific instructions to organize roadblocks at the three main approaches to the city. While Team Desobry headed three miles straight north to Noville, Team Cherry wheeled east to Longvilly and Team O'Hara pivoted southeast to Bras. The remaining CCB forces were kept in Luxembourg to prevent the Germans from hitting Bastogne from the south. These three teams would be the first line of defense around Bastogne until reinforcements arrived.

Wayne Wickert of C Company, 55th Armored Engineer Battalion, 10th Armored Division joined Team Cherry out at Longvilly. He recalled, "When we arrived at Longvilly, a captain asked me, 'Are you an engineer?' 'Yes, sir,' I replied. 'In that case I may have a bridge for you to blow up'. In my truck I had about 25 landmines with 8lb of TNT, and pipes full of TNT in it to shove into roadblocks to clear the way, [I also had] a couple of five-gallon cans of TNT for bridges. When the Germans began firing I went across the road and got up a real steep hill on the hill because the Germans were aiming at my truck. I got behind an evergreen tree, and I lay down in a prone position with my rifle. Next thing I knew I felt something on my neck, and I thought I was going to get the bayonet. When I pulled myself up my arm started flapping around, shrapnel had hit me. Then as small arms tore up the ground, medics just grabbed my shirt and started running down the hill, and they were not a bit careful. I was holding my arm, and the bone was sticking out as they carried me down [and] the bone got stuck on a tree.

"I jumped on a halftrack and held on but asked if I could sit down, I was exhausted. I backed up to the door as blood congealed in my sleeve. There was a solid clot of blood that slid out, and when it hit the floor, the radioman threw up. As he jumped outside a machine-gun cut loose, and I could hear the tinning on the side of the halftrack. There was a tank there, a Sherman, which silenced the machine-gun. When I got to an aid station in a house, they put some dressing and a steel rod on my arm, and wrapped it up close to my body. A medic stuck

"WHEN I WOKE UP, THE FIRST THING I LOOKED FOR WAS MY ARM, WHICH THANKFULLY WAS STILL ATTACHED. I RECEIVED SEVEN PINTS OF BLOOD AFTER THAT AND WAS TRANSFERRED TO ENGLAND"

Three American M4 Sherman tanks at St Vith during the Battle of the Bulge

Two Infantrymen at Bastogne, Belgium, during the Battle of the Bulge

US soldiers fire at German positions to relieve besieged airborne troops in Bastogne, Belgium

a needle in my vein that was spurting, and I was going to ask him about the needle, but I passed out. When I woke up, the first thing I looked for was my arm, which thankfully was still attached. I received seven pints of blood after that and was transferred to England."

"Hold at all costs"

After his meeting with Middleton during the late afternoon of 18 December, Roberts connected with the vanguard of his column one mile south of the city whereupon, after briefly scanning a map and choosing a favorable position for the armored artillery, he relayed Middleton's orders to the respective team commanders. Physically getting into the city was no easy matter because access to the southern approach roads was becoming severely impeded by corps personnel and an increasing number of stragglers homing in from the east. Some of these were assigned as military police to supplement the MPs already assigned to CCB. They would be dispatched to intersections to the south and southeast of Bastogne armed with strict instruction to prevent any soldiers attempting to escape the coming battle and turn them back to the CCB area.

At 6.15pm as the long winter night descended on Bastogne, CCB, now under the direct control of VIII Corps, were provided with additional units, the 35th and 158th combat engineer battalions to augment their forces. These two units were designated as infantry to enhance the defense of the city. Remnants of various other units who were drifting back to Bastogne would be allocated later. Roberts sent out a detail to retrieve these stragglers and billet them at locations in proximity to his CP at the Hotel LeBrun on the Rue Marche just a few yards from the city's main square. He managed to assemble around 250 men, mostly from the 28th Infantry Division and some from the 9th Armored Division. Collectively this ad hoc reserve became known as the SNAFU unit (Situation Normal All Fouled Up).

The three teams, supported by three batteries of the 420th Armored Field artillery battalion, would be tasked with establishing defensive blocking positions to hinder or prevent the advancing enemy forces from capturing this key city, with specific instructions from Middleton to "hold at all costs". They would face the full force of that German onslaught alone until reinforcements from one of the airborne divisions reached the city.

"When we got into Noville around midnight we heard that the enemy was coming down the road and they fired on the outpost," said Jerry Goolkasian, B Company, 3rd Tank Battalion. "This was the first connection with the

Two captured German SS soldiers from the command of Otto Skorzeny. They had been caught while wearing American uniforms, a deliberate tactic intended to create confusion behind Allied lines

OPERATION GREIF: SS BEHIND THE LINES

Operation Greif was part of an abortive attempt by a number of German soldiers dressed in captured GI uniforms to infiltrate American lines

During the Battle of the Bulge the man known to the allies as 'Hitler's assassin', SS Obersturmbannführer Otto Skorzeny, commanded Panzer Brigade 150. At the start of the Battle of the Bulge he was given the task of orchestrating Operation Greif (Griffon) with the purpose of infiltrating US lines and causing as much disruption as possible. He later said that, "Operation Greif was an abject failure." Owing to delays and miscalculations, only a small number of his men actually infiltrated behind the Allied lines, while the remainder were compelled to fight as regular soldiers. During the planning, Skorzeny

requested 20 Sherman tanks and at least 30 British or American scout cars. He was given two Sherman tanks and a few American Jeeps, some of which were not considered roadworthy.

Of the 2,500 men in Skorzeny's unit only about 400 could speak any form of colloquial English and only ten of those were actually fluent. Nevertheless the psychological effect on the US forces was profound and the ensuing paranoia among the Allies even reached Eisenhower who doubled the guard at the SHAEF HQ. Skorzeny's men never got within proximity of Bastogne but the US 10th

Armored were aware of rumors of 'Krauts dressed as Joes'.

At check points all along the Bulge front GIs stopped any vehicle or soldier they didn't recognize and attempted to establish their identities with questions such as 'who was Mickey Mouse's sister?', 'who won the World Series in 1934?' and 'what's the name of President Truman's dog?'. However, Operation Greif wasn't a total failure. Even Field Marshal Montgomery was temporarily detained when he crossed the River Meuse south of Liege and some of these infiltrators managed to delay the 84th Infantry Division by three days.

German troops advancing past abandoned American equipment

Germans around the area of Bastogne on the night of the 18th. The Germans pulled back because they believed they had run into a bigger force than they actually had. The halftrack behind us got hit and that was flaring up all night. Ziggy, my driver, and I got some .50 caliber ammunition from the burning halftrack because we were desperate for ammunition."

"Never heard of Bastogne"

Precisely why Bastogne was so important to the Germans became self evident during the battle. OKW had identified the strategic location of the city during the initial planning stages for the offensive. It had been generally agreed that the two key cities of Bastogne and St Vith needed to be taken within the first 24 hours of the offensive if they were to succeed in their intended objective of recapturing Antwerp. Many of Hitler's generals at the time had been reduced to obsequious nodding sycophants who didn't dare to voice their reservations about the plan known as 'Wacht am Rhein' (Watch on the Rhein). Field Marshal Otto Moritz Walter Model was one of the very few who openly disagreed with the whole plan at a time when Hitler's temperament was at best unpredictable and at worst murderous.

One of the reasons for this may have been the abortive attempt on his life that occurred in July 1944 instigated by General Von Stauffenberg and other high-ranking military

men. It was while recuperating from injuries sustained during this failed assassination attempt that the Führer ruminated on the prospects of going on the offensive in the west. General Hasso-Eccard Freiherr von Manteuffel, general of the 5th Army, also harbored serious reservations, which he voiced to von Rundstedt, who secretly concurred but neither dared to openly state their opinions. The semantics and machinations of the planned Nazi offensive were superfluous to the 10th Armored CCB as the teams arrived to take up positions at their pre-designated locations.

"I remember going through the town of Arlon in the afternoon of December 18th. It was a scene out of a Christmas card. It was snowing, but the Christmas lights were on, people were shopping and it was about the prettiest scene you could ever imagine. After passing through Arlon we made a turn in the road and the truck headlights showed a sign saying 'Bastogne', white letters on a dark blue background. I had never heard of Bastogne, but something told me that it was a name that I would never forget," recalled Phil Burge, C Company, 55th Armored Engineer Battalion. "We reached Bastogne by 7.00 or 8.00pm, we spent the first night in the railroad station."

"Put those tank destroyers on point and gather all the ammo you can lay your hands on. Good luck and God be with you," shouted Major William Desobry to his advance guard,

comprising an intelligence and reconnaissance Platoon, 20th AIB, and a section of 1st Platoon, troop D, 90th Cavalry Reconnaissance Squadron (CRS). They had entered Noville at around 10.00pm. At the time nobody suspected that the 'perfect storm' was about to break. A soldier from an armored platoon that had fallen back into Noville near midnight provided Desobry with a graphic description of the enemy forces moving in their direction, and added, "The whole goddam German army is heading this way, major."

In the thick of the fog

Team Cherry had been warned that they might encounter elements of the US 9th Armored Division's CCR along the way. When they arrived in Longvilly they were dismayed to discover the whole village jam-packed with CCR vehicles retreating in apparent disorder. Tanks, trucks, and troop-filled halftracks produced a nigh-on impossible traffic situation on the narrow approach road as Team Cherry endeavored to get up to the line. The 9th Armored had been badly mauled while attempting to stem the German advance and had suffered terrible casualties, but it had been a valiant effort. "When anyone asks me where I was during the battle I tell them 'hell I was everywhere'," said Bob Sheehan, veteran of the 9th Armored.

Just three miles southeast of Bastogne in the village of Wardin, Team O'Hara established a

"THEY DIDN'T KNOW HOW MANY WE HAD AND WE DIDN'T KNOW HOW MANY THEY HAD, WE JUST HAD TO FIGHT LIKE HELL"

road block on the high ground but the elevation didn't provide any real advantage due to the all-encompassing fog that reduced visibility to ten yards in some places. They had no idea that they were in the path of General Fritz Bayerlein's dreaded Panzer Lehr and General Kokott's 26th Volksgrenadier division currently striking out for Bastogne from the east.

All three team commanders were essentially faced with the same inclement weather problem. One Belgian/Congolese nurse named Augusta Chiwy, who had returned from up north to spend Christmas with her father in Bastogne, described the weather, "The fog was so thick you could cut it with a knife." As long as it persisted, tactical air support was impossible. This 'Hitler Weather' was a potentially serious impediment, but some US forces managed to turn it to their advantage. "They didn't know how many we had and we didn't know how many they had, we just had to fight like hell and hope for the best," said Bob Parker, C Company, 21st Tank Battalion. "There were a couple of divisions that had been overrun and they were retreating back through our lines. We had set up a roadblock and the next thing I knew, I saw something similar to our halftrack or a

truck, I shot it and I hit it. We lost a couple of tanks that first day. I think we had three left in our platoon at the end." Bob would later be re-assigned to Team SNAFU.

The 101st Airborne 'Screaming Eagles' were originally designated to go to Werbomont on the northern shoulder to check the advance of the SS in that sector, but were redirected to Bastogne when the 82nd Airborne got ahead of them on the road north through Luxembourg. With the commander General Maxwell Taylor back in Washington, DC, attending a conference, Brigadier General Anthony McAuliffe assumed command of the division. As lead elements of the 101st Airborne Division reached Bastogne late on 18 December, McAuliffe immediately went to VIII Corps headquarters in Bastogne to talk with Middleton. The 101st received direct orders to take up positions in support of the CCB teams who were already in place.

Desobry said, "O'Hara had been sent out to the southeast to block a road coming to the town of Wiltz which was a high speed road, and Cherry was moving out to the town of Longvilly to block that road, and I was going due north to a town of Noville and I was to block that

road. They really didn't know what the situation was, except the Germans had broken through the 28th Division and somewhere to the east of us; that Germans were using American equipment and some of them were dressed in American uniforms and some of them civilian uniforms. So you had to watch out for that."

A company of paratroopers from the 1st Battalion, 506th, commanded by Lieutenant LaPrade was ordered up to Noville to assist Team Desobry. When they arrived a slight altercation occurred between LaPrade and Desobry's regarding who was in charge. Such details were superfluous to Phil Burge as he observed the paratroopers arriving in Bastogne, "They had come in by truck, since it was impossible to drop them in by air. Eventually the whole division of the 101st Airborne was in Bastogne. But we were there first."

Ten to one against

The fighting in Noville began in earnest at 5.30am on 19 December when a group of German 2nd Panzer Division halftracks emerged from the fog. GIs manning an outpost on the Bourcy road that converged on the village of Noville couldn't determine whether they were friend or foe. In an attempt to discover the identity of the approaching vehicles a GI sentry shouted 'Halt!' four times. Suddenly a voice responded in German. That was the timely cue for Desobry's men to shower the lead vehicle with hand grenades. Several explosions followed as agonized, feral howls of pain and derision emanated from the halftrack as spurts of blood and severed limbs were ejected into the freezing air. The GIs immediately dispatched the bloodied survivors who attempted to crawl out. Close-quarter fighting ensued for around 20 minutes as the opposing forces hammered away with grenades and small arms. It was 'game on'.

Despite overwhelming odds of around ten to one, in two days team Desobry disabled 31 tanks and halted the entire 2nd German Panzer Division, which had assumed it was opposing a much stronger force. During the fighting Desobry was wounded and captured and LaPrade was killed outright when a bomb impacted their CP. Col Roberts repeatedly refused to give Desobry permission to fall back on Bastogne even when he was personally visited by Desobry, whose left eyeball was resting on his cheek due to the percussion from the blast that destroyed his CP. On 20 December Roberts finally acquiesced.

On 21 December the survivors of Team Cherry were ordered back to Bastogne and assigned to 101st Airborne Division's mobile reserve. Team O'Hara held out until Patton's 3rd Army arrived on 26 December. All three team leaders survived the battle.

General Troy Middleton's expert delaying tactics and the 10th Armored CCB teams severely disrupted the German timetable. Bastogne would hold against repeated German attacks and the gargantuan efforts of the men who got there first would be overshadowed by the exploits of the 101st Airborne Division.

General McAuliffe would later remark, "It seems regrettable to me that Combat Command B of the 10th Armored Division didn't get the credit it deserved at Bastogne. All the newspaper and radio talk was about the paratroopers.

"Actually the 10th Armored Division was in there a day before we were and had some very hard fighting before we ever got into it, and I sincerely believe that we would never have been able to get into Bastogne if it had not been for the defensive fighting of the three elements of the 10th Armored Division who were first into Bastogne and protected the town from invasion by the Germans."

The 10th Armored Division left Bastogne for good on 17 and 18 January and headed to the Saar-Moselle Triangle to continue their fight against the Third Reich. They would fight on through Germany and eventually cross the Danube in Czechoslovakia with Patton's 3rd Army. When the war concluded they were in the Austrian Alps 20 miles from Innsbruck.

A US soldier shortly after returning from the frontlines, December 1944

IWO JIMA

IWO JIMA, SOUTH PACIFIC 19 FEBRUARY – 26 MARCH 1945

After an arduous slog through the Pacific, US Marines mounted one final
assault on Japanese forces in an attempt to unlock the mainland

WORDS JOSH BARNETT

201

The US Navy Sixth Fleet photographed during the Battle of Iwo Jima

After the decisive naval victory at the Battle of Midway in June 1942 (the first significant triumph in the Pacific for the Allies since Japan instigated the war at Pearl Harbor in December 1941), the US Navy was afforded some time to rebuild during 1943. Ships were in need of repair and refitting, seamen and ground troops required rest, and armaments needed replenishing.

It was during this lull that Chief of Command for the US's Pacific Fleet, Admiral Chester W Nimitz, refocused the tactics employed against the Japanese in the Pacific. Rather than take on the enemy direct, a campaign of island-hopping was instigated. Imperial forces had become heavily entrenched on certain key islands, making them difficult and costly targets for the Allies to capture. Instead, Nimitz's plan was to skirt around this nuclei, taking the less fortified islands in the Pacific as the US advanced towards the Japanese Home Islands.

The war was taking its toll on the Japanese as the US gained the upper hand in both the sea and the air. To make matters worse, Japanese cyphers were easily decoded by US intelligence, who kept Allied forces one step ahead of their enemy at all times. It was this advantage that led to the death of Marshal Admiral Isoroku Yamamoto (Nimitz's opposite number) in April 1943.

After the Japanese defeat at Guadalcanal, Yamamoto decided to go on a morale-boosting inspection of the South Pacific. Word of the Japanese Commander in Chief's plans reached US Navy intelligence, leading President Franklin D Roosevelt to give the order: "Get Yamamoto". On the morning of 18 April 1943, the commander's plane was shot down by US forces, dealing an embarrassing blow to the Imperial Japanese Navy.

By April 1944, with momentum firmly on their side, US forces recaptured the Marshall Islands. Later the same year, it was the turn of the Mariana and Caroline Islands to fall into Allied hands, as plans for the invasion of Okinawa continued apace. The Japanese mainland was, metaphorically, in sight, with just one remaining target: Iwo Jima.

Located 750 miles south of Tokyo in the Volcanic Islands cluster, Iwo Jima was home to two Japanese airstrips (with a third under construction at the north end of the island). The United States believed this small island, just eight square miles in size, to be a strategic necessity for mainland attacks. If it could be captured, the island would be used as a base for escort fighters, as well as a landing patch for damaged B-29 bombers returning from the mainland.

The Japanese had also recognized the importance of Iwo Jima and, under the command of General Tadamichi Kuribayashi, began constructing numerous inland bunkers in the summer of 1944, a noted departure from the usual beach fortifications used by the Imperial Japanese forces. US aerial and submarine reconnaissance showed the supposed scale, with 642 pillboxes, blockhouses and other gun positions identified prior to the assault.

A summer-long barrage designed to incapacitate the staunch Japanese defenses

"UNKNOWN TO THE US FORCES, KURIBAYASHI'S 109TH INFANTRY DIVISION WAS HOLED UP IN A NETWORK OF OVER 5,000 CAVES AND TEN MILES OF TUNNELS"

ensued. For 74 days straight, US bombers pummeled this tiny blot of volcanic rock, while in the 72 hours running up to the invasion, the US Navy peppered Iwo Jima with shells, shattering the peace of this once idyllic South Pacific island.

The invasion begins

Codenamed 'Operation Detachment', the invasion proper began on 19 February 1945. The assault was tasked to the V Amphibious Marine Corps, led by General Holland 'Howlin' Mad' Smith, commanding general for the expeditionary troops once ashore. H-Hour was set for 9am, with the initial wave of armored amphibian tractors coming ashore at 9.02am followed, three minutes later, by the first troop-carrying vehicles.

Spilling down the ramps, the 4th and 5th Marine Divisions (led by Major General Clifton B Cates and Major General Keller E Rockey respectively) waded through the ankle-deep volcanic ash of Iwo Jima's southwestern shore unopposed. The pre-invasion bombardment appeared to have cleared the island. However, unknown to the US forces, Kuribayashi's 109th Infantry Division was holed up in a network of over 5,000 caves and ten miles of tunnels around Iwo Jima, waiting for the

landing force's shelling to cease before showing their resistance.

There were murmurs among the US troops that the Japanese forces had been wiped out as the beach remained eerily quiet – a marked departure from previous infantry battles in the Pacific where shorelines were staunchly defended. The landing plans tasked the 5th Division's 28th Regiment with taking Mount Suribachi, the 554-foot dormant volcano at the island's southernmost tip, by the end of D-Day. Likewise, the 4th Division was scheduled to take Airfield 1 the same day. In the calm of the initial landing, both plans seemed achievable yet, as the leading battalions crested the terrace at the end of the beach, General Kuribayashi gave the order to take up weapons.

The unmistakable chatter of machine gun fire from hidden Japanese emplacements cut down the initial waves of US troops, as artillery and mortar fire now began to pound the beaches. The soft volcanic soil, churned by the pre-invasion barrage, proved difficult to move through at pace, slowing the US advance. To make matters worse, fortifications on Mount Suribachi (protected by reinforced steel doors) rained down shells on the troops below.

Despite landing some 30,000 men, progress was slow and, by the time the US advance

was called to a halt at 6pm, the Marine line fell well short of their D-Day targets. Still, Mount Suribachi's northeastern side had been surrounded by the 28th Regiment. The 5th's 27th Regiment had been able to push towards the northwestern coastline but had taken heavy casualties in doing so, while the 4th Division skirted around Airfield 1's southern perimeter, securing a line towards the quarry near East Boat Basin.

During previous battles, Japanese banzai charges had caused considerable chaos throughout the night and, expecting similar attacks, US forces remained vigilant during darkness. General Kuribayashi did not believe in the usefulness of such tactics, though, feeling the banzai charge was a needless loss of life. This allowed the 3rd Battalion, 13th Marines (the artillery support for the 28th Regiment) to launch mortar and 105mm Howitzer shell attacks on Mount Suribachi during the evening of 19 February in preparation of an ascent the next morning.

Capturing Mount Suribachi

Formulated by the 28th's leader, Colonel Harry B Liversedge, the 2nd and 3rd Battalions plunged forward at 8.30am on 20 February, with the 1st Battalion remaining in reserve.

With regular gunfire proving useless against the Japanese emplacements, US troops turned to their trusty flamethrowers and grenades to flush defenders out of their foxholes. However, the Japanese (thanks to their comprehensive tunnel network) soon re-manned each supposedly clear pillbox. It would be a tactic that kept US forces fighting on all fronts across the island, keeping the Marines' progress to a minimum.

Just 200 yards of Mount Suribachi had been taken by 5pm on D+1. The following day, Liversedge's Marines attacked again after a 40-plane airstrike. With all three battalions heaving forward on one front, and with effective support from tanks and artillery, the 28th Regiment surged to the foot of the mountain. With the naval support covering the western side, the Marines had Suribachi surrounded by 22 February.

Finally, a day later, after recon from 2nd Battalion, a 40-man combat patrol was sent to the summit upon the orders of Lieutenant Colonel Chandler W Johnson. Under the command of First Lieutenant Harold G Schrier, they stormed the summit, raising a small US flag while under intense fire from the remaining Japanese troops. Later that day, a larger flag would be raised in order to boost the morale of Marines across the island.

While the 28th Marine Regiment was still on Suribachi, the 26th and 27th Regiments of the 5th Division had pushed to Iwo Jima's western coast with suicidal rapidity, beginning their journey to the island's north sector on 20 February. Meanwhile, the 4th Division's 23rd, 24th and 25th Regiments had secured 'Motoyama 1', the southernmost airfield. With the 5th Division surging the Marine line forward by around 1,000 yards, only the 23rd Regiment (fighting on the 4th Division's left flank) could keep advancing at a similar pace.

Compared with the southern half of Iwo Jima, the northern sector was extremely well fortified, thanks to the efforts of Kuribayashi's men during that summer of 1944. The US Marines were finding the rocky terrain tough to negotiate, with every cleared pillbox and fortification soon reoccupied by Japanese forces, who were putting up a staunch and bloody resistance. Any gain was seemingly met with renewed fire from the shellproof artillery emplacements and well-hidden tanks.

To aid the 4th Division's charge, General Cates called the 21st Regiment of the 3rd Division ashore on 21 February. However, with Japanese forces pinning down the 25th Regiment on the eastern shores, the beach was congested, forcing the 3rd Division's relief through the center of the Marine Corps line in

BATTLE OF IWO JIMA
19 FEBRUARY – 26 MARCH 1945

02 On 22 February, during the siege on Suribachi, the US support carrier, USS Bismarck Sea is sunk after being stung by a string of kamikaze attacks from Japanese planes. A day later, though, Marines raise the flag atop the mountain, with the moment immortalized on camera by Associated Press's Joe Rosenthal.

03 The northern half of the island sees much more Japanese fortification. Many of Baron Nishi's tanks have been buried up to the turret, providing camouflaged emplacements that decimate the 4th Division's progress and require General Erskine's 3rd Division to be brought on shore en masse on D+4.

06 With the fighting all but done, the 5th Division's 28th Regiment find themselves faced with a gorge full of caves and some 500 ill-organized Japanese infantry. Two prisoners of war are used to translate a surrender appeal but, despite returning alive, the US troops are forced to pick off Kuribayashi's remaining troops one-by-one.

04 After four days in 'the meat grinder', the Marines focus their efforts on Hill 382, north of the 'Amphitheater'. Naval guns, artillery and air strikes aid the 24th Regiment's attack but, despite gaining a footing on 'Turkey Knob', the US forces have to retreat under the cover of a smoke screen just before dark on 1 March.

01 Although the amphibious invasion will begin on Iwo Jima's southern beaches on 19 February 1945, the first US air strike against the island hits the black, volcanic soil on 15 June 1944, with US bombers based in Saipan flying hundreds of offensive sorties.

05 Finding a 300-strong Japanese stronghold just a few hundred yards from the sea, the 4th Division delays an attack at 7am on 12 March to try and coax the Imperial forces to surrender. However, a problem with the generator-powered loudspeaker sees snipers pick off a number of Marines, provoking the US troops to fight back at 9am with grenades and flamethrowers.

"THE US MARINES WERE FINDING THE ROCKY TERRAIN TOUGH TO NEGOTIATE, WITH EVERY CLEARED PILLBOX AND FORTIFICATION SOON REOCCUPIED BY JAPANESE FORCES WHO WERE PUTTING UP A STAUNCH AND BLOODY RESISTANCE"

The original US flag raised on the top of Mount Suribachi once it had been taken

place of the 23rd Regiment. By the morning of the 22nd, frontline units were beginning to be relieved, with the fresh Marine forces able to grind out short territorial gains. Yet, Kuribayashi's men were alert to the fresh threat, pinning down units that were about to be replaced.

On D+4, V Marine Corps' Major General Harry Schmidt came ashore to survey the damage, ordering an attack the following morning. 24 February dawned with tanks thrusting through toward the second airfield, supported by the 21st Regiment. The 5th Division's tanks flanked Motoyama 2's western edge, while the 4th Division armor edged forward on the airstrip's east perimeter. Aided by a 76-minute naval bombardment, the US Marines were advancing once again.

Into the meat grinder

The same day, the remaining regiments of Major General Graves B Erskine's 3rd Division were committed to Iwo Jima. The veteran division was tasked with advancing through the supposedly flat center line of the island, going head-on into Kuribayashi's main defensive line on 25 February. With flamethrowing tanks incinerating the enemy (and 50 per cent of the corps' artillery missions aiding the 3rd Division) three days of toil finally paid off on the evening of 27 February.

The Japanese line cracked, and the 9th Regiment found itself controlling two hills north of the second airfield, while the following day, the 21st Regiment stormed through the remnants of Motoyama village to seize two hills commanding over the unfinished third airfield. Elsewhere, the 5th Division had secured 'Hill 362A' after initial resistance from the Japanese proved deadly. 224 of the Division's Marines were killed or wounded on 1 March, but the hill's access to Nishi Ridge on the northwest edge of the island was too important to bypass.

While many hills had fallen with relative ease, Hill 382 on the eastern edge of the island was proving a more difficult proposition for the 4th Division. Honeycombed with Kuribayashi's tunnels, the hill's approach was guarded by hidden tanks, while the crest had been fortified into a huge artillery-proof bunker.

South of the hill was a series of ridges, topped by 'Turkey Knob', while further south of this massive rock was a natural bowl known as the 'Amphitheater'. The fighting here was bloody, with 1 March the fourth day that the division's Marines had hurled themselves at the Japanese forces. Such was the relentlessness of this quadrant, it became known as the 'meat grinder'. It wasn't until 10 March that the Japanese defenders around 'Turkey Knob' were

A Marine takes cover next to the body of a Japanese soldier

Marine calls in for artillery support to counter enemy mortar attacks in his area

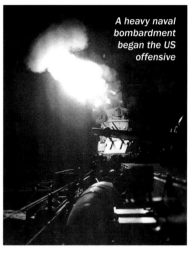

A heavy naval bombardment began the US offensive

eliminated. Naval fire, carrier air strikes, heavy shelling and many Marine lives were needed before Hill 382 finally fell into US hands.

In this time, the 5th Division's 26th Regiment had succeeded in securing 'Hill 362B' on 3 March, before the 3rd Division readied itself for the assault on 'Hill 362C' four days later. Under cover of darkness (a departure from the usual US tactics in the Pacific), General Erskine's men advanced beyond the unsuspecting Japanese forces. It was a blow for General Kuribayashi, yet his men remained to resist strongly in their lasting areas of occupation.

Unfortunately for Imperial Japan, their attacks were becoming increasingly uncoordinated, allowing patrols from the 3rd Marine Division to reach the northern coast by 9 March. The following evening, there was only one final pocket of Japanese resistance left in the division's sector, although the tunnels underneath the ground gave many more fanatical infantry a hiding place.

In the eastern sector, home of the 4th Division, Japanese troops launched a counterattack on 8 March. Under the cover of heavy artillery fire, the men attacked the Marine forces, worming their way through the 23rd and 24th Regiment's lines. Some attacked with the blood-curdling banzai cry, though many chose a stealthier approach, attempting to impersonate wounded US soldiers. Despite the counterattack's ingenuity, it was an ultimately hopeless effort that saw 650 Japanese killed by noon the following day. The end result was that, on 10 March, the Turkey Knob/Amphitheater salient was completely destroyed as Marine forces pushed Kuribayashi's defenses right back to the northern coast.

Clearing up the north

For the remainder of Operation Detachment, each Marine division would be faced with isolated pockets of resistance dotted around Iwo Jima. The 3rd Division was tasked with

Iwo Jima was a key
strategic target for the
US in the Pacific

Japanese prisoners are taken aboard a US transport ship

"AFTER 36 DAYS, THE BATTLE OF IWO JIMA BECAME A MANHUNT, WITH AT LEAST 223 JAPANESE SOLDIERS HUNTED AND KILLED"

the grim job of destroying a heavily fortified resistance southwest of Hill 362C (eventually achieved on 16 March), while the 4th Division focused on an enemy stronghold between East Boat Basin and Tachiiwa Point.

Across the island, 5th Division bore down on Japanese forces around Kitano Point, the last point of defense in the Iwo Jima campaign. Joined by two battalions of the 3rd Division's 21st Regiment, the final Marine drive began on 11 March with naval shelling and airstrikes. The US artillery again had little impact, though, making initial progress painstaking.

Despite being ravaged since the initial landing on 19 February, the 5th Division carved through 1,000 yards between 14-15 March, as many of the Japanese troops met a fiery end at the hands of the Marines' flamethrowing tanks. The following day, the 21st Regiment flanked the Japanese on the right, providing the US forces with two attack fronts to decimate the remaining Imperial forces.

By 25 March, organized enemy resistance was declared over. However, Kuribayashi's men had one final assault up their sleeve. In the vicinity of Motoyama 2, some 300 men assembled that evening. On the morning of

26 March 1945, they stormed the US camp, killing sleeping Marines at will until a defensive line was formed by the Americans as dawn broke, sending the remaining Japanese into hiding. After 36 days, the Battle of Iwo Jima became a manhunt, with at least 223 Japanese soldiers hunted and killed. General Kuribayashi was rumored to have been among those slain, bringing to an end a bloody conflict that saw more than 70,000 Marines deployed.

Of the 20,060 Japanese troops on the island, only 216 were ever captured, with roughly 300 left hiding in the tunnels for the remainder of the war. On the US side, 5,931 Marines were killed, with a further 17,372 injured – the only time in the Pacific Theater that American casualties outnumbered those of the Japanese. General Holland Smith had "thrown human flesh against reinforced concrete" in taking Iwo Jima. Yet, in the ensuing aerial war against the Japanese mainland, over 2,200 heavy bombers made unscheduled landings on the island's airstrips, saving 24,761 US airmen from potential disaster.

Iwo Jima was a grim yet inspirational victory for the Americans that demoralized their enemy. Mainland Japan had never seemed closer to the United States. A final victory in the Pacific was in sight.

Images: Getty, Alamy

OKINAWA

OKINAWA, RYUKYU ISLANDS 1 APRIL - 22 JUNE 1945

The last campaign of World War II in the Pacific required an
arduous 82 days for the Allies to claim victory

WORDS MIKE HASKEW

Marines of 2nd Battalion, 1st Marines maneuver at Wana Ridge

I t was a curious coincidence – Operation Iceberg, the Allied invasion of Okinawa, was scheduled for 1 April 1945, both Easter Sunday and April Fool's Day. Short of an invasion of Japan itself, the island in the Ryukyu archipelago was the last objective of the Allied campaign across the Pacific Ocean during World War II. Only 340 miles from the Japanese Home Islands, Okinawa would provide the sternest test of the war for the Marine III Amphibious Corps and the US Army's XXIV Corps, comprising the Tenth Army under Lieutenant General Simon Bolivar Buckner, a veteran army officer and the son of a Confederate general from the American Civil War.

The invasion date was designated Love-Day (L-Day) to avoid confusion with the 1944 D-Day landings in France. Actually, the Allied build-up was larger than that of D-Day. The US and British Royal Navies brought 1,300 warships and support vessels, along with 750,000 tons of supplies to the waters off Okinawa.

Buckner's Tenth Army included more than 180,000 troops. Marine Major General Roy S Geiger led the III Amphibious Corps, including three divisions – the veteran 1st Marine Division, the 6th, and the 2nd in reserve. Major General John R Hodge commanded the XXIV Army Corps, including four infantry divisions – the 7th, 77th, 96th, and reserve 27th.

"GRABBING A THIRD RIFLE AND A CLUTCH OF GRENADES, HANSEN CHARGED FORWARD AGAIN, KILLING EIGHT ENEMY SOLDIERS AND SMASHING A MORTAR POSITION"

The carnage at Iwo Jima remained fresh in US minds and a bloodbath was also expected at Okinawa. During the week before L-Day, navy guns fired 13,000 shells and aircraft flew 3,095 missions. The L-Day landings were to hit the Hagushi beaches on Okinawa's southwestern shore. After the anticipated fight to gain a foothold, the Americans intended to advance eastward across the Ishikawa Peninsula, seizing Yontan and Kadena airfields. Splitting the island in two, they would swing north and south, fighting their way to opposite shores, completing the conquest of Okinawa. Another worrisome aspect of Operation Iceberg was the kamikaze threat to the host of Fifth Fleet ships obliged to remain offshore. Japanese suicide planes were expected to assault these rich targets with unprecedented vigor.

82 days of fighting on Okinawa and the nearby cluster of small islands also seized yielded an immense harvest of destruction. By the time the island was declared secure on 22 June 1945, American deaths totaled 7,374, while 31,807 were wounded and 239 were missing. The navy suffered 4,907 casualties, 120 ships were damaged, and 29 had been sunk. Marines and soldiers earned 23 Medals of Honor, many of them posthumous.

The Japanese garrison, under Lieutenant General Mitsuru Ushijima, commander of the 32nd Army, fielded over 100,000 troops – only 11,000 prisoners surrendered. A total of 2,373 kamikaze pilots died and thousands of sailors perished in the Imperial Japanese Navy's last substantial offensive action of the war. Many died when the super battleship Yamato sank under a fusillade of bombs and aerial torpedoes. An estimated 150,000 Okinawan civilians lost their lives.

Storming the beaches
Under a canopy of aircraft and naval bombardment, the invasion rolled forward on the morning of 1 April, landing craft engines stirring white wakes extending 7.5 miles across. Virtually no resistance was encountered. By the end of L-Day, 60,000 US troops occupied a beachhead 2.9 miles deep and 8.7 miles wide.

Torpedo bombers and fighters of the Royal Navy Fleet Air Arm occupy the flight deck of the carrier HMS Implacable

The Japanese sometimes pressed teenagers and young boys into service. Here, an American soldier attempts to communicate with two of them

Ushijima watched the awe-inspiring sight from his command post at Shuri Castle, the ancient abode of the kings who once ruled the Ryukyus, as the Americans put 16,000 troops ashore in an hour. A firm advocate of defense in depth, he conceded the beachhead and airfields to draw the Americans inland, where he would defend the island to the last man. His forces included the 9th, 24th, and 62nd Divisions. Independent brigades and artillery, engineer and naval troops were also attached. For the death struggle, the Japanese constructed three defensive lines across southern Okinawa.

Early progress was swift. In four days, US troops took territory they thought would require three weeks of combat. Both airfields were captured on the first day. By 3 April, the 1st Marine Division crossed the Ishikawa Isthmus, captured the Katchin Peninsula, and cut Okinawa in half. The airfields were quickly operational. Marine Air Groups 31 and 33 flew in from aircraft carriers and an Army Air Force fighter wing also arrived.

Soon enough, the Marines found stubborn resistance. Five battalions of the 4th and 29th Marines attacked 1,200-foot Mount Yae-Take and 2,000 enemy troops under Colonel Takesiko Udo. The Marines were stonewalled by enemy machine guns and mortars. The 14-inch guns of the battleship USS Tennessee barked, and Corsairs of Marine Fighter Squadron 322

(VMF-322) bombed and strafed. The Udo Force was slaughtered while the Marines took 964 casualties clearing the area.

The 7th and 96th Divisions hit the first defensive line on 19 April. The 27th Division was soon committed. Minimal gains could not be held and the attack faltered, meaning that Sherman tanks got separated from supporting infantry while advancing near Kakazu and enemy guns knocked out 22 of the 30 that were sent forward. On 23 April, Admiral Chester W Nimitz, commander in chief of the Pacific, arrived on Okinawa and voiced his concerns for the Fifth Fleet as kamikaze attacks intensified. Hammering Buckner to energize the offensive, Nimitz snarled that if Buckner was not up to the task, "We'll get someone here to move it… I'm losing a ship and a half each day out here."

Nimitz was blunt for a reason – Japanese Operation Ten-Go was unleashing 4,500 kamikazes against the Fifth Fleet, filling the skies with ten mass sorties nicknamed Kikusui, or Floating Chrysanthemums, each including 350 or more aircraft. The sailors of the Fifth Fleet endured, earning the nickname of "the fleet that came to stay". Two kamikazes ripped into the aircraft carrier USS Bunker Hill on 11 May, its 58th day on station.

US fighter pilots shot down scores of kamikazes. On 22 April, three Marine Corsairs of VMF-323 flamed 16 in 20 minutes.

Nevertheless, some got through. The stand of the Fifth Fleet (redesignated Third Fleet when Admiral William F 'Bull' Halsey relieved Admiral Raymond A Spruance on 27 May) wrote a stirring chapter in US naval history.

After three weeks of fighting, Ushijima pulled surviving defenders out of the first line. In early May, the Tenth Army was poised to assault the second, or Shuri Line, four divisions abreast across a 5.1-mile front. On 2 May, the 1st Marine Division assaulted the Awacha Pocket. The 5th Marines advanced through a downpour but ran into enemy fire from concealed positions. It took a week to clear Awacha.

Private Dale M Hansen of the 2nd Battalion, 1st Marines, lost his rifle as it was shattered by an enemy bullet during his single-handed destruction of a Japanese pillbox on 7 May. He picked up another weapon and ran up an adjacent ridge but six Japanese soldiers blocked his path. Hansen shot four – but then his rifle jammed. The two survivors pounced. Hansen swung the rifle's butt and slipped away. Grabbing a third rifle and a clutch of grenades, Hansen charged forward again, killing eight enemy soldiers and smashing a mortar position. More Marines followed, claiming the ridgeline. Hansen was killed by a sniper four days later. On 30 May 1946, his parents accepted his posthumous Medal of Honor.

The 1st Battalion, 7th Marines, reached the top of Dakeshi Ridge twice on 11 May but was forced to retire. A day later, three Sherman tanks, two mounting flamethrowers, charged ahead of the riflemen spitting flame and machine-gun bullets and claimed the high ground. The Marines atop Dakeshi Ridge looked southward towards the rocky jumble of Wana Draw and nearby Wana Ridge. The 1st Marine Division flung itself against the outcroppings, cliffs, and caves. Progress was measured in yards. Through 19 days of horror, Marine casualties averaged 200 for every 100-yard advance.

Marine and army tanks fired 5,000 75mm shells and 175,000 rounds of .30-caliber ammunition on 16 May alone. The 3rd Battalion, 7th Marines, lost a dozen officers in four days. The 7th Marines took 700 casualties at Dakeshi Ridge and 500 more in five days at Wana Draw.

500 replacements reached the 1st Marines, which relieved the 7th Marines, and renewed the attacks on Wana Draw, 1,200 feet wide at its mouth but narrowing southward toward Shuri Ridge, funneling Marines into interlocking fields of fire. By 20 May, the 5th Marines had taken Hill 55 west of Wana Draw but at the end of the month, the 1st Marine Division was bogged down one ridgeline short of Shuri.

Battle for Sugar Loaf

Meanwhile, to the west, the 6th Marine Division crossed the Asa River on 10 May, advancing 2,950 feet in 36 hours. By 12 May, it had drawn up around a nondescript hill rising precipitously 230 feet. The riflemen nicknamed it Sugar Loaf. Sugar Loaf was flanked by two more small hills dubbed Half Moon and Horseshoe. The Marines did not initially realize that the complex was the western command nexus of the Shuri Line. 2,000 Japanese soldiers defended Sugar Loaf and another 3,000 held Half Moon and Horseshoe.

The battle for the Sugar Loaf-Half Moon-Horseshoe triad extended for ten harrowing days. Captain Owen G Stebbins of Company G, 2nd Battalion, 22nd Marines, led his command towards Sugar Loaf. In seconds, two platoons were pinned under a torrent of enemy fire. Stebbins and executive officer Lieutenant Dale W Bair kept the third platoon moving. 28 of the 40 men were quickly killed or wounded.

Stebbins was hit in both of his legs. Bair was shot in the left arm but still he persevered, gathering 25 Marines and charging to Sugar Loaf's crest, although he was ultimately unable to hold it. Five attempts had come up short. Just 75 of the original 200 Marines in Company G were unscathed.

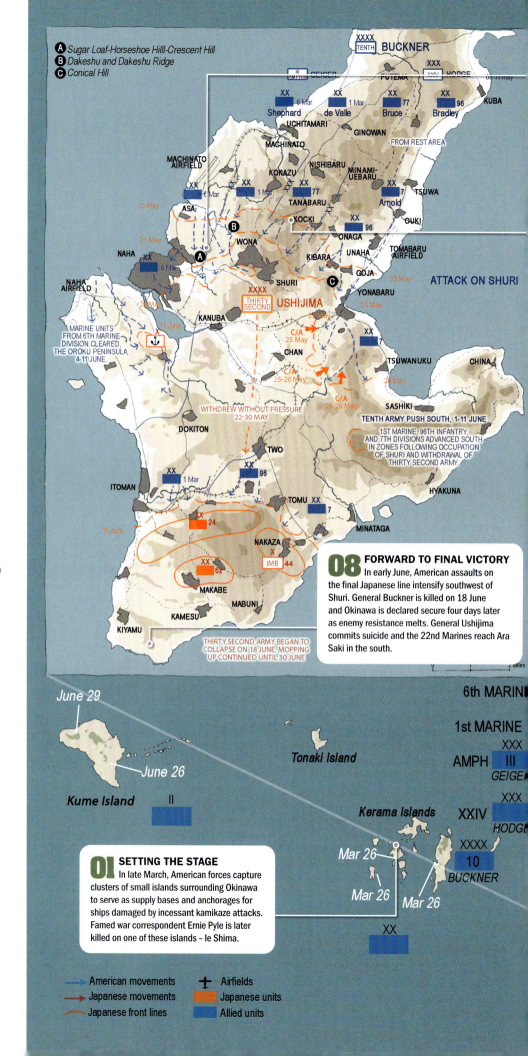

08 FORWARD TO FINAL VICTORY In early June, American assaults on the final Japanese line intensify southwest of Shuri. General Buckner is killed on 18 June and Okinawa is declared secure four days later as enemy resistance melts. General Ushijima commits suicide and the 22nd Marines reach Ara Saki in the south.

01 SETTING THE STAGE In late March, American forces capture clusters of small islands surrounding Okinawa to serve as supply bases and anchorages for ships damaged by incessant kamikaze attacks. Famed war correspondent Ernie Pyle is later killed on one of these islands – Ie Shima.

American movements
Japanese movements
Japanese front lines
Airfields
Japanese units
Allied units

BATTLE OF OKINAWA
1 APRIL – 22 JUNE 1945

06 SAVAGERY AT SUGAR LOAF
In late May, American forces finally capture the Sugar Loaf-Half Moon-Horseshoe complex of mutually supporting hills, significant progress against the Shuri Line. After losing nearly 3,000 men, the Americans compel the Japanese to abandon strong positions at Shuri Ridge and Shuri Castle.

07 KAMIKAZE RAIN OF STEEL
For weeks, the US Navy's Fifth Fleet and British warships are subjected to Operation Ten-Go, an onslaught of Japanese suicide planes that ravages Allied ships, including picket line destroyers and aircraft carriers. More than 300 ships are damaged before Ten-Go blows itself out. The fleet remains on station.

05 FIRST LINE BREACHED
For three weeks, the Americans batter the first of three Japanese defensive lines, finally forcing an enemy withdrawal and proceeding toward the second, or Shuri Line, where determined defenders have fortified a labyrinth of caves, crevices, hills, and valleys. By the first week of May, casualties begin to mount on both sides.

04 RAPID RUN NORTHWARD
The Americans bisect Okinawa and then turn north and south. Japanese resistance in the north is sporadic and sacrificial, and many enemy troops are bottled up and annihilated in the Motobu Peninsula. By 13 April, the 22nd Marines have occupied thumb-shaped Hedo Misaki Peninsula at the extreme northern tip of the island.

03 CAPTURING KEY AIRFIELDS
Kadena and Yontan airfields, keys to continuing support of the American ground offensive, are captured on the first day. Marine, navy and army aircraft are soon flying combat air patrol, interdiction, and ground support missions from these airfields, facilitating the advance, which nevertheless grows sluggish as enemy resistance intensifies.

02 STORMING ASHORE
On 1 April 1945, US Marines and Army troops splash across the Hagushi beaches on southwestern Okinawa, while the 2nd Marine Division creates a diversion at sea. Although a tough battle is expected at the water's edge, the Japanese have withdrawn to the south, and early progress is brisk.

EAST CHINA SEA

JAPAN

Yoron Island

Iheya island

Izena Island

Hedo Cape

Apr 13

Apr 15
Apr 23

Apr 12

Apr 21/22

Apr 19

Aha

Apr 21

Bise

Tako

Apr 13

Apr 16

Motobu Peninsula

XX 77

Nago

Apr 7

Okinawa

Apr 4

Apr 1

Kurawa

Kin

XX

XXXX 32 USHIJIMA

XX

XX

N

Chimu Bay

Yokatsu Islands

PACIFIC OCEAN

XX

Hagushi

Chibana

XXX

Kuba

Apr 1

Apr 4

XX

Tsugen Island

Apr 10

XX

Japanese resistance in north ends, Apr 20

Shuri

XX 62

May 31

X

44

XX 27

14

Itoman

XX 24

Apr 11

XX 2nd MARINE DIVISION

attle
-Jun 30

Demonstration Group
WRIGHT

Map: Rocío Espín

10km

10miles

After dark on 14 May, the 29th Marines reinforced the 22nd Marines. 44 men were marooned on Sugar Loaf's slope with at least 100 bodies lying around them. Major Henry A Courtney Jr, executive officer of the 2nd Battalion, 22nd Marines, decided that his men could not remain where they were but withdrawal would invite a hostile response. He reasoned that the best option was to attack so he roused Marines of Companies F and G and asked for volunteers. Courtney led all 44 Marines again to Sugar Loaf's crest. They held until after dark, when 15 survivors scrambled down. Courtney, however, died when a mortar fragment slashed his neck. He received a posthumous Medal of Honor.

Corporal James L Day's seven-man squad from Company F, 2nd Battalion, 22nd Marines, had followed Courtney up Sugar Loaf. Quickly, five men were shot. Day and Private Dale Bertoli were alone on the western slope. For four days and three nights the pair peppered rifle bullets and tossed grenades at the Japanese – Day was wounded and Bertoli was killed later. In 1984, Major General James L Day would return to Okinawa and take command of its Marine garrison. The 22nd Marines had lost 400 casualties, nearly half its number, in three days.

On 17 May, Company E, 2nd Battalion, 29th Marines, charged Sugar Loaf four times, losing 160 men but holding the hill for several hours before withdrawing at dusk. On 18 May, Company D, 2nd Battalion, 29th Marines, under Captain Howard L Mabie, assaulted Sugar Loaf while suppressing fire, keeping Japanese heads down on Half Moon and Horseshoe. Mabie's Marines skirted both flanks, negotiated minefields and emptied their weapons into clusters of Japanese soldiers emerging from bunkers on the reverse slope. Company D's grip on Sugar Loaf held.

The 4th Marines relieved the 29th and by 20 May, its 3rd Battalion controlled most of Horseshoe, while the 2nd Battalion held most of Half Moon. The 6th Marine Division had lost nearly 2,700 casualties fighting for Sugar Loaf.

While the Marines battled in the west, the 96th Division took Conical Hill and the 7th Division were able to secure Yonabaru. Ushijima's flanks were vulnerable and his positions at Shuri Ridge and Shuri Castle were untenable. He finally withdrew to the final line across the Kiyamu Peninsula under a cloak of steady rain and fog.

Foul weather slowed the American advance – nevertheless, 6th Marine Division tanks probed the village of Naha on 28 May. The next morning, Company A, 1st Battalion, 5th Marines, managed to reach the crest of Shuri Ridge without firing a shot, crossing into the 77th Division zone to occupy the much-coveted Shuri Castle.

Ushijima's 3.7-mile front then stretched across Kunishi Ridge in the west to Hill 89, the site of his last command post, and to Hill 95. Meanwhile, the 6th Marine Division secured the Oroku Peninsula and Naha Airfield in a joint land and amphibious craft assault, decimating 5,000 Japanese defenders under the command of Rear Admiral Minoru Ota.

The 7th Division's 32nd Regiment captured Hill 95 on 12 June, while the 17th Regiment took the eastern end of the Yuza Dake escarpment, unhinging Ushijima's right flank. The 96th Division claimed the rest of Yuza Dake the next day and the 1st Marine Division concurrently began its assault on the western anchor of the Japanese line. With Colonel Edward Snedeker's 7th Marines in the lead, initial assaults on Kunishi Ridge on 11 June were repulsed. Snedeker ordered a night attack and two Marine companies reached the crest near sunrise, mowing down surprised Japanese troops who were cooking breakfast and preparing for the day.

Campaign climax

The Japanese mounted some heavy counterattacks. Three attempts to reinforce the Marines atop Kunishi Ridge were thwarted but the 1st, 5th, and 7th Marines slowly made gains. In five days, the last heavily defended ridgeline on Okinawa was finally subdued. On 18 June, the 7th Marines finally trudged rearward to be relieved by the 8th Marines, 2nd Marine Division.

General Buckner climbed Mezado Ridge to observe the 8th's deployment. Five Japanese artillery shells crashed down, spraying rock and shrapnel – a splinter the size of a dime struck Buckner in the chest. One of the highest-ranking American officers killed in action in World War II, he died in ten minutes. General Roy Geiger handled the Tenth Army for five days until Army General Joseph Stilwell arrived to take over the command.

Geiger declared Okinawa secure on 22 June, while elements of the 7th Division took Hill 89, and the 77th Division captured Hill 85. That same day, as 7th Division troops neared the entrance to his headquarters in a cave on Hill 89, General Ushijima committed ritual suicide along with Rear Admiral Ota. The 6th Marine Division turned south from the Oroku Peninsula, occupying Ara Saki, Okinawa's southernmost point. Company G, 2nd Battalion, 22nd Marines, raised the Stars and Stripes. The great battle of Okinawa, the climax of the Pacific land campaign, was over.

A Marine glances at the body of a dead Japanese soldier as he passes through a shattered Okinawan village

Images: Alamy

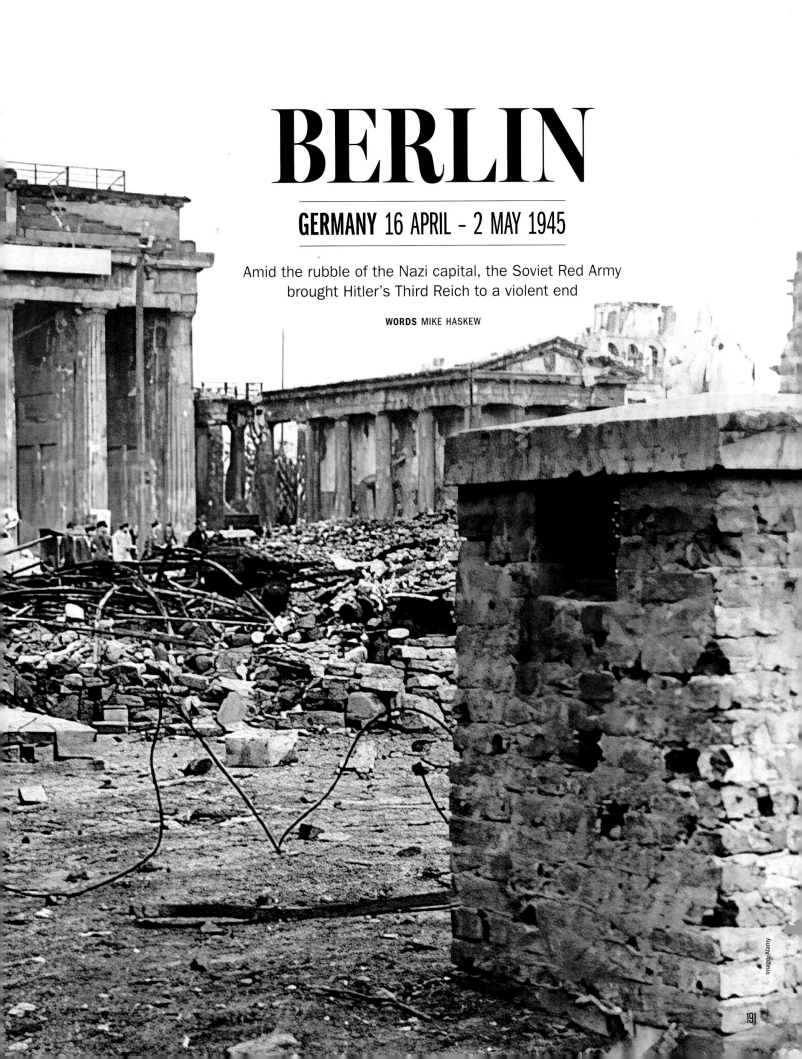

BERLIN

GERMANY 16 APRIL - 2 MAY 1945

Amid the rubble of the Nazi capital, the Soviet Red Army
brought Hitler's Third Reich to a violent end

WORDS MIKE HASKEW

By the spring of 1945, World War II was in its sixth year. The once mighty war machine of the Third Reich had been brought to its knees. Assailed from both East and West, Nazi Germany was in its death throes.

Since the beginning, Allied forces had been buoyed by the cry, "On to Berlin!" Now, however, practical considerations weighed heavily on the conduct of the final weeks of the war. General Dwight D Eisenhower, supreme commander of the American and British armies advancing across the western German frontier, breached protocol and contacted Soviet Premier Josef Stalin directly, informing him that the Western Allies did not intend to fight for Berlin. For several reasons, both political and military, the battle for the Nazi capital and whatever wisps of glory might come with its capture would be left to the Soviet Red Army.

Indeed, since Hitler had launched Operation Barbarossa – the Nazi invasion of the Soviet Union on 22 June 1941 – the Soviets had suffered mightily and borne the brunt of the fighting on the European continent. Millions of Soviet military and civilian lives had been lost before the Nazi juggernaut was even stemmed only 12 miles from the Soviet capital of Moscow, Russia. German generals peered at the gleaming onion domes of the city's buildings but could get no closer. Winter set in, and the Germans literally froze to death, while weapons and equipment failed to function in such inhospitable conditions.

The following spring, a renewed German offensive was met by a resurgent Red Army, and then the great Soviet victories at Stalingrad and Kursk occurred in 1943. Seizing the initiative, the Soviets pushed the Germans westward across thousands of miles, reaching Warsaw, the Polish capital, in the summer of 1944. Soviet offensives from Leningrad in the north to Odesa in the south were known as 'Stalin's ten blows'. By early 1945, East Prussia, the Baltic States, and Pomerania were in Soviet possession. The Red Army advanced from the River Vistula to the River Oder, and then to within 37 miles of Berlin.

Conference at the Kremlin

On 1 April, Stalin and two of his top commanders, Marshal Georgi Zhukov of the 1st Belorussian Front and Marshal Ivan Konev of the 1st Ukrainian Front, met at the Kremlin in Moscow. "Who will take Berlin?" Stalin asked. "We will!" Konev answered. Stalin proceeded to give the two commanders their orders. Zhukov was to attack Berlin from the north and east, while Konev approached from the south. The two immense Fronts would surround Berlin in a giant pincer and destroy the opposing forces in an ever-shrinking defensive perimeter.

Two weeks later, the final offensive began with the thunder of thousands of Soviet guns. Konev's advance across the River Neisse gained ground steadily, but Zhukov failed to accurately assess the strength of the main German line of resistance before Berlin at Seelow Heights just west of the Oder, where elements of Army Group Vistula, outmanned and outgunned but full of fight and Nazi fervor, made a stand along a ridgeline. Under the command of Colonel General Gotthard Heinrici, the defenders pulled back from frontline positions just as the Soviet artillery bombardment erupted; therefore, most of the shelling failed to inflict heavy casualties. German tanks and tank-killing infantry squads saw the silhouettes of Red Army armored vehicles and troops illuminated by their own searchlights and took a fearful toll, stalling Zhukov's advance.

After four days of fighting, Zhukov broke through the defenses, but the cost was high. No fewer than 30,000 Red Army soldiers were dead, along with 12,000 Germans. Stalin was enraged by the delay and ordered Konev to abandon his wider swing around Berlin and send his armored spearheads directly towards the city. The existing rivalry between Zhukov and Konev became heated as both vied for the prestige of capturing the Nazi capital.

A memorable birthday

20 April 1945 was Hitler's 56th birthday, but there was little revelry in the Führerbunker beneath the Reich Chancellery in Berlin that

A soldier of the Volkssturm holds a Panzerschreck anti-tank weapon on the outskirts of Berlin

2nd Lt William Robertson, US Army, and Lt Alexander Sylvashko, Red Army, shown in front of an East Meets West sign symbolizing the historic meeting of the Soviet and US Armies, near Torgau, Germany

OPPOSING FORCES

SOVIET RED ARMY

MARSHAL GEORGI ZHUKOV, 1ST BELORUSSIAN FRONT

MARSHAL IVAN KONEV, 1ST UKRAINIAN FRONT

6,250 TANKS

2,700 AIRCRAFT

2.5 MILLION TROOPS

41,600 GUNS

GERMAN ARMY

GENERAL HELMUTH WEIDLING

COLONEL GENERAL GOTTHARD HEINRICI

10,400 TANKS

3,300 AIRCRAFT

1 MILLION TROOPS

1,500 GUNS

day. Soviet long-range artillery began shelling the capital, and the guns would not cease firing until the city had fallen. Word reached the Führer in his subterranean command center that three defensive lines east of Berlin had been breached, including Seelow Heights. Zhukov was advancing. Konev was in open country and moving steadily with the 4th Guards Tank Army and 3rd Guards Army leading the way. A third Red Army Front, the 2nd Belorussian under Marshal Konstantin Rokossovsky, had broken through the 3rd Panzer Army's lines. Inside Berlin, the remnants of Army and Waffen-SS units prepared makeshift defenses. Old men and boys joined these soldiers for a fight to the death once the Soviets entered the city.

Territorial gains brought Berlin within range of field artillery on 22 April. A Red Army news correspondent came upon several guns preparing to unleash a storm of shells on the German capital. He later wrote, "'What are the targets?' I asked the battery commander. 'Center of Berlin, Spree bridges, and the

northern Stettin railway stations,' he answered. Then came the tremendous words of command: 'Open fire on the capital of Fascist Germany.' I noted the time. It was exactly 8.30am on 22 April. 96 shells fell on the center of Berlin in the course of a few minutes."

Both Zhukov and Konev ordered a continued westward advance, and on 25 April, the leading elements of a Guards rifle regiment from the 1st Ukrainian Front made contact with troops of the US 69th Infantry Division at Torgau on the River Elbe, splitting the Third Reich in two. On the same day, the encirclement of Berlin was completed. Both the German 9th and 4th Panzer Armies were surrounded, and efforts by the 12th Army under General Walther Wenck to move to the relief of Berlin were thwarted by the westward movement of the 1st Ukrainian Front.

Defending the doomed

As the Soviet noose tightened around Berlin, probing attacks tested the city's defenses. The Germans had divided three concentric rings into nine sectors. About 60 miles in

circumference, the outermost ring ran across the outskirts of the capital. Flimsy at best, it consisted primarily of roadblocks, barricades of rubble and vehicles, and shallow trenches. It was compromised rapidly in numerous locations prior to the main assault on the city.

The second circle ran about 25 miles and made use of existing buildings and obstacles, including the S-Bahn, Berlin's public transportation railway system. The inner ring included the massive buildings that once housed the ministries and departments of the Nazi government. These were turned into machine-gun and anti-tank strongpoints with firing positions on each floor.

Six huge flak towers, studded with guns and virtually impervious to anything but a direct hit, were also part of the inner circle. Eight of the pie-shaped dividing sectors, labeled A through H and radiating from the center of Berlin, crossed each of the rings to the outer perimeter. The ninth sector, named Z, was manned partially by a fanatical contingent of Hitler's personal SS guard.

Images: Alamy, Getty

The city of Berlin itself comprised 210 square miles, and defensive positions along the barriers of the River Spree and the Landwehr and Teltow Canals were particularly fortified. The main objective of the converging Soviet forces was the complex of government buildings known as the Citadel, north and east of the Tiergarten, a large park and residential district that was home to the Berlin Zoo.

Estimates of German strength vary from roughly 100,000 to 180,000, including SS, Army, Volkssturm (People's Militia), and Hitler Youth, under the command of General Helmuth Weidling, appointed by the Führer on 23 April to lead the last-gasp defense.

On 26 April, the final chapter of the battle for Berlin began with a fury. The Soviet 8th Guards and 1st Guards Tank Armies fought their way through the second defensive circle, crossing the S-Bahn line and attacking Tempelhof Airport. To the west, elements of the 1st Belorussian Front entered Charlottenburg and drew up to the River Spree after two days of bitter combat. The Soviets advanced inexorably toward the center of Berlin on four primary axes, along the Frankfurter Allee from the southeast, Sonnenallee from the south toward the Belle-Alliance-Platz, again from the south toward the Potsdamer Platz, and from the north toward the Reichstag, where the German Parliament had once convened and which had not been in use since a devastating fire had gutted the building in 1933.

On 28 April, the Potsdamerstrasse Bridge across the Landwehr Canal was taken, and fighting spread into the Tiergarten. The next morning the 3rd Shock Army crossed the Moltke Bridge over the River Spree. The Reichstag lay to the left fronting the Königsplatz, which was mined and heavily defended by machine-gun nests, artillery, several tanks, and a mixed bag of roughly 6,000 Germans. Attacks on the Interior Ministry building progressed sluggishly, and by dawn on 30 April, Red Army soldiers occupied Gestapo headquarters on Prinz Albrechtstrasse for a brief time before a heavy counterattack pushed them out. The Soviets did capture most of the diplomatic quarter that day.

Meanwhile, the 79th Rifle Corps began a concerted effort to take the Reichstag. Troops of the 150th Rifle Division ran a gauntlet of fire across the Königsplatz in a frontal assault. Other divisions attacked the flanks of the large building, and three attempts were beaten back between 4.30am and 1pm. The defenders were aided by 128mm guns atop one of the reinforced concrete flak towers at the Berlin Zoo firing from over a mile away. Soviet tanks and self-propelled assault guns lumbered into

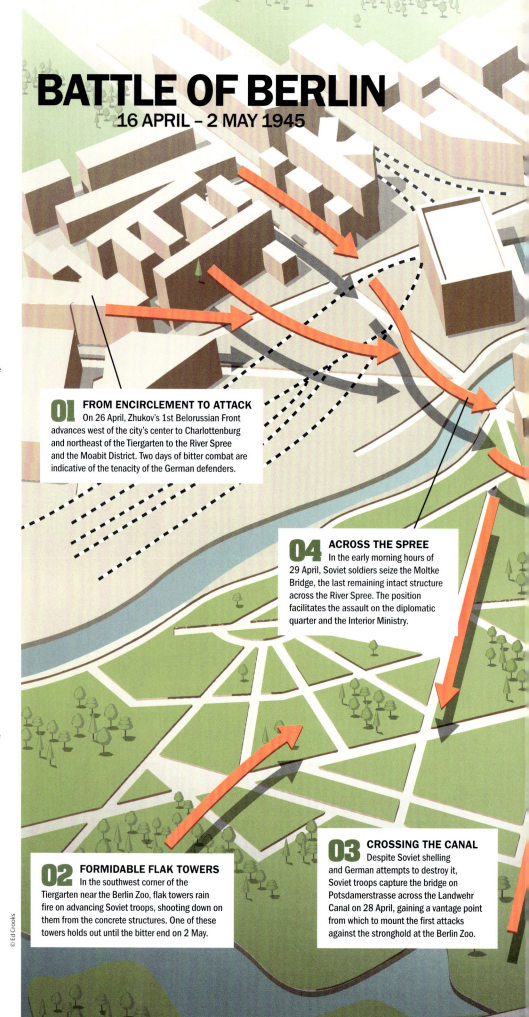

BATTLE OF BERLIN
16 APRIL – 2 MAY 1945

01 FROM ENCIRCLEMENT TO ATTACK
On 26 April, Zhukov's 1st Belorussian Front advances west of the city's center to Charlottenburg and northeast of the Tiergarten to the River Spree and the Moabit District. Two days of bitter combat are indicative of the tenacity of the German defenders.

04 ACROSS THE SPREE
In the early morning hours of 29 April, Soviet soldiers seize the Moltke Bridge, the last remaining intact structure across the River Spree. The position facilitates the assault on the diplomatic quarter and the Interior Ministry.

02 FORMIDABLE FLAK TOWERS
In the southwest corner of the Tiergarten near the Berlin Zoo, flak towers rain fire on advancing Soviet troops, shooting down on them from the concrete structures. One of these towers holds out until the bitter end on 2 May.

03 CROSSING THE CANAL
Despite Soviet shelling and German attempts to destroy it, Soviet troops capture the bridge on Potsdamerstrasse across the Landwehr Canal on 28 April, gaining a vantage point from which to mount the first attacks against the stronghold at the Berlin Zoo.

© Ed Crooks

08 SURRENDER AND SUBJUGATION

On the morning of 2 May, General Helmuth Weidling meets Soviet soldiers at the Potsdamer Bridge and surrenders to General Vasily Chuikov shortly thereafter. Some of the defenders of Berlin attempt to break out of the encirclement to the west. However, most are killed or forced to surrender.

07 TO THE REICH CHANCELLERY

After reaching the Potsdam rail station and moving across Lanbergerstrasse to the east on 1 May, Soviet troops advance along the Unter den Linden toward the Reich Chancellery, occupying the structure early the following morning. They also discover the Führerbunker and the charred remains of Hitler and Eva Braun.

06 ASSAULTING THE REICHSTAG

On 30 April, the Soviet 79th Rifle Corps, commanded by Major General SI Perevertkin, begin a series of assaults on the Reichstag, which commands the Königsplatz. Late that evening, soldiers scramble to the roof of the building and plant the Soviet flag there. The building is secured on 2 May.

05 HITLER COMMITS SUICIDE

Deep beneath the Reich Chancellery, Hitler commits suicide in the Führerbunker at 3.30pm on 30 April. Eva Braun, his longtime mistress whom he married hours earlier, dies with the Führer. Their corpses are doused with gasoline and set aflame in the garden of the Reich Chancellery.

Soldiers raise the flag of the Soviet Union above the Reichstag in a symbolic gesture of the fall of Berlin

the Königsplatz to blast German positions. A false report that a red banner had been seen flying above the Reichstag was issued at mid-afternoon when the attackers had managed to advance only partially across the Königsplatz. Fearing the repercussions that might ensue if the report were found to be inaccurate, Major General VM Shatilov, commanding the 150th Rifle Division, ordered a redoubling of the effort.

By 6pm, the fight for the Reichstag had raged 14 hours. Soviet soldiers renewed the attack, carrying small mortars to blast open entryways that had been covered with brick and mortar. Once inside, the Soviets clashed with Germans in hand-to-hand combat throughout the building. A small group of Red Army soldiers worked their way around the back of the Reichstag and found a stairway to the roof. Sergeants Mikhail Yegorov and Meliton Kantaria rushed forward with a red banner and found an equestrian statue at the edge of the roofline. Minutes before 11pm, they jammed the staff into a space in the statue.

Although the hammer and sickle flag of the Soviet Union flew above the Reichstag on the night of 30 April, the building was not secured until 2 May, when the last 2,500 German defenders surrendered. The famed photos and footage of the flag raising were actually taken during a reenactment of the event on 3 May.

Crumbling center

The Germans still forlornly defending Berlin were exhausted and running low on ammunition. General Weidling informed Hitler on the morning of 30 April that in a matter of hours the Red Army would be in control of the center of the city.

The Soviet 5th Shock, 8th Guards, and 8th Guards Tank Armies advanced down the famed Unter den Linden, approaching the Reich Chancellery and the Führerbunker. Hitler authorized General Weidling to attempt a breakout from the encirclement that had formed, and then with his longtime mistress, Eva Braun, who had become his wife only hours earlier, committed suicide in the underground labyrinth.

By this time, only about 10,000 resolute German soldiers remained in defensive positions, and Soviet troops and tanks were closing in from all sides. Soviet artillery pounded the remaining defenders, relentlessly shelling the Air Ministry building on the Wilhelmstrasse, a strong position that had been reinforced with steel, concrete, and barricades. The 3rd Shock Army advanced along the northern edge of the Tiergarten and battled a cluster of German tanks while maintaining pressure on the Reichstag and

the surrounding area. In concert with the movement of the 8th Guards Army, the 3rd Shock Army cut the center of Berlin in half.

On 1 May, General Hans Krebs, chief of the German General Staff, contacted General Vasily Chuikov, commander of the 8th Guards Army, informing the Soviet officer of Hitler's death and hoping to arrange surrender terms. The attempt failed when Chuikov insisted on unconditional surrender and Krebs responded that he did not have such authority. Meanwhile, some of the German troops began attempting to break out of embattled Berlin, particularly toward the west and a hopeful surrender to British or American forces rather than the vengeful Soviets, whose people had suffered so much at the hands of the Nazis. Only a relative few succeeded after crossing the Charlottenbrücke Bridge over the River Havel. Many were killed or captured when they abruptly encountered Soviet lines.

On the morning of 2 May, Red Army troops took control of the Reich Chancellery. Weidling had already sent a communiqué to General Chuikov at 1am, asking for another meeting. The German general was instructed to come to the Potsdamer Bridge at 6am. He was then taken to Chuikov's headquarters and surrendered within the hour. Weidling issued orders for all German troops to follow suit and put the directive in writing at Chuikov's request. He also made a recording of the order, and Soviet trucks blared the message through the shattered streets of the city. Some pockets of diehard SS troops resisted until they were annihilated. At the troublesome Berlin Zoo flak tower, 350 haggard German soldiers stumbled into the daylight of defeat. The Battle of Berlin was over.

Counting the cost

Casualties were staggering. During the drive from the Oder to Berlin, at least 81,000 Soviet soldiers had died and well over a quarter million were wounded. German losses are estimated at 100,000 killed, 220,000 wounded, and nearly half a million taken prisoner. At least 100,000 civilian residents of Berlin had also perished.

Red Army soldiers raped and murdered countless German women. They destroyed and pillaged in retribution for the horrors previously inflicted on their Motherland by the Nazis. For some Berliners who survived the battle, the nightmare of Soviet vengeance was – perhaps – a fate worse than death.

Within a week of the fall of Berlin, World War II in Europe ended with the unconditional surrender of Nazi Germany. The Third Reich, which Hitler boasted would last 1,000 years, had ended in fiery ruin in only 12.